FROM ONE OF OUR MOST DISTINCTIVE LITERARY MINDS

A cerebral debut novel about panic attacks, rituals, and the subconscious thoughts that make us human

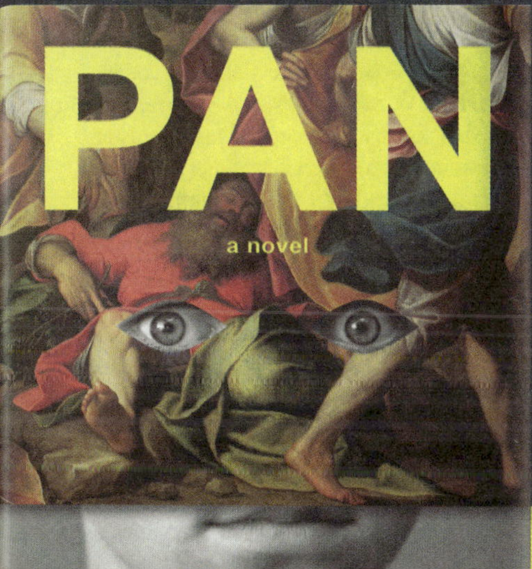

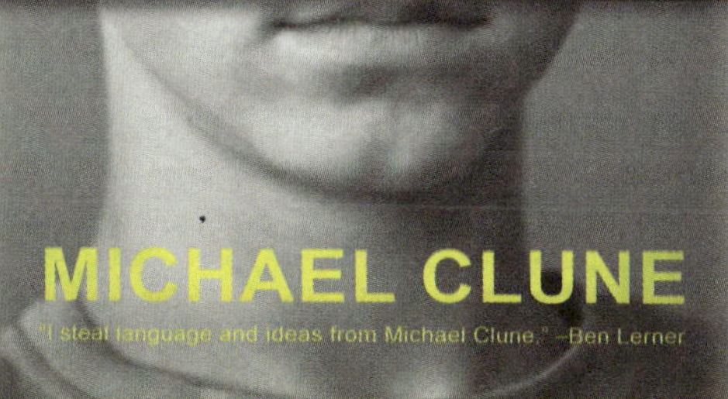

"THERE IS NO OTHER WRITER LIKE HIM."
—Maggie Nelson

"I DIDN'T WANT THIS BOOK TO END."
—Blake Butler

"I STEAL LANGUAGE AND IDEAS FROM MICHAEL CLUNE."
—Ben Lerner

"A STRANGE, VIVID, AND INTENSE NOVEL."
—Tao Lin

"AN ONTOLOGICAL COMING-OF-AGE STORY FOR, WELL, THE AGES."
—Paul Tremblay

PenguinPress | prh.com/pan

GRANTA

12 Addison Avenue, London W11 4QR | email: editorial@granta.com
To subscribe visit subscribe.granta.com, or call +44 (0)1371 851873

ISSUE 172: SUMMER 2025

EDITOR	Thomas Meaney
MD & DEPUTY EDITOR	Luke Neima
SENIOR EDITOR	Josie Mitchell
MANAGING EDITOR	Tom Bolger
ASSOCIATE DESIGN DIRECTOR	Daniela Silva
ASSOCIATE EDITOR	Brodie Crellin
EDITORIAL ASSISTANT	Aea Varfis-van Warmelo
PHOTOGRAPHY EDITOR	Max Ferguson
COMMERCIAL DIRECTOR	Noel Murphy
OPERATIONS & SUBSCRIPTIONS	Sam Lachter
MARKETING	Simon Heafield
SPECIAL PROJECTS	Janique Vigier
PUBLICITY	Pru Rowlandson, publicity@granta.com
CONTRACTS	Margaux Vialleron
ADVERTISING	Renata Molina-Lopes, Renata.Molina-Lopes@granta.com
FINANCE	Suzanna Carr
SALES	Rosie Morgan
IT SUPPORT	Ravi Dhir
PRODUCTION & DESIGN DIRECTOR	Sarah Wasley
PROOFS	Katherine Fry, Jessica Kelly, Jess Porter, Will Rees, Francisco Vilhena
CONTRIBUTING EDITORS	Anne Carson, Rana Dasgupta, Michael Hofmann, A.M. Homes, Rahmane Idrissa, Karan Mahajan, George Prochnik, Leo Robson
PUBLISHER	Sigrid Rausing

This selection copyright © 2025 Granta Trust.

Granta (ISSN 173231 USPS 508) is published four times a year by Granta Trust, 12 Addison Avenue, London W11 4QR, United Kingdom.

Airfreight and mailing in the USA by agent named World Container Inc., 150–15, 183rd Street, Jamaica, NY 11413, USA.

Periodicals postage paid at Brooklyn, NY 11256.

Postmaster: Send address changes to *Granta*, ESco, Trinity House, Sculpins Lane, Wethersfield, Braintree, CM7 4AY, UK.

Subscription records are maintained at *Granta*, c/o ESco Business Services Ltd, Wethersfield, Essex, CM7 4AY.

Air Business Ltd is acting as our mailing agent.

The manufacturer's authorised representative in the EU for product safety is Authorised Rep Compliance Ltd, 71 Lower Baggot Street, Dublin D02 P593, Ireland (arccompliance.com)

Granta is printed and bound in Italy by Legoprint. This magazine is printed on paper that fulfils the criteria for 'Paper for permanent document' according to ISO 9706 and the American Library Standard ANSI/NIZO Z39.48-1992 and has been certified by the Forest Stewardship Council (FSC). *Granta* is indexed in the American Humanities Index.

ISBN 978-1-909-889-74-3

The Destination
for Art and Culture

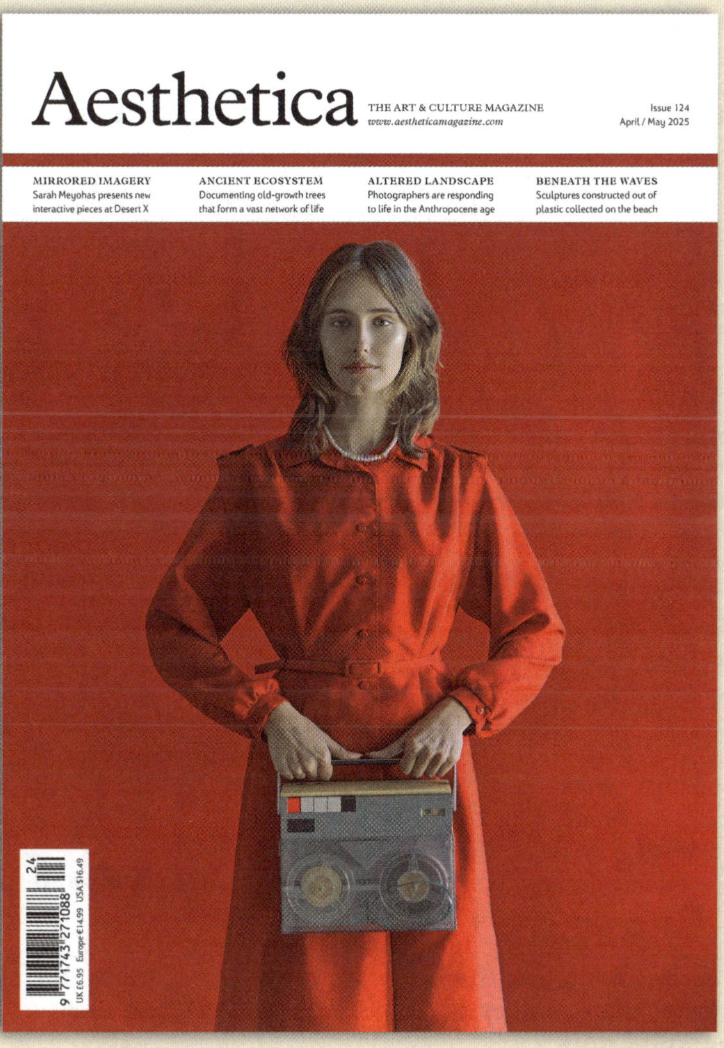

Since 2003, Aesthetica has published in-depth features and visual narratives with today's most innovative practitioners.
Be Inspired! Save 70%. £12 for 12 months.

CONTENTS

That's how it was then! Everything that grew took long to grow; and everything that ended took a long time to be forgotten. Everything that existed left behind traces of itself, and people then lived by their memories, just as we nowadays live by our capacity to forget, quickly and comprehensively.

– Joseph Roth, *The Radetzky March*

Badlands

Mauvaises terres à traverser. That is what French traders and trappers in the eighteenth century called the mud-rock highlands that blocked their passage through present-day South Dakota. They may have picked up the phrase from the Lakota name for the territory: 'Mako Sica' – 'Badlands'. I grew up in the flatlands not far away. The Badlands National Park looked like skin grafted from another planet. Remnants of ancient river channels, red-brown folds, blinding patches of white: the rock seemed unwilling to cooperate with any human activity except photography. 'Badlands' itself has hardened into a term of geomorphic science: it now refers to any highly eroded landscape.

The badlands of this issue refer to inhospitable terrain, whether on land or in the mind. Eighty years after the end of the Second World War, multiple times the firepower inflicted on Hiroshima has been dropped on Gaza in savage pursuit of Palestinian oblivion, while the Houthi dissenters in Yemen continue to break world records: first combat exchange in outer space, highest number of US drones destroyed, first non-state actor to down an F-18. In the Democratic Republic of the Congo, the mineral-rich eastern region of Kivu, an area the size of Western Europe, has been a geopolitical badlands for three decades. In Sudan, a deadlocked civil war fractures the country anew. These are only some of the areas on Earth whose uninhabitability is accelerating.

And Europe? A proxy war still rages there between Russia and the United States, with the Ukrainian people paying the price. What is remarkable is how much of the devastation has been confined within the national borders of pre-2014 Ukraine. Bombings and assassinations in Moscow are, at the time of writing, still rare, and the counter-invasion of Kursk by three Ukrainian brigades has come to naught. Mystifyingly, in the sleepy town of Wiesbaden, Germany – the de facto headquarters of the Western alliance, where NATO officials and Ukrainian commanders coordinate targets – the Russians have not raised a finger. In Berlin in 2022, I remember seeing the dead tropical fish on Karl-Liebknecht-Straße in the aftermath of the explosion of the AquaDom, widely speculated to have been the result of a Russian attack at the time, and thinking: this is what the war will be like when Moscow starts coloring harder outside the lines. But both the US and Russia have an interest in keeping the conflict confined to Ukraine. For the US, the ongoing war underlines the terms of European dependence on American arms and energy. For Russia, it has helped put the economy on a new, more autonomous footing. If the oft-dangled peace arrives, it will be the result of sated appetites as much as exhaustion. At some point Russia will want to consolidate its gains, while the US wants to keep open capacities that may be needed in the Midde East and East Asia.

For this issue, *Granta* sent William T. Vollmann into the drone-infested Ukrainian badlands. Vollmann describes himself as a writer low on fitness but high on endurance. In 1982, when he was twenty-two, he joined the Afghan mujahideen fighting against the Soviet invasion (a portion of his account appeared in *Granta* 40). Vollmann has staged collisions of his innocence with rough country ever since: Sarajevo, Fukushima, the Korean DMZ. 'I went to help [Ukraine] in my helpless way, with journalistic good intentions which sorrowed into love,' he writes. The good intentions would verge on naive if Vollmann did not hitch them to sober-eyed appraisals of his surroundings. There are few writers of contemporary reportage who see as many shades of color beyond the windshield. In Ukraine, Vollmann finds distraught mourners, hardened dog-lovers, defensive literary critics, and wised-up drone pilots. His chief interlocutors, however, are the two modernist giants of the region: Joseph Roth and Isaac Babel. In his affectionate way, Vollmann confronts a puritanism among some Ukrainians he meets that recalls Soviet history-scrubbing excesses: the pressure to purge vestiges of a shared past, in an effort to decontaminate Ukraine from the taint of Russian culture. While trying to summon reasons for leaving a statue of Babel intact, Vollmann asks: 'Isn't genius enough?'

Vollmann once supplied a dark clue for the origins of his strenuous attention to detail. In 1968, when he was nine years old, he was told to watch over his sister at a pond in New Hampshire. The pond had a steep drop-off and his sister drowned. 'I just stopped paying attention at one point,' Vollmann recalled. 'I was lost in some sort of daydream.' For a decade afterward, he describes having 'nightmares practically every night – of her skeleton chasing me and punishing me'. Part of the way out of being pursued for Vollmann has been to become a great noticer of everything around him.

There are badlands of the Earth, but also badlands of memory – whited-out areas that the mind fills in as best it can. Like Vollmann, Annie Ernaux also lost a sister, but one she never knew. So effectively was the existence of the dead sibling kept secret that Ernaux only found out about her through an aunt's slip of the tongue. The older sister – Ginette – died two years before Ernaux was born. In 'The Other Girl', Ernaux tells the story of her relations with her lost sister, a kind of double who has followed her in life, or rather crept slightly ahead of her. As in much of Ernaux's work, the past is a place of repression, where society ensures the realities of the body and sex and death cannot be adequately understood. Ernaux's parents seem to have believed that their younger daughter would not be able to bear the burden. They visit Ginette's grave, but they whisper about the rituals they have made around her, to the point that the young Ernaux feels outside their circle. One of the lingering questions of the account is whether this veil of ignorance cast over Ernaux's childhood might not be at the origin of her art.

For the photography for this issue, George Prochnik talks to the old master Joel Meyerowitz about how he recovered his aesthetic orientation amid the shadows of Franco's Spain. Julián Herbert considers the balance of myth and material labor in the hallucinatory photographs of Cian Oba-Smith, which document the annual firework festival in Tultepec, outside Mexico City. Sana Badri, closer to home, finds islands of solace and care in London's corner shops, 'the final great equalisers in a neighborhood', where everything seems to be available except for copies of *Granta*.

Frederick Seidel conjures a season of his childhood ('Summer in St. Louis mothers me') and a time of bliss on Long Island which refuse connection to moments of his present and the American past.

This is the poetry of imperial twilight. 'The United States has been a great disappointment,' Seidel declares. In five linked poems, Sharon Olds makes sorties into sexual and emotional memory, giving the reader the sense she has whittled down the past to the most essential flashes. Paul Muldoon delivers a jocular poem from the badland of Alcatraz, where the inmates yield a rich haul of associations. The younger poet Nasim Luczaj provides us with a close-up of the Mavic drone that hovers in Vollmann's report as well as miniature biographies of Marc Chagall, himself a child of the badlands known as the Pale of Settlement.

Outside of Diane Williams's supremely compressed stories, where botched intimacies give way to playful revelations, our fiction canvasses a selection of younger writers, all of them straying from the pastures of received style. Natasha Stagg draws out a getaway among friends and lovers into a blurred pattern where no one listens enough, stories are stranded in their own telling, and people are condemned to be individuals. Stephanie Wambugu's is a dry-witted story about following the unknown with detached abandon. Brittany Newell presents a starkly original narrator from the American south-west who navigates a thicket of friendship and desire, ending up in a salon that offers the most unusual services. Finally, in 'Carousel', by Leopold O'Shea, a retired flight attendant moves through the rituals of her life – applying makeup, walking to Lidl – while rehearsing the steps she would take to leave her husband. Yet each time she packs a suitcase and plans the exit, time starts to slip, and she finds herself once again in the kitchen sifting flour for crêpes.

Future geographically focused issues of *Granta* will be devoted to Scandinavia, the Koreas, Nigeria, and the American Berserk. But next, India. ∎

TM

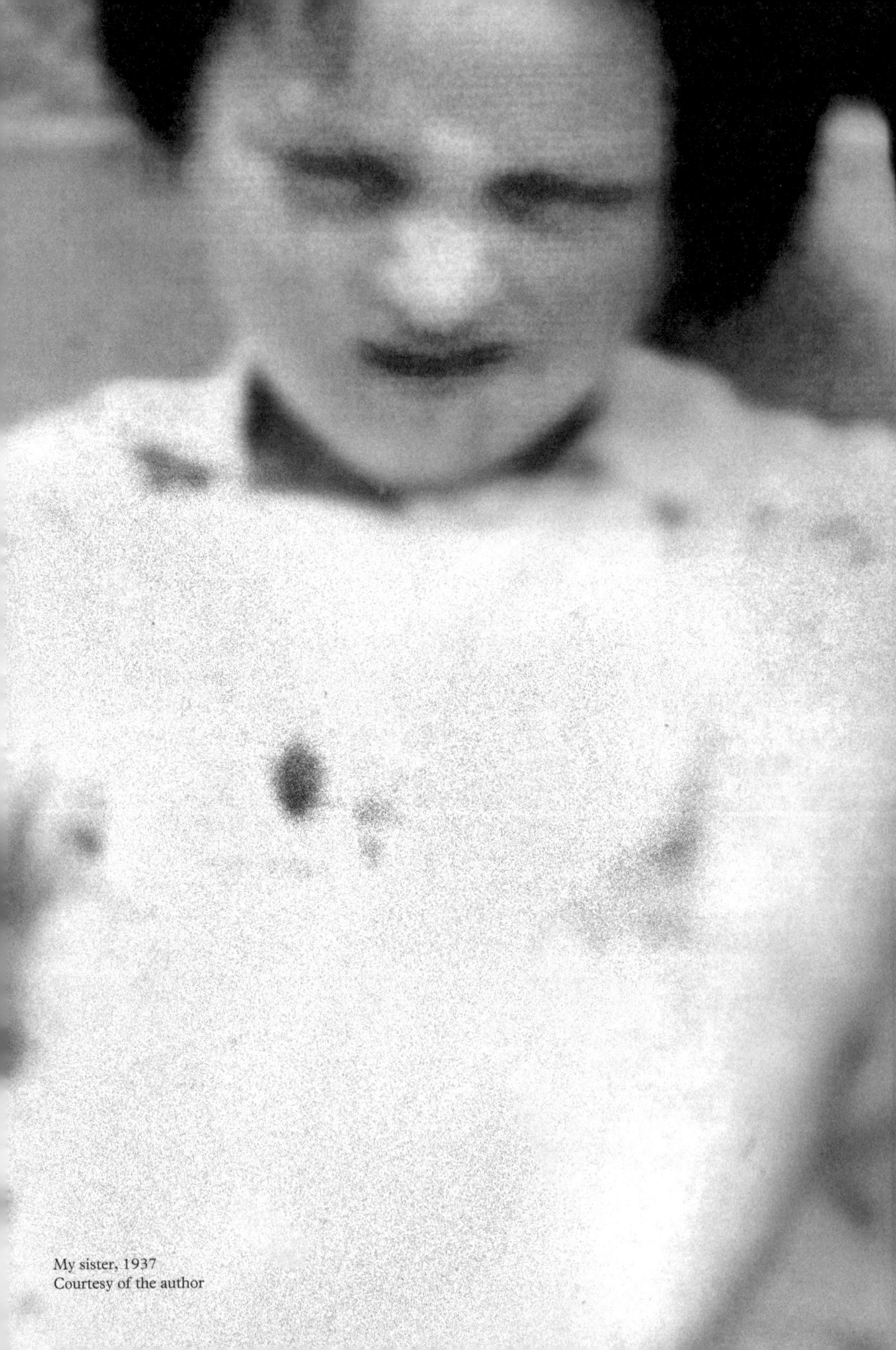

My sister, 1937
Courtesy of the author

THE OTHER GIRL

Annie Ernaux

TRANSLATED FROM THE FRENCH BY ALISON L. STRAYER

It is a sepia photo, oval-shaped, glued inside a yellowed cardboard folder, showing a baby posed in three-quarter profile on a heap of scalloped cushions. The infant wears an embroidered nightdress with a single, wide strap to which a large bow is attached, just behind the shoulder, like a big flower or the wings of a giant butterfly. The body is long and not very fleshy. The legs are parted and stretch out toward the edge of the table. Under the brown hair, swept up in a big curl over the protuberant forehead, the eyes are wide and staring with an almost devouring intensity. The arms, open like those of a baby doll, seem to be flailing, as if she were about to leap from the table. Below the photo, the signature of the photographer (M. Ridel, Lillebonne), whose intertwined initials also appear in the upper left-hand corner of the front cover, which is heavily soiled and coming unglued.

When I was little, I believed – I must have been told – that the baby was me. It isn't me, it's you.

There was another photo, taken by the same photographer, of me on the same table with my brown hair pulled up in the same sort of roll, but I appear to be plump, with deep-set eyes in a round chubby face, my hand between my thighs. I don't remember ever being puzzled by the – obvious – differences between the two photos.

*

Around All Saints' Day, I go to the cemetery in Yvetot to lay flowers on the two graves, the parents' grave and yours. From one year to the next, I forget where they are but find my bearings with the tall and very white cross that can be seen from the central pathway and which looms over your grave, right next to theirs. I place a potted chrysanthemum of a different color on each grave, or sometimes a pot of heather on yours, working it into the patch of gravel put there for that purpose at the foot of the tombstone.

I don't know if people spend much time thinking in front of graves. I linger for a moment before my parents' grave. It's as if I'm saying, 'Here I am', and showing them what has become of me in the past year, what I've done, written, hoped to write. Then I move on to yours, to the right. l look at the headstone and read the inscription in big, too-shiny gilded letters, crudely repainted in the nineties over the old ones, which were smaller and had become illegible. The marble mason took it upon himself to remove half of the original inscription, leaving a single entry under your first and last name, certainly because he considered it to be of utmost importance: DIED ON HOLY THURSDAY, 1938. That is what struck me too the first time I saw your grave. Like proof carved in stone of your being chosen by God, of your saintliness. In the twenty-five years I've been visiting the graves, I've never had anything to say to you.

According to the civil registry, you're my sister. You have the same surname as me – Duchesne, my 'maiden name'. We are listed one after the other in the parents' family record book, almost in tatters, under the heading 'Births and Deaths of Children of the Marriage'. You are above, with two stamps from the Mairie of Lillebonne (Seine-Inférieure), I am below with only one. The box for death will be filled out for me in another record book that attests to my reproduction of a family, under another name.

But you're not my sister, you never were. We did not play, eat, or sleep together. I never touched you, or kissed you. I don't know the color of your eyes. I've never seen you. You have no body, you have no voice. You're just a flat image in a few black-and-white photos. I have no memory of you. You'd already been dead for two and a half years when I was born. You are the child of heaven, the invisible little girl that no one ever talked about, the absent one in every conversation. The secret.

You have always been dead. You entered my life dead the summer I turned ten. You were born and died in a story, like Bonnie, Scarlett and Rhett's little girl in *Gone with the Wind*.

I have only six photos of you, all of which were given to me by cousins, some after my mother's burial, others very recently. I'd only known of two, which my mother kept in a drawer in her wardrobe and which disappeared around 1980, probably thrown away in one of the outbursts of destructive rage that were early signs of Alzheimer's.

In these photos, apart from the one of you as a baby, you must be between four and six. No doubt they were taken with the camera they said they'd won at a fair before the war, and which they kept until the end of the fifties. I used it often. You almost always have your head down and are grimacing, or shielding your eyes with your arm, as if the light hurts you – as if it were unbearable. In a recent letter, my cousin G, who also noticed this, remarked: 'She doesn't look as if she likes herself much.'

I am violently disturbed by this remark. Were you happy? I've never asked myself the question, as if it were an absurd, outrageous thing to ask about a little dead girl. As if their pain at losing you and their missing your niceness – proof of their love – guaranteed your happiness. If there is truth to the belief that happiness comes of being loved, you must have been happy – you couldn't have been otherwise. Saints are happy. But maybe you weren't.

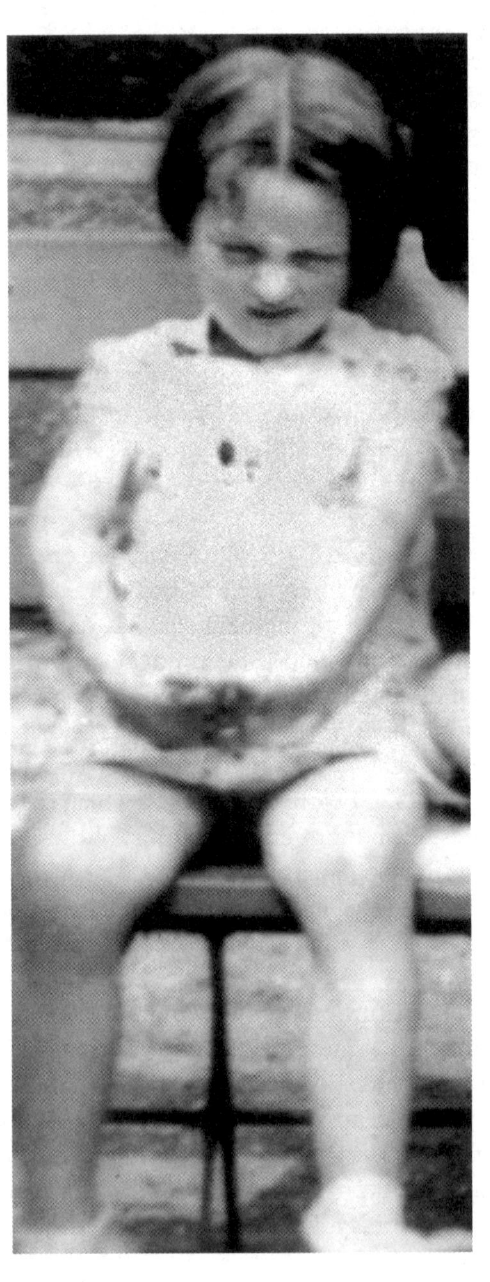

I've been unable from the start to write *our mother,* or *our parents* – to add you to the trio of my childhood. There is no possessive we can share. (Is this a way of excluding you, of responding in kind to my being excluded from the story told on that summer Sunday?)

From one – significant – perspective, that of time, we were raised by different parents.

When you were born in 1932, they were young, scarcely four years married, workers with ambitions who had taken on debt the year before to set up a business in the Vallée, the spinning mill district of Lillebonne. He continued to work outside the business, on a construction site in Hode and then at the refineries in Port-Jérôme. The hopes awakened by the Front Populaire bubbled inside and around them. The stories of those years of living hand to mouth, of evenings spent working in their café until three in the morning, always ended with 'but we were young then'.

In an undated photo from before the war, he holds her by the shoulders, smiling. She wears a dress with big polka dots and a pale lace collar. A thick lock of hair falls over her eyes. She still resembles the sleek and rebellious young bride of 1928. I never saw her in that dress or with that hairstyle. I did not know the woman of that time, of your time.

At the beginning of mine, in photos in which I also appear, probably from the spring of 1945, although they are smiling there is no longer anything youthful or carefree about them, but something broken. Their features are marked, heavy-looking. She's in a striped dress that I saw her wear for a long time. Her hair is swept up in a roll. They have lived through the Exodus, the Occupation, the bombings. They have lived through your death. They are parents who have lost a child.

You are there between them, invisible. Their pain.

They must have used the expression 'when you grow up', listing the things you'd learn to do – read, ride a bicycle, walk to school by yourself – and said, 'next year', 'this summer', 'soon'. One evening, instead of a future there was only emptiness. They said the same words again, to me. I was six, seven, ten; I'd overtaken you. There was no longer any way for them to compare. Obscurely, I believed she was angry with me for ceasing to be a child, 'becoming a young woman', as she said, on the day of my first period, with disproportionate embarrassment, verging on distress, as she handed me a sanitary towel.

The story that I overheard was the first and last I ever heard. Neither of them ever talked to me about you.

I don't know when it was that they hid your photos in the wardrobe, and the family record book in a rusty strongbox in the attic, where I read it one day – I was at least eighteen – when the box was left open. Every week they took turns cycling to the cemetery with flowers from the garden. Sometimes one would discreetly ask the other, *Have you been to the cemetery?* Long before they knew they'd be going back there, seven years later, in 1945, it was in Yvetot – where almost all the members of the two families lived – that they'd wanted you to be buried, and not in Lillebonne, probably so that people would go often to visit your grave.

I never heard them say your name. I learned it from my cousin C. As an adolescent, I thought it seemed old-fashioned, almost ridiculous. None of the girls at school had that name. Even now, on hearing it, I feel uneasy, vaguely repelled. I hardly ever say it, as if to do so were forbidden. Ginette.

They never said anything about the things that had belonged to you and they had kept.

They had me sleep in your rosewood cot until I was about seven. After that, they bought me a corner unit, a single bed with shelving, and the cot was dismantled, the four panels, wooden frame, and metal bedsprings put away in the attic, reassembled from time to time for a visiting child to sleep in. When my mother came to live with us in Annecy, she brought it with her other furniture. I stored it in the basement, from where some moving men mistakenly transported it to my parent-in-law's in Charente, who, without telling me, hastily disposed of it, as they told me with an offhand laugh in the summer of 1971.

Until the start of secondary school, they made me go to class with the brown Morocco leather briefcase that you had started school with. No one else but me had one like it, and it was awkward to use. When the bag was opened, both compartments had to be flipped over in one sharp movement, otherwise the pencil case and notebooks would tumble out and scatter. Because I'd always seen it around the house, I thought it had been bought for me, years in advance of my first day of school. I must have been over twenty when I realized that the briefcase – which she always kept for storing papers in – was yours.

I find this written in my journal of August 1992: 'As a child – is this the origin of writing? – I always thought I was the double of another girl living in another place. That I wasn't really living, either, and that this life was "writing", a fiction about another girl. This absence of being, or fictional being, needs to be explored further.'

Perhaps this is the purpose of this fake letter; for the only real letters are ones that are written to the living.

Only today do I ask myself the question, so simple yet it never occurred to me before: Why did I never, at any time, ask them about you, even as an adult and a mother myself? Why did I never tell them that I knew? At a certain point, all that is revealed by a delay in asking a question, whether private or collective, is the very impossibility of doing so. In the fifties, an implicit rule forbade us from asking our parents, or adults in general, about things they didn't want us to know but that we knew. On that Sunday in the summer of my tenth birthday, I was given both the story and the law of silence. I wasn't supposed to ask them anything because they didn't want me finding out about you. I was supposed to comply with their desire for me not to know about you. It seems to me that breaking that law (but I did not even imagine doing so) would have been tantamount to uttering obscenities in front of them, or doing something even worse – bringing on a kind of cataclysm and an unusual punishment that I associate here with the phrase of Kafka's father to his son, who relates it in his 'Letter to His Father', and which I immediately copied down the first time I read it, at the age of twenty-two, on my bed in the university halls of residence: *I will tear you apart like a fish.*

I remember the terror I felt at age sixteen, while visiting my aunt Marie-Louise, who, in her usual Sunday state of drunkenness, forgot what she wasn't supposed to talk about and said, *That's your sister,* pointing to you in a photo that I didn't even look at in my haste to move on to the next one, panic-stricken at the thought that the two of them, standing nearby, had heard what she'd said and therefore learned that I knew their secret.

We maintained the pretense beyond a point anyone would have believed possible.

In June 1967, my father's coffin was lowered into the fresh grave dug next to yours, which she and I pretended not to see. The following summer, while on holiday at her house, I went to lay flowers from the garden on my father's grave. I didn't put any on yours, since she hadn't told me anything. Even the place where you are buried was never named. ■

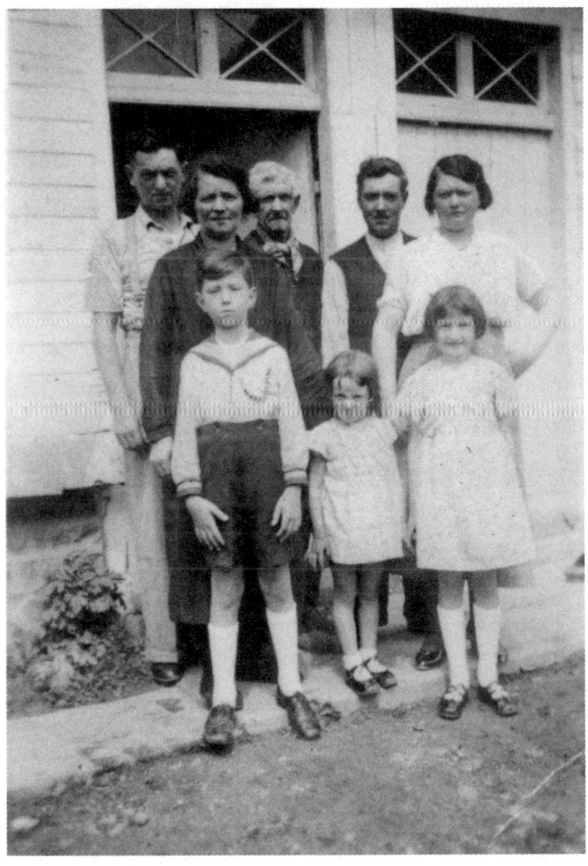

Valliquerville (near Yvetot), 1935. Standing left, my father; an unknown woman; my grandfather; Uncle Henri, my father's brother; Cécile, his wife; in front, Jean, Uncle Henri's son; my sister Ginette; an unknown child

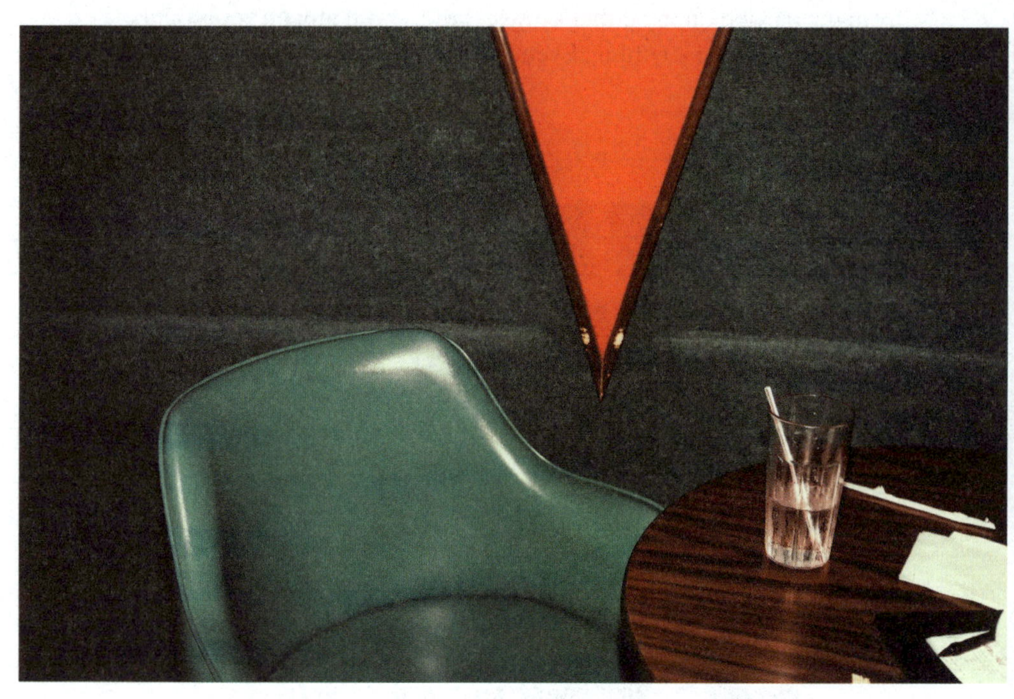

LORENA LOHR
Untitled (Nebraska Bar Room), 2018

HAPPY ENDING

Brittany Newell

Hunter was hot but she made me feel stupid.

It was my fault, not hers. She was patient with me. We'd been dating for three months and the stupid feeling still hadn't gone away, not even when we kissed, not even when she looked at me under a streetlamp and said with her hands on my hips, *You're an angel from God.* I didn't know what to say so I just looked at her, her skin tinged green by a nearby EXIT sign. We stood there, weirdly quiet, until she touched me on the forehead and murmured, *Knock knock,* and I said, automatic, *Who's there?*

I felt stupid when she told me she'd started working at a massage parlor and without thinking I said, *How come you never practice on me?* We were drinking at a tiki bar and her group of friends burst out laughing, then covered their mouths.

Being around Hunter's friends only made me feel stupider. Their lives seemed so robust, urbane, full of rotating love affairs and semi-legal gig work. When they spoke, it was like they were handing out business cards – this is me, here are the things that I'm good at, that get me hot, that piss me off. They chain-smoked but had perfect skin or else the wrinkles suited them, made them look cowboy-esque. They were never home and yet their apartments were full of tropical plants that flourished in their absence. They wore complicated rompers to the gym and dirty T-shirts to parties. I suppose they were nice to me, in their own way. They recommended things for me to try – the soup dumplings from that place on Clement, EMDR, bangs.

It didn't help that Hunter had told them I'd never dated a woman before. As a group their understanding made me squirm, their soft-focus waterproof eyes. I didn't know how to explain myself. I practiced, sometimes, in the bathroom mirror: *I don't like labels, I'm from bumfuck Nevada, I've never had a boyfriend either . . .* but everything reeked of cliché so I just said nothing, mute in my seat, while Hunter and her friends spoke about movies that I'd never seen and who was fucking who.

When I asked Hunter to explain, her voice was serene. *Surely you've heard of a happy ending massage?* She was eating leftover noodles, standing in her bedroom with one sock on, the other foot bare. Nothing seemed to make her shy; she never doubted the world's ability to accommodate her and her shapeshifting desires. I was just another casualty to her old-world bravado, to the way she wore her jacket over her shoulders with her long arms bare, to the way she called everyone baby. She had a way of making you feel chosen when she touched you on the inner wrist, like some porno nurse taking your pulse – *there, there.* Her friend Ducky once told her, *If you hadn't turned out gay as fuck, you would totally be evil,* to which they both cackled. Kept afloat by a trust fund, she was always into something new: noise music, numerology, performance art. There was the winter of mime, the self-imposed stick-and-pokes zigzagging her thigh. She spent hours every day in her studio, from which I was barred. That month, a blue June, her thing was collage. The floor of her apartment was covered in thrashed fashion magazines and bottles of Elmer's glue I liked to sniff when she wasn't around; the back-to-school smell made me nostalgic.

Of course, I said. *You mean those skeezy places where dudes go to get off?* I sat on her bed and picked up a magazine, a weather-beaten *Vogue*; as I pretended to study it, I saw that each page had a woman-shaped hole in it. This made me uneasy, like I was a rookie detective in a cop show and I'd found something damning.

Sure, Hunter said. *That's the gist of it. Genevieve told me about this place downtown, Angel Palace Spa, they'll hire anyone with tits. I've been craving more structure in my life, as you know, so I picked up some daytime shifts.*

And you like it?

She smiled, cilantro in her teeth. *I do.*

What else was there to say? She wound her arms around my neck. There was chili oil under her nails and it made my eyes sting. We took off our clothes and slid into bed, a California king she'd pushed up against the window so that I sometimes dreamed of suicide. She had a squishy white duvet I associated with privilege, as if coziness was something, like table manners or French, she'd been taught as a child by some lanky au pair. Meanwhile I rented a room in the Sunset from two dental students who dabbled in kink; on weekends they hosted sex parties and their friends would arrive in cop uniforms while they themselves wore their actual dental scrubs. Sometimes I heard a drill from behind their closed bedroom door. More perversely, they boiled three dozen eggs every Sunday night without fail. For this reason Hunter and I spent most nights at her apartment in Russian Hill, having sex on her oh-so-breathable sheets.

As we lay down, I could sense that we would never talk about this again. It would be neatly off-limits, like how her family made money (they were tied up in oil and guns) or the fact that she liked me for being a little bit broken. The last thing I could think to ask was, *What days do you work?*

Tuesdays, ten to three, she said, her voice thick with sleep. Like every mega-babe I'd ever known, she slept with a stuffed animal, in her case a gnarled hippo named Boom Boom. *They said I have the makings of a top earner.*

I scratched her scalp the way she liked. She had recently shaved her head and we were still finding shreds of hair everywhere. With her golden curls and puffy lips, she'd looked the part of an angel;

now, freshly buzzed, she was angular, troubling. She got even more attention from men in the street. *Oh,* I whispered. *Good for you.*

Four days later she was leaving. Her college roommate Zero was getting top surgery and would be convalescing in his family's Nantucket beach house; Hunter had volunteered to fly out, drain his tubes, wrangle the Roku, and reminisce on the past.

He won't be able to lift his arms or walk the dogs, she explained, throwing clothes in a duffel bag. *He needs me right now.* I wondered why she was packing bikinis if the plan was to putter around a dank, smelly room. I tried to picture Zero: muscular forearms, a wide-ranging knowledge of queer literature. I fought the urge to ask if they'd fucked. I didn't want to hear her airy proclamation, *Of course! But that was, like, a million years ago. Who even were we?* Instead I said, *I'll miss you.*

She pulled me in for a kiss; her lips tasted of Emergen-C. *I'll miss you too, Laney. Really, I will.* She put Boom Boom in her bag. *Will you hold down the fort while I'm gone? Water my plants, stay out of trouble?*

I nodded, trying not to laugh; what trouble was there without her? I'd been in San Francisco for all of four months. Before Hunter and I matched on a dating app, I'd spent my nights alone. I lay in the bath and read my textbooks front to back, until my fingers went pruney and the dental students banged on the door. *Some of us need TO GO #2!* I'd moved to California to finish my degree, but really, the desert no longer suited me. In college I studied engineering but I stopped going the spring semester of my junior year. I floated around for a while, then found work as a receptionist at a Reno hotel called The Nugget. I liked the thirty-minute drive into Reno, when the desert was still purple, hushed; I liked the little black dresses they made us wear, bland enough to fit anyone's fantasy.

It was there that I first kissed a girl, in a double room full of cigarette smoke, while her boyfriend sat on the opposite bed and filmed us with his phone. That was the rule: he had to stay on his bed, us on ours. I remember how the cheap green bedspread crumpled under my ass, how the girl spilled her Tecate on the bed and it just slid right off, like an oil slick. I'd first seen the couple by the pool on my lunch break; the next evening, they came looking for me at the front desk. The woman wore a snakeskin bikini both times, giving me the impression that she never took it off. You might call this my wild era, a smeary year of sleeping with people I met at The Nugget. I marked the third anniversary of my sister's death by fucking a traveling salesman who specialized in robotic vacuums. *It's the future,* he promised, *the future is here.* Every day after work I changed into the clothes I kept in the trunk of my car and permitted myself one martini at the hotel bar. If someone fuckable didn't materialize by the time I finished my drink, I went home.

I never told Hunter about this. My encounters felt seedy compared to her tangled summer romances, her exacting terminology – polycule, edge play, stone. Her love life was a novel while mine was a pamphlet handed out by Jesus freaks (*repent!!*). Sometimes Hunter's preoccupation with love made her seem worldly and sometimes it made her seem babyish, a little girl looking around her birthday party and wondering, *who will pick me up next?* She didn't know who she was if she wasn't in love, like the boys in my engineering classes who wept when they got a B+ or the veterans at The Nugget who guarded their favorite slot machines – we each sought something God-shaped to define us. I thought of the career-assessment tests I'd taken as a senior in high school, administered by a woman in buttoning sneakers. The tests were supposed to lay bare our passions and aptitudes. My results were inconclusive; I'd gotten stoned during lunch and decided to bubble my answers in the shape of a heart.

The proctor had squinted at my test for a long, long time. *Does the letter S mean something to you?* she said finally. *I'm getting a name that starts with S.* I stared at her, horrified; my sister's death was still fresh. *I moonlight as a psychic on the strip,* she explained with a devilish smile.

Whatever, I said, then cut class for the rest of the day, driving in circles with my AC on high.

I'll be good, I said into Hunter's deliciously unwashed hair. *Don't have too much fun without me.* Then I shouldered her bags and walked her outside, where the taxi was already waiting.

It was nice to be on my own at first. I watered Hunter's ferns, I slept in her bed, I did my shitty data entry job from the tub. I took a long walk every afternoon and concocted baroque stir-fries using things I found in her pantry. On the third day I made blondies, thinking of her. I opened a kitchen drawer and found an official-looking form amid rubber bands and takeout menus. It was a list of rules, xeroxed on pale pink paper; on the back of it, the name JULIET had been scribbled. I read it in the kitchen, letting the oven warm my hip –

> *Who are the ANGELS, you ask? ANGELS bring*
> *pleasure & relief to our discerning customers. ANGELS*
> *provide an important service to the men who visit us. Our*
> *clean & discreet Spa is a temple for many, located at 666*
> *Stockton, open 24/7*
>
> *ANGELS are timely & punctual*
> *ANGELS are clean, presentable, smooth. NO heavy*
> *perfumes*
> *ANGELS are selfless*
> *ANGELS are vectors of light*
> *ANGELS are always happy to see you no matter WHAT*
>
> *Congratulations! You are now an ANGEL in our clean*
> *& private Palace Spa. Please show up to your shift in a*
> *WHITE dress or skirt, spaghetti straps OK. Please note:*
> *we keep the Palace at a comfortable 72 degrees so long*
> *sleeves are not necessary.*

I turned off the oven, forsaking my blondies.

From then on the Palace was all I could think about. It followed me like a ghost, like BO. When Hunter texted me selfies from Zero's guest bedroom, I texted back: *missing you!!* I didn't let her in on my turmoil. But every walk I took brought me closer and closer to that side of town until one afternoon, a week after Hunter had left for

Nantucket, I went out for some air and found myself at 666 Stockton.

It was the last building on the block, next to the mouth of a smoggy tunnel. A handwritten sign had been taped to the pale pink door – A TOUCH OF ECSTASY? 3RD FLR. I rang the bell and the grate buzzed open; I stepped into a small, dark lobby. The floor was covered in junk mail. I read the fake-sounding names of the other businesses on their mail slots: Life Options Inc., Favorite Models & Talent, Forevermore Financial. There was no elevator, just an empty shaft with a chair placed in front of it and another handwritten sign that said BROKEN!!!!, so I took the stairs. I didn't have a plan; I felt swimmy and blank, like when I drank after work at The Nugget and emptied my mind, wearing a tank top that still smelled of cum because I didn't see the point in washing something that would be dirtied again and again. I would sit at the bar and become a vessel, a whistle, a ceramic dog on a shelf – useless until used.

I reached the third floor and entered a room, high-ceilinged and airy. It was furnished by neutral-hued beanbags and white shag rugs. White plastic roses had been strung vertically from the ceiling, causing me to stoop. Along the far wall was a series of closed doors, each labeled with a plaque: LOVE ANGEL, TOUCH ANGEL, MY ANGEL, GO ANGEL. It smelled of baby powder and expensive shampoo. A horde of tan, leggy girls lounged about, clad in white tube tops, knee-socks, tennis skirts, scrunchies, gossiping crisscross-applesauce. One girl sat by the window, blanched by the late-afternoon light, knitting a baby hat in a white microkini. I felt like I'd walked into a casting call for a Xanax commercial and/or a porno so softcore as to be holy. A limby older woman with long blonde hair sat on an exercise ball behind a desk, writing in a diary with an actual lock. She beamed at me as I entered. *Welcome!* she called in a clipped Slavic accent. She wore the key to the diary on a chain around her neck. *How can I help you, my love?*

Oh . . . I glanced around; the girls had formed a chorus line in the center of the room. I felt lurid as a stop sign in my dirty pink sweatpants, unsure of what I wanted or why I had come. *I was j-just wondering . . . if y'all are still hiring.* I wiped my palms on my ass. *My friend Juliet referred me.*

Oh! The woman clutched her throat. She wore a loose white slip that gave away the shape of her ass when she stood in a sunbeam. *We love Juliet!* The girls bobbed their heads, a breeze through a cornfield. Even the floor-length lace curtains swelled at her name. *Any friend of Juliet's is a friend of mine. We are pretty fully staffed these days, but let me see what I can do . . .* She floated to her desk and began to flip through the diary. *And Juliet told you what we do here at the Palace? It's, how you say, specific.* Her voice was level, betraying nothing.

Yes, I said slowly. *She showed me the, um, rules.*

The woman smiled. *Guidelines, not rules.* She jabbed her finger at the diary. *Would you look at that! Camilla called out sick tonight. She works nights, 10 p.m. to 3 a.m.; that's when we get the broken hearts' club. Could you come back then?*

Sure, I heard myself saying. *I could do that.*

Perfect! the woman cried. *The universe works in mysterious ways.* She handed me a packet of papers to sign, all pale pink and smelling of vanilla. *You can call me Phaedra. And you are?*

I answered without thinking. *I'm Laney,* I said, then felt a clunk in my gut, like I'd made a mistake, like I'd given something away.

Laney, she said, fingering the key at her throat. *I feel good about you, Laney.* She touched my hair, before quickly retracting her hand. *I think you'll be a natural.*

Thank you, I muttered, edging toward the door. I agreed to return later that night, then saw myself out. The girls called goodbye as I took the stairs two at a time, their raised voices like a lullaby when you're trying to stay awake.

D id I stop to consider what this experiment entailed, this double doggy dare? I did. Pacing Hunter's apartment, I knew it was a bad idea. I knew that I could walk away. And yet I returned at 9.50 p.m. in a white eyelet sundress I'd found in Hunter's give-away pile, smelling of orchids and dread.

I'd assumed Phaedra would train me herself, that I'd spend my first shift in the shadows. Instead I was once-overed by a wispy knockout named Demi, who wore bridal lingerie and her hair in two buns. *Howdy partner,* she said. That was all. There were six other girls on the schedule for the late shift. Phaedra had already gone home for the night.

So we just … wait? I said, toying with a plastic rose. I hadn't thought to bring a book; I'd thought only of Hunter and the weird ways she touched men for pay. That fixation had brought me here, to the scene of the crime, which no longer seemed so criminal. Behind me, two girls played Twister, their full mugs of tea dangerously close to the mat.

Demi glanced at me over the top of her *Architectural Digest* and shrugged. *Pretty much,* she said. A little dust-colored dog lay in her lap. *Ninety percent of our business is walk-ins. Until someone comes, we just chill.*

The first customer arrived at 10.20 p.m. As soon as the doorbell rang, the girls around me sprang to their feet and formed a semicircle in the center of the room. The man who entered was nondescript, wearing a hoodie and jeans; he smelled vaguely of refried beans. He immediately pointed to a surfer-y chick on the end and said, *C'mon over here, Kylie.* She took him by the hand and led him to the room marked MY ANGEL, the two of them murmuring like sweethearts.

Over the course of the night, men drifted in and out; though we displayed ourselves each time, the vast majority called out the name of their favorite girl and barely glanced at the rest of us. I tried to detect a change in the men as they left but they generally looked the same, perhaps a bit pinker in the cheeks.

I felt invisible until almost midnight, when an older gentleman walked in. He was smartly dressed, as though on his way to the opera, with some sort of woodsy oil in what was left of his hair. Unlike the other customers, he took his time appraising us, making thoughtful little grunts. When he saw me, he clapped a hand to his mouth in pretend surprise. *New girl?* he said. Demi nodded and said, *She's filling in for Camilla.*

Well then, he said, *I'd be happy to show her the ropes.*

I stared at Demi. Her face was smooth, vacant, as though we worked at a pretzel place in the mall. *This way,* she said, leading us both to the room marked THEE ANGEL. She held the door open and whispered to me, *Don't worry, he's a regular. He knows the rules.* Then she smiled and cooed, *Enjoy yourselves!* before shutting the door.

A salt lamp cast soft rippled light on the walls of our room, which was barely bigger than a closet. Everything was dim and pink. The room contained a massage-bed covered in waxy white paper that made me think doctors, a folding chair, and an end table with a clock and a box of tissues. The tissues perturbed me most; I tried to think of the last time I'd dealt in cum, that spidery goo, its chlorine aftertaste. The room itself smelled of cloves and cinnamon, no trace of bodies past. The folding chair, I learned, was for the customer's clothes.

I'm Ernesto, the man said, taking my hand in both of his. He reminded me of a professor. Then he turned his back to me and dutifully stripped to his boxers, which were surprisingly dingy, frayed at the hem. He folded his coat over the back of the chair, then sat on the table. *I'm all yours,* he said with a pep that unnerved me. He swung his legs back and forth.

OK, I whispered. *Great.* My heart ping-ponged inside my chest. I was sweating so badly that little capital Ds had formed under the arms of my dress. *So,* I said, laboring to sound normal, *what are you looking for tonight?*

An ending, he said matter-of-factly. *The soup du jour.*

A . . . I could barely get the words out *. . . happy ending, you mean?*

He chuckled, not unkindly. *Not necessarily,* he said. *Whatever comes naturally. We'll see how it goes.*

I reached out to touch him, then withdrew my hand. His skin was alarmingly hot. Sensing my hesitation, he stood. *Are you nervous?* he said. His smile was gentle.

I nodded. *A little.*

I get it, he said. *It takes some getting used to.* He gestured to the table. *Lie down.* His chest was like a diner pancake, squishy and beige. *Just try not to move.*

Oh, I said, feeling my stomach twist. *OK* . . . I lay face down on the massage table, feeling the paper crinkle under me. He'd warmed it up with his thighs. I closed my eyes and tried to empty my mind, prepare myself. I waited for his touch, slimy or dry. I could smell his piney hair oil and anti-itch cream. I can always overpower him, I thought to myself. I weighed at least thirty pounds more than he did; this thought comforted me.

But he didn't touch me. I heard him circling the table. He was suddenly agitated, unsettled. *Oh*, he whimpered. *Oh, oh, oh.* He gripped the edge of the table with unexpected ferocity. *No!* he cried out, his voice both childish and ancient. I felt something wet on the back of my neck. Ernesto was crouched over me, weeping into my hair. *Why?* he moaned. *Why?* He sounded so sad that I began to cry too. *What will I do without you?* he moaned. *I don't want to live without you. I don't want to be here anymore.* When he took a jagged inhale, he made the table shake. I wanted to comfort him but I sensed this would forfeit the game; instead I held my breath and tried not to move, letting my snot drip to the floor. I played dead while Ernesto beat his chest; the sound was like lemons plopping onto a lawn. *It isn't fair*, he kept blubbering, *it just isn't fair.*

He grieved for what felt like a long time. Eventually his wails petered out into sighs, until the room was quiet but for the occasional sniffle. I felt his papery hand on my shoulder. *That was good*, he said hoarsely. *Very good.*

I sat up and was surprised to see that he'd already put his clothes back on. I looked at the clock on the table; only twenty minutes had passed.

Are you OK? I asked. I felt lightheaded.

He nodded, buttoning his coat. *Oh, yes! That was just what I needed. I feel so, oh, what's the word?* He clapped his hands together. *Refreshed.* And it was true that his eyes were shining, his cheeks heartily flushed. *What a rush, huh?*

I nodded, unsure if I should smile or continue to act somber. *Can I . . . do anything else for you?*

No can do, kiddo. He floated across the room. *Gotta go. My wife is waiting up for me.* He stuffed a wad of cash in my hands before waltzing out the door. *Till next time, angel.*

I sat in the folding chair after he left, thumbing through my money. I couldn't name what I was feeling. A keen sense of accomplishment, a tingle in my cunt. A piercing loneliness. Residual longing, as though his had flaked off. It was all mushed together in me, a feeling both glitzy and dire. I had expected to feel closer to Hunter but instead I felt distant, zipped into my sadness, like when I used to get stoned and ride the bus alone, pretending to be sober; I would look at the people around me and think, no one knows the truth but me. It was a cozy solipsism, my pain like lucky underwear, meaningful only to me.

Eventually I got up and finger-combed my hair. In the main room I found an empty beanbag by the window and sank down. A stick of incense burned into a teacup on the windowsill. The girl next to me was looking at her phone, laughing without making a sound. When she noticed me, she held out her screen: it showed a picture of a wet cat with the caption BAD HAIR DAY. I closed my eyes and held my breath. I practiced slowing my pulse, quieting my body's cycles. I felt certain that the next man who walked in would pick me. He would clock my sloped shoulders, grave eyes; he would see that I was made for this, this game of aping death. Behind me, the dust-colored dog gnawed on a rose. I could hear his little grunts of pleasure, but I didn't turn to look.

For the rest of the week, I worked the night shift at the Palace. On Friday I went to a party thrown by Hunter's friend Ducky. I didn't want to go but I knew it would make Hunter happy. *He likes you,* she'd assured me over the phone. *Everyone likes you. What's not to like?*

I showed up early in jeans that I'd hacked into shorts. *Oh, honey,* Ducky said, *look at you!* I drifted around his apartment and pretended to drink a cocktail he'd named Cher the Blame. Beautiful girls draped themselves into doorways, talking about Last Night. *You won't believe where we ended up last night* . . . There was always something happening in their lives that needed to be dissected. *No!* her friends screeched. *You fucking stupid slut!* I waited in line for the bathroom and watched two boys make out against a wall. I found myself soothed by the straightforwardness of their actions, the trusty linearity of lust, until one pulled back and said, *Are you really chewing gum?* They began to bicker; a pile of babes emerged from the bathroom, having apparently all swapped shirts.

I lasted fifteen minutes at Ducky's. Then I dug out my coat from the heap on the bed and made my way downtown, practicing death on the bus: eyes slitted, mouth ajar. The woman sitting next to me shook my shoulder. *Hey,* she said, *you OK, honey? Hello?* Her shopping bags banged into me, a butterfly-like battery, and she looked annoyed when I sat upright. *Jesus,* she snapped, *I thought you had OD'd or something.* She gathered her bags and moved to a different seat. I rode the rest of the way with a glow in my gut. I made $900 at the spa that night and slept until well after noon.

Then came the morning when I awoke to a new text from Hunter. *Good news!! Z is all healed so I booked a flight home. See you tomorrow my angel!!* She sent a selfie, looking Vaseliney but radiant, wearing a shirt I didn't recognize. My heart swelled at the sight of her: I still couldn't believe she wanted me. *Kiss kiss to my Laney love. You'll soon be in my arms.*

I wasted no time. I cleaned her apartment in a manic spurt. I took a taxi to the gourmet grocery store to get the fancy coffee beans she liked, the weapon-like rye bread. I stripped the sheets and washed everything but the white dress I'd been wearing to work. I needed it for one more night.

I got to the spa at 9.45 p.m., my wet hair in two braids. Things picked up quickly. By 1.30 a.m. I'd seen five dudes and made enough money to pay rent for two months. When the doorbell rang again and we scrabbled into place, I felt focused, lit up. I angled my body toward the door and was surprised to see a woman walk in. Phaedra greeted her fluidly, petting her hand. *Welcome!* she sang. *Make yourself comfortable, no rush, no rush.* Everyone acted normal as the woman appraised us, worrying the strap of her purse.

It was difficult to gauge her age; she'd had a lot of work done. The skin of her cheeks was stretched taut, her lips like deflated party balloons. She had a sullen feline look, her green eyes flecked with yellow, her body poky and small in a neat black skirt suit. Her legs had the slightly wet look of nylons, something I hadn't seen since I worked at The Nugget, guiding retirees to the smoking floor. It was impossible to tell what this woman was feeling, if she'd be sweet and melty in a room or demanding, punitive. I'd been lucky in my week at the spa; all my customers had been easy sells. The fact of my breasts hushed them. These men responded well to my directness; as soon as we entered a room, I asked if they wanted an ending, then lay down on the table and let the mourning begin. I felt sure of my skills as a corpse. I'd eavesdropped on enough of the other girls' conversations, however, to know that men could get greedy; sometimes they wanted more, something splashy and brutal, a more obvious violence. They sought a haunted house, not a drowsy sorority. Some of them demanded refunds from Phaedra because their girl 'fidgeted' or 'didn't sell it', because her skin was too warm or that she was ticklish. They came for gore and got freeze-tag instead. *Child's play,* I heard one man grumble on his way out. *Too light, too fluffy. What fucking happened to darkness?*

Now the woman pointed at me with a French-tipped nail. Her blonde hair was streaked with silver. *You,* she said meekly. *I think I'd like to see you.* Then she turned to Phaedra and stage-whispered, *Just so you know, your elevator is broken.*

I led her into LOVE ANGEL. *After you,* I said, remembering to smile. *You can take your clothes off, if you like.*

She held her purse with both hands, like she was boarding a bus in the bad part of town. *All right,* she murmured. She took off her kitten heels first, lining them up under the chair; she had trouble with her skirt's zipper but didn't ask for help. There was a shyness to her movements, a skittish femininity that felt almost teenaged, like she'd not yet acclimated to fleshiness, like her hips might be a hoax. She had to sit down on the chair to take off her nylons, which she then held in her hand like two snakeskins. *I'd prefer to keep my underwear on,* she said, *if it's OK with you.*

Whatever you like. I tried not to stare at her strappy beige girdle. The skin of her legs was smooth and white, like a new tub of ice cream. Perhaps because she was a woman I could pick up on her fear; I heard it in her pauses, I saw it in the way she smiled without meaning to. It made me uncomfortable though I tried to speak calmly. *Have you been here before?*

Oh, no. She looked at the ceiling, still gripping her nylons. *My husband used to come here. Quite a lot, actually. I found the name of this place in his diary. Over and over. He was rather ... obsessed.*

Did he die? I asked before I could stop myself.

She smiled, then covered her mouth with her hand. *No,* she said. *He left me.* She forced a laugh. *I suppose he could be dead by now. Who knows?* She touched her throat. *Anyway, I was curious.* She left it at that.

Well, I'm happy you're here. I smoothed out my dress. *Why don't I get on up the table and we'll take it from there?*

Oh. Her eyes flashed with panic, as if I'd gone in for a kiss. *Perhaps I misunderstood. I was hoping I could ... be the one to lie down?* She gestured to the table. *I'd like to try it that way, if it's OK with you.*

Of course! My voice was too loud; I felt my heart skitter. *Whatever you like!*

I helped her onto the table, the paper barely puckering under her weight. She was so dainty, so thin; she reminded me of a ballerina, that studied frailty. She lay face down, her arms at her sides; some of her gray hairs stuck straight up from static. *Like this?* she said.

Perfect. I took a long breath. *Now just relax and stay still.*

The room went silent. For one moment I blanked. Then I closed my eyes and thought of the things I tried not to. I thought of Nevada at night, the black desert cleaved by neon. I thought of the first house we grew up in, the gravel yard, the yellow plaque above the kitchen sink that read DOGS EAT FIRST. Everywhere we moved, this plaque came too. I thought of the La-Z-Boy my mother would sleep in, stinking of menthols and tiger balm. Sometimes I rubbed her feet while Sophia rubbed her shoulders. *My sweet girls*, Mom would mutter before she became incoherent. I thought of the bunk bed I shared with Sophia, put together by a so-called friend of our mom's we both found so handsome we'd go mute when he visited. *It's the skinny twins*, he teased us. He and my mom drank Twisted Teas and watched TV; when *American Idol* was on, they let us watch too. One summer he painted butterflies on the walls of our bedroom, something we'd later get in trouble for with the landlord. Trouble, trouble. Nevada was sunsets, nervy and pink; it was oranges for dinner because it was too hot to cook, it was driving while smoking and getting in trouble with people who did far worse.

When I was in high school, my mother asked me, *Did Jeremiah ever touch you?* That was the name of her friend. *No way!* I cried. *Never!* I felt angry at her for suggesting it, for scrambling my memory of a man who'd been kind. It felt unfair of her to pin him as our family's bogeyman, as if by singling him out she could undo her own failures, as if he could be blamed for my lack of ambition and Sophia's depressive spells, which got longer each time. We both knew Sophia felt sad but I never thought it was serious. *She's wound up*, I would say when friends asked why she wasn't eating or speaking. *Too many Red Bulls.* I wouldn't find out until Sophia's memorial that our father had killed himself too. *Runs in the family*, a distant aunt sighed. *Chemical imbalance and all that jazz.* She licked egg salad off her fingers. *Take care of yourself, love.* He even did it the same way as she did: slit wrists in a shower stall because we didn't have a tub.

I touched my cheek; it was damp. The little pink massage room went wavy as I wept. *Sophia*, I whispered. *I miss you. I miss you.* It was all that I could think to say. The woman on the table lay perfectly still. When I looked at her back, I didn't see Sophia. I just saw a body, hard angles, crimped skin. I got closer and studied the sunspots on her shoulders, little cappuccino stains. I wondered if my mother had them too; she loved to sit in the yard on her one day off, sunbathing with the dogs. *Sunscreen is for narcs,* she'd bark, her skin turning the color of rotisserie chicken. Even on triple-digit days she wore jeans. I never once saw my mother in shorts; a lifer waitress at a big-shot steakhouse, she was embarrassed of her varicose veins. She and this woman could be the same age. I let my gaze linger on the woman's bare legs, a pink rash on her upper thighs as if they had been touched too much. For the first time I wondered: did my mom shave her legs? Did she ever wear a bathing suit? Did she have a secret tattoo, a rose or the initials of an ex-lover on the crook of her thigh? My eyes drifted up and I noticed blonde fuzz on the back of the woman's neck. It struck me that everyone must have this, a soft spot, a hinge; she had had that fuzz there since she was a baby. I began to cry harder, thinking not of Sophia but of my mother's dumb plaque. The last time I'd been home the plaque was hung up over the sink, which was cluttered with the baby bottles she used to feed her dogs. That was many years ago now but I didn't need to go back to know it was still there. So much shredded, lost to time, and that was what remained.

I managed to stop crying with five minutes left on the clock. *You can get up now,* I said. *Take your time.* I extended my hand and helped the woman off the table. Her eyes were glassy.

Thank you, she whispered, slithering into her skirt. For the first time, she struck me as ravishing. I tried not to stare as she put on her tights. Her lips were the color of a box of chocolates.

I hovered by the door, snotty tissues in my hand. My teeth were chattering, my cheeks ablaze. There was something I wanted to say to her but I didn't know what. I felt the giddiness of a crush, the neediness of a kitten; perhaps this was the post-grieving rush Ernesto so craved, a zippy sense of having been flayed.

At last the woman was dressed; she fluffed her hair and stood up. *Well,* she said. She seemed embarrassed, as if I were a stranger who had fainted in her lap. Neither of us knew how to name what we had shared. She licked her lips and forced a smile. *How much do I owe you?*

My heart cramped but I managed to smile back. *$400,* I muttered, *not including tip.*

I looked at the floor as she scrounged in her purse. Suddenly she couldn't leave fast enough for me. I wanted to go home, take off this damp dress, disappear in Hunter's bed. I wanted to fill her apartment with roses, real ones that would die. I wanted to pick her up from the airport and kiss her on the throat and say, *Don't leave me alone again.* I no longer cared who Juliet was; Hunter was touchable, warm in the night. She often went to bed in pajamas and awoke in the nude. The woman handed me a wad of twenties. *That should do the trick*, she chirped, not looking at me.

I took the cash. *Thanks.*

Thank you, she echoed, her voice soft and far. And that was that. I held open the door and she left. I listened for the sound of her kitten heels on the stairs; instead I heard the elevator creaking to life. Phaedra must've finally called a handyman, I thought. Just my luck; it gets fixed on my very last night at the Palace. But by the time my shift ended and I was on my way back to Hunter's, the elevator was out of service again, a hasty sign taped to the doors – DON'T GO. ∎

Sharon Olds

While the Bear

While the bear was walking
slowly
past the porch,
he looked the size of the porch – his nose
out of sight beyond the baluster rails
before his tail had come into sight.
My eyes had made an O and an O
and my mouth made an O.
The neighbors had said he weighed 300 pounds but he looked
    like 500,
swaying from side to side, exhausted in the heat,
his muzzle the brown velvet of a child's dress,
his back feet small and close together like the flippers of
    a walrus.
He made me think of Carl,
his shy frown and the width of his chest.
I ran around to the side window
and watched him lumber into the woods.
I thought of Carl yawning and stretching in his coffin,
the pine cracking apart, the ground breaking open.
I went out under the sky this morning
and found a big, warm, heavy
blackberry, and buried it in my mouth
where it would never see the sky again.

First Date, with Little Summer Shower

They reminded me of something, and I could not remember –
the drops close together all over the pane,
lit from behind by the sodium streetlamp –
maybe the drops, they drop into eyes at birth.
The elm and the locust in the fitful midnight
wind were making the droplets seem to
stir, I did not stop walking
from one end of the apartment to the other and back,
on a long oval,
I was not drunk and I was not sober,
I was not in love with him because I did not
know him, I walked, not restless but had no
intention to stop, till I had orbited,
several times, the table bearing my
water tumbler and his water tumbler,
mine the old highball glass
spotted with crystal dots like little
jacquard mirrors – like drops splattered
on the pane – and his lowball glass with one
flattened teardrop in the thick base,
I held it up to the ceiling light in
hopes there would be the big wet
print of a lower lip, and there was, it was
huge – as children say, it was

ginormous, seared like Eros, and the striae of his
mouth were there, the cool feathered
lightning that joins the earth and the cloud,
and near this was a hedge of cumulo-
nimbi, a cauliflower bouquet
of fingerprints, each floret
particular, like no other on the hand,
or on the other hand, or on the earth.
And he'd held it, and put it down onto his
shirt until a darkness appeared
over his heart – then picked it up and
kiss-sipped, and put it down
again, the thumb of his other hand
back and forth over my neck and
seed pearls of the necklace on my neck,
until I had to say Have mercy, and he'd
stop and move away and then
start, I loved being the ground
that drew the figure of his fingers and palm –
unstoppable, in them, the desire to
go where you desire them to go,
gravity magnetism,
looking into my eyes while rubbing and
rubbing my skin, as if I am done for,

into the mesh hedge of whoever he
is I am plunging. But not tonight,
tonight he is walking across the park,
under my umbrella, case in his hand
the print of my hand. And when he left
I thought a bit before I picked this pen
up, but there was the rose patch briar of his
identity on my mind – and the dense
tiny bullseyes of the storm on the window,
the still life in motion.

Sex as Between

I have thought of sex as between two people –
though for some it might be three, or four, or twenty-four –
but I know that sex is by itself within each one of us
    also,
tolling its hours and seasons, the way in the
grandfather clock, in the curved slot
above the face, the moon came up
crescent, full, then waning as lust
waxes on its own in each body, as well
as within a couple. When I feel desire,
when he is not there, immediately
I think of him, as if he has caused it,
but sometimes it's just sex's timepiece,
within me, both hands straight down, or straight up.
But I like it to be connected to him
in its origin, as it will be in its
completion and exhaustion, as if the link between
it and him is like what keeps my
feet on the earth. I used to feel
as if my eyes sort of made the things
they saw. The thought of the things alone,
unseen, waiting to exist – I think that
reminded me of the dread chill
of some childhood hours.
If you were not loved – which you were not – you were
    nothing.
In his arms, in his burly embrace, that nothing
seems to cease to exist,
though not as if it never had existed.

When I Fell Forward

When I fell forward, ankles tangled
in his oxygen tubing, hands by my sides,
I turned my face, so when the floor came up
it struck me on the cheek,
and the next morning I had a purple
raccoon eye, and a purple parenthesis
beneath my mouth.
A month later, the swelling has gone from
pear to plum to walnut to olive
to an olive pit. I want to say
my mother never beat me. Beat me has a wild aura.
She punished me by requiring that I wait
half naked on the center of her rug, a half-hour or so,
and there was the stile bridge of her lap
over which a soul would bend. The back of the
hairbrush was the shell of a murdered being
who had swum, and laid eggs. The blows were
smithy-anvil hard, 4/4 time,
they stopped only when my sobbing was coming in
rolling combers, 'the child's spirit
has to be broken', a Wasp beating
in an elegant room, an opera in which
one person brought out the song
in another. It was a lesson in being
the possession of another, as she had been
the possession of her mother. I was beaten by the dead
who had been beaten by the dead, until we howled. My mother
was a singer. Once again, I am singing her here.

Flash Memories

Of the things I so liked about him – how evenly
he bears his weight on the balls of his feet, how
easily he turns immediately
to either side – the ways I knew he was the
one for me, for this life. And when they're
the one, there is something about the sex
with them which seems over the top of the mortal,
into the future history of the earth
when he and I will no longer exist. When I say eternal,
I mean intensity, and duration,
when you think <u>I will never sleep with anyone
else in my life</u>, and pump your fist.
When you're sitting on the bedroom floor, taking off your
stockings, lacooning with them, and his back is to you,
and he's bending down, naked, to finish
taking off his second sock,
what you look up and see is what you always
wanted to see, and what follows is what you always
wanted to follow. And even if
you don't know how to live with him and still
have your own inner life,
still you feel, under the keel
of your soul, open ocean – the steady
sweet slaps of the chop of his soul coming
in, under you, with the tide going
out, as if human possibility,
for you, including the suffering, is summed up in this man.

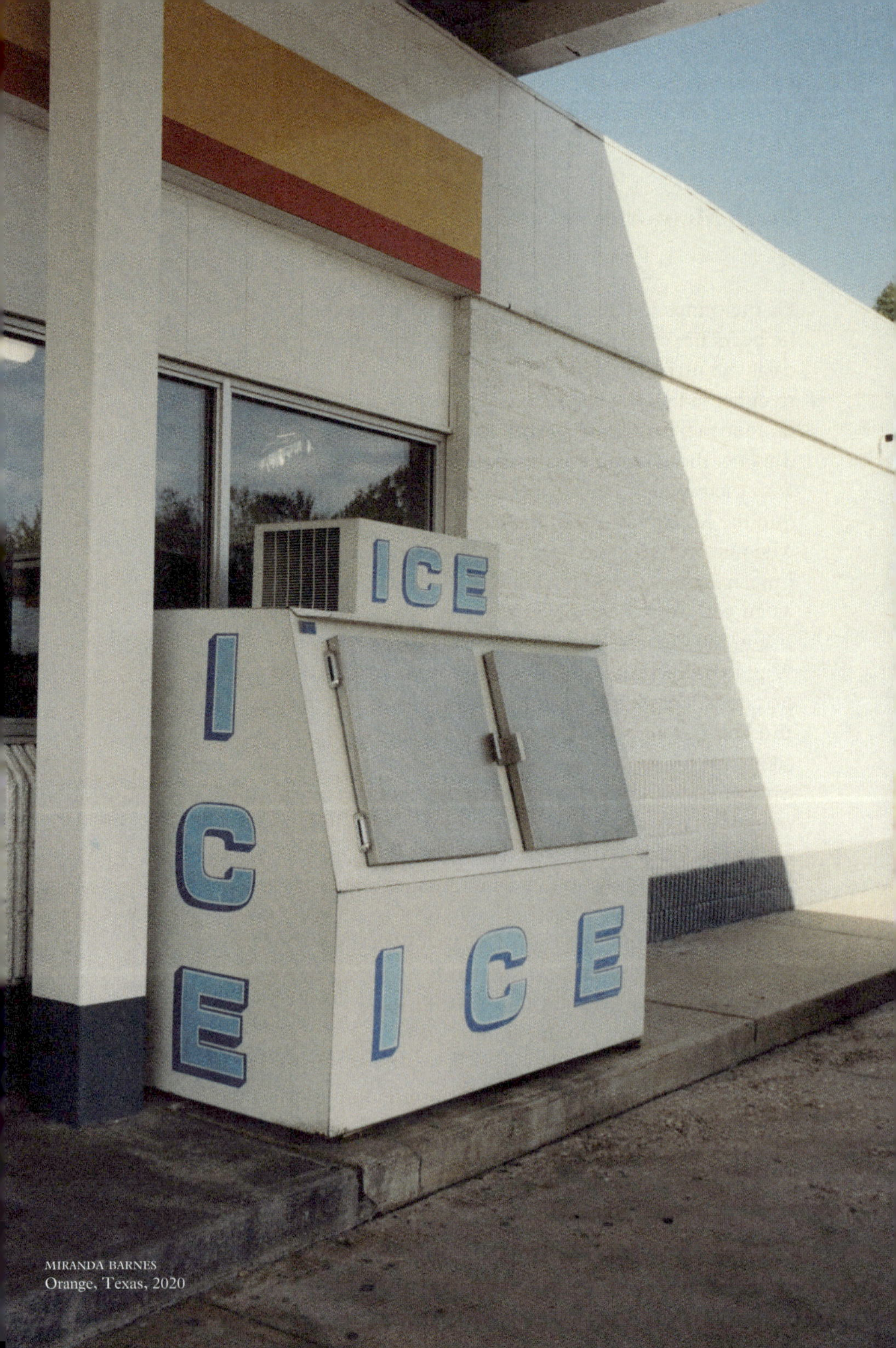

MIRANDA BARNES
Orange, Texas, 2020

NOTHING NEW HERE

Natasha Stagg

As Nance told it, it sounded like nothing.

Heath was half listening from the back seat of the car. 'Ancient history, though, right?'

'No,' said Nance. 'No. This was only last week.' Only last week, she had awoken in a cold sweat, alone. She had reached for her phone and found it charging on the nightstand as usual, but without a second phone next to it. 'Is that normal? Heath? Was he like this in college?'

'Nance,' Don interrupted from the driver seat. 'Are we really doing this again?' He looked back at Heath in the rearview mirror. 'She's gonna tell the story as if I'm a monster.'

'No,' said Nance, 'I'm gonna tell it as it happened, to me.'

Heath looked down at his phone. Nothing new. The girl hadn't posted or messaged him, so he couldn't reply. He searched through his other threads. Maybe he'd left someone else hanging. Not really, or at least not recently. It would be hours before they got to the house.

Nance had never once reached for Don in their bed and not found him there, she told Heath. 'It was disconcerting.' More than that. 'Terrifying.'

'Alright,' said Don.

She called him – he was always the last call on her phone, top of the list, easy. He didn't answer. She tried again. She thought she might be dreaming. But in dreams, phones don't work. Numbers are not names – they're scrambled captchas or license plates, glitching or unmoving. No, it was not a dream, it was just nightmarish. She called fifteen times, texted, messaged on apps in case his phone was dead and he had access to someone else's. Nothing.

Now, thought Heath, would be a good time for Don to jump in to spare him the full rant – they were on this trip together, so the story would necessarily end happily. Don was focused on the road, although it was straight and uncrowded. Indecipherable crops rolled by, offering Heath no distraction. When he gazed out the window, he was revisited by a slight carsickness not experienced since childhood.

Nance had got out of bed and put on shoes, she said. Still in a T-shirt and sweat shorts, because changing her clothes felt wrong, she had walked down the stairs and out the front door. Don's car was gone. It was after three. She went back upstairs and opened the shutter to their shared closet, as if some gap in the row of clothes would clue her in to where he'd gone.

Nance and Don must have made up within a few days of this argument, thought Heath. And then today, they'd loaded up the Explorer, driven downtown together and picked up Heath from the parking lot of his apartment building, overnight bag in hand, on their way to a weekend rental in the country.

'Want to see me tomorrow?' asked a text sent to Heath. The number wasn't saved, but he scrolled up and recognized the conversation. 'Out of town, but what about next week?' He remembered how her hair felt. Every part of her was softer than the pads of his fingers, which now gripped the phone, a portal away from this couple and the couple they'd be meeting at the house, another friend from school and his new girlfriend. An ellipsis signaled typing. It disappeared.

Minutes before, they had been laughing at the names of roadside diners and gossiping about the alcoholic boyfriend of a mutual friend. In fact, the discussion about the night Don went missing had only started because Heath had said something like, 'I don't think I've ever seen you two argue.' He'd meant it as encouragement, not a provocation. Don had responded with something like, 'Oh, you'd be surprised,' and then, like the revving of an ignition, came the too-familiar buzz of bickering starting up. It was a noise Heath usually did everything in his power to avoid. This was why he was still single, his sister would say, to which he'd nod, pretending to understand.

'Sure,' said the text, which had taken a beat too long to arrive. Sure? He was somehow already disappointing her. 'Forget it,' he wanted to text back, but instead sent a cartoon face with a stupid smile. He was reminded of a sound she made, a moan inside of his mouth. He pulled up a selfie she'd posted with pleading eyes. 'Sure,' he could hear her sigh. The tiny photo trembled with the motion of the car.

Don breathed through his nose so loudly it turned Nance's head. 'Nothing to say?' she hissed.

'But you got ahold of him in the end,' Heath said to Nance.

'No,' Nance shook her head. 'He just came home, after I'd fallen back asleep. I could've called around or filed a missing person's report. Who doesn't answer their phone?'

'And where were you, Don?' Heath asked, understanding his role as the child they didn't have, the entertainment and the entertained. It was a game that had started before his arrival and would continue after his departure, but he couldn't sit it out – the third wheel's function in arguments was always pivotal. The landscape outside tilted into tall orchards, silhouetted leaves that caused the sunlight to glisten too quickly. Heath closed his eyes and still saw the pattern flashing through their lids. His stomach inched closer to his throat.

'Where was I?' Don repeated. Nance shrunk into her seat and stared ahead.

'Why don't you say where I was?' said Don. 'Go ahead.'

'I went back to sleep,' said Nance, quieter. 'When I woke up, you were back. You never told me.'

'I did, though,' said Don. 'I told you.'

Heath could hear the strain of springs and opened his eyes. Nance had turned around and put her head between the driver's and front passenger's seats. Her expression was softer than he'd imagined. She blinked slowly. This was a very Nance blink, usually utilized for comic effect.

'He was at his ex's house,' said Nance. 'Don woke up in the middle of the night, didn't tell me where he was going, got dressed and drove to another woman's house, a woman who has kids –'

'They were with their dad,' said Don.

'On a night she didn't have her kids, because you know that. You know her fucking schedule and you understand, and she understands, that if you go over there in the middle of the night –'

'She called *me*.'

'Right, and it's normal to call someone else's man in the middle of the night –'

'She has a history of mental instability.'

'And she can't call her own ex-husband or her own – whoever –'

'She called me.'

'Yeah, so Don was helping his ex –'

'My friend.'

'His friend. He was helping his friend. Someone he used to date.'

'We never dated.'

'Someone he used to fuck. Whatever. Right? He went all the way over there to talk her out of a suicide attempt, or I don't know, was she trying to kill herself, or just having a panic attack?'

Don's silence curdled Nance's question. She was not speaking correctly about psychological disorders, Heath gathered. Don was out saving someone. What difference did it make who it was? Everything became spiked with accusations once the initial excitement made room for domesticity: negotiating schedules, family visits on Christmas, groceries every Sunday. Inevitably someone forgot to get eggs, someone drank all the beer. This was one more misunderstanding, amid the many others.

No one spoke for some time. Heath noticed that no music played, that it had been like this the whole trip. He wondered if Nance had fallen asleep.

Don took them onto an exit, announcing the need for gas. They rolled up to a pump and with the tap of a large button the SUV turned off. Nance, very much awake, hopped out and crossed the lot to the convenience store with one arm wrapped around the strap of her purse, the other swaying. Heath followed her, hands in pockets, through the automatic doors. He stood outside a locked bathroom and watched as Nance stared at a display. She didn't look up, but the forced serenity of her face told him she knew that Heath was there.

They had first met at a sports bar downtown, what, six years ago? She was half the size of anyone in their group but took up more airspace altogether, darting from the bartender to her new boyfriend to his friends, showing a genuine interest in IPAs and football while meeting the gaze of each man, impressing upon everyone a brown-eyed mischief. At the end of the evening, she had held Don's hand as they walked to his car, pulling his arm in the way of a child leaving a toy store, excited to go home but sad to leave.

Watching them depart, Heath had – because he couldn't help it – pictured Don and Nance having sex.

Each following encounter was fortified by that first impression. Heath and Nance spoke at other games and other get-togethers until the initial frustration at her unavailability wore away, and she became his friend.

Over the last six years, birthmarks and kitchen burns became noticeable. With familiarity, postures were loosened, necks were lined, and waists bloated. Heath wondered how she would appear to him from across a gas station mart if he'd never seen her before in his life – would she now be in the category of women who didn't do it for him? Would he, if seeing her for the first time, in their current states, picture her naked? Maybe at that very moment she was wondering the same thing. She crossed her arms, which had gained a ruddiness behind the biceps. Her eyes were glassy and sullen, unimpressed by the selection.

An industrial-strength flush sounded and the bathroom door opened. Heath turned to let a dust-blonde woman hand him the knob. He glanced backward before stepping in. Nance was holding a Cheetos bag with both hands, blocking her entire head. A life-sized Chester Cheetah face glared at Heath, sunglasses and smirking snout pointed in his direction. Nance twisted the bag from side to side like a sock puppet over a partition.

Inside the Explorer, they returned to the standoff and sat listening to one another's silence. Highway traffic thickened as clouds evaporated beneath a midday sun. Vehicles emptied into every lane. Don was, Heath noted, a smooth and confident driver. Had he always been? In college, cars were mostly used for going home to parents' houses on laundry days or breaks. Don, the philosophy major, didn't offer rides the way Matt would. Heath remembered that Matt, who would presently be joining them for the weekend, had driven a souped-up cherry-red truck in college, but he couldn't picture the type of car Don had driven. That was something he could ask to break the ice.

'Didn't have a car,' chirped Don, his voice falsely upbeat.

'Hm,' Heath said, trying again to smooth the tension. 'I thought everyone had a car.'

Nance had not been listening. She turned to Heath. 'You probably know her,' she said.

This again. Yeah, if he thought about it, surely Heath would know of a woman Don had slept with, someone who now had kids and what sounded like a pill or alcohol problem. In fact, there were a few options. He would need some more clues to narrow it down.

'He doesn't,' said Don.

'Who does then?' Nance asked.

Heath received another text, the word 'Bored' and a selfie. In this one, her head was wrapped in a towel and water from a shower was clinging to a bare collarbone. She'd put on lipstick for it. 'Sexy,' he wrote back, knowing she wanted more than that. It was called a trap for a reason. He wanted more too. He wanted to know that the image was only for him. He wanted to sit her on his lap in a big empty house with giant windows facing a lake. He wanted a boat.

'Why do none of us know her?' Nance said.

Don and Heath met in their first semester of college. The friendship hardened on the infamous night they liked to talk about not talking about. 'We do not discuss the infamous night,' was a refrain he and Don and Matt would still say, making a zipper motion over their lips. There had been a house party, likely at some dilapidated, shared Victorian with a torn-up yard but appearing in their memories as a mansion with never-ending kegs. They had conspired before arriving to lie about being freshmen. Every one of them ended up with a girl or two that evening, in bathrooms or bedroom closets. At one point Heath zeroed in on two girls and elegantly brought Don into the conversation, dividing to conquer. Don never wanted to hang out with the philosophy students again. Heath could still see him cheering, holding an open bottle of whiskey over his head as they walked up the street away from that house, the sun rising.

'He was my wingman from day one,' Don would tell new acquaintances, an arm over Heath's shoulder. That was before Nance, who asked Don to move in with her as soon as his lease was up, less than a year into their relationship. It didn't make sense, him finding a new place, when she had a whole inherited house. There were ball-and-chain jokes here and there, but otherwise, Don seemed, more than most of the guys Heath had seen settle down, genuinely happy.

Once they were alone, Heath would ask Don what was up – how he was really doing. Because if Don had indeed gone to a woman's home after some midnight cry for help, the possibility of an affair had to have crossed his mind. But what constituted an affair? Were the rules of a relationship, in this milieu and moment, such that no one was allowed to lean back into the past, that everyone was always obligated to stoop forward? Heath had always wondered if there wasn't a way to auto-renew some girls, restarting the process of knowing them, with adjusted settings. If he thought about it, every girl still meant something to him, and maybe always would. And if they aligned sexually but not otherwise, did it follow that they couldn't go on aligning in that one way?

These were people, after all, not train cars. One did not simply transfer to the next, heading always in the so-called right direction. Life and time weren't like that; each instant contained every instant that had ever and would ever occur. Even if he couldn't quite grasp it, Heath believed this with all he had.

Girls would often lean on him after their breakups with subsequent men, happy at first to wiggle back into his arms, this time without expectations. But then, in bed, a conversation about stability would start, and in due course they would leave with a new determination to not contact him. Sometimes, they would return yet again. It was sad, he decided, that such women were so accustomed to breaking things off the moment they didn't get their way. Still, he knew it wasn't entirely their fault.

Nance opened a bag of Corn Nuts. 'What does she look like?' Her crunching forced a casual tone.

'You wouldn't be jealous.'

'No?' Nance threw another handful into her mouth. 'Can I see her?'

'And what would that do?' Don's voice had a squeezed composure to it too now. Heath had heard of couples embracing infidelity as a coping mechanism. If they forgot he was there, maybe they could take a huge step in their relationship.

'What does she look like?'

'Ugly,' said Don.

Nance bunched the Mylar bag in one hand and dropped it in the footwell. Heath saw Don glance at the freshly vacuumed mat under her feet, his mouth just open enough to let out a fricative. From the back seat, he watched as Nance lunged sideways, grasping at Don's shoulder, clawing at his wrists, finally launching herself up onto her knees and crashing down, pro-wrestler style, into the driver's seat. Heath saw Don's hands let go of the wheel in confusion. He watched as Nance took over steering, thrashing them left and right until they hit a metal guardrail, and the sound blocked out any of the words they were screaming, any of the thoughts Heath had, any other instant that had occurred in his life or ever would.

Heath came back from the kitchen and settled on a corner of the rug near Matt, handing him the beer he'd requested. He sipped from his own, a hoppy local brew with green and pink spirals on its label. Don rose from his seat in the big armchair and fetched a piece of wood for the fire. The absent hosts had left a pile of perfectly chopped logs, as clean as sliced Gouda with brown wax rinds, in an iron basket next to a set of hanging tools.

Nance entered from the half-bathroom and stood near Don. She picked up a pair of firewood tongs that accordioned apart and together. 'These are nicer than ours,' she mumbled to herself, continuing a pattern of scrutinizing each of the house's communal objects, from serving spoon to towel rack. All the guests did this, owing to the inevitable contrasts and parallels that could be made to the things they had at home.

The car was all scraped up on one side, and that was the first thing anyone saw when it pulled up. Don said that they'd gotten into an accident. Nance had helped him come up with a story about someone drifting into their lane and running them off the road. Had they been going any faster, the party decided, things could have been much, much worse, and so the annual reunion was also a celebration of their survival. No one was injured, only rattled, and the adrenaline made them better than ever, more than fine, happy to be alive, together again, approaching middle age, away from Matt's kids and their mother. Matt's girlfriend, Leandra, was meeting everyone for the first time. To her, nothing could be off, because she had nothing with which to compare.

Leandra was, contrary to everyone's expectations, a normal person, with pores that pulled straight when she smiled and a few grays at the temples growing out of their latest dye treatment. The discrepancy between her and the old college friends was only recognizable in the details of a braided twine bracelet threaded with amber beads and a silver anklet made from tiny, linked paperclips, each hinting at a history of impulsiveness, travel, and street food on cloud-level terrain.

'Tomorrow, we can take the canoe out,' said Matt. He'd made the arrangements and read through the laminated binder of instructions. The boat, oars and life jackets were in the garage and part of the deal. There was a chest filled with half-empty bottles of bug spray and sunscreen, too, he informed them. It was amazing, the way things accumulated at the secondary homes of others. He had noticed doubles of books on the shelves.

Heath wondered if Matt saw how quiet Don and Nance were after dinner, but then, Matt was never known for his perceptiveness, and besides, fires tend to permit, even beckon silence. Nance, cross-legged on the carpet, stared into the hearth and the wet of her eyes reflected its movement, resembling the quiver of tears. Don sat on an ottoman and held an iron poker in both hands, face lowered, eyelids and forehead reddening, lips folded inward. As the air around them changed temperature and density, Heath saw them all as meat being smoked and sealed, their outsides crisping and their insides tenderizing. Leandra cleared her throat, sipped from a wineglass, and laughed, or said a word that was the sound of a laugh.

'I was in a car accident once. I was seventeen. Sixteen? I was with my dad, in Mexico. My dad isn't Mexican. I mean, he also didn't live in Mexico. I didn't know him as a kid, and then, once we met, we'd go on these trips instead of me visiting him. Or him visiting me. I've never asked him why.'

Heath felt sorry for Leandra, not because she hadn't known her father growing up or because she'd been in a car accident, but because her expectations for the weekend were likely nowhere close to being met. He wondered how she and Matt would discuss the group dynamic that night in bed. Then, of course, he pictured them having sex.

'We were on this vacation with his girlfriend and the whole thing was strange because they were basically strangers to me. My grandparents lived in Boston, so I thought I knew what Catholic churches were like, but the ones in Mexico looked like birdhouses on

Christmas trees. It was hard to take anything seriously – everything was like a toy, even their places of *worship*.

'But so, we were driving along these cliffs, and we smashed into the back of a car that had smashed into another car, one after the other, all crumpled into each other, with smoke everywhere, dust, horns blaring, people yelling, dogs barking. This is how I remember it. Somehow, I'm seeing it from an aerial view, which of course I couldn't have had.

'I was wearing my seat belt, and it snapped my stomach. I thought I was going to throw up. I remember the sound, like a smack, like someone slapping both your ears at once. I guess we were the last in the pile-up. There were cars driving around us. We played a game, guessing the color of the next one to pass by.

'We waited there for hours, in the heat, with no AC. Eventually the police came, and a tow truck, and pulled us all apart one by one, and my dad had to speak with someone in his terrible Spanish. It was dark by the time we could be towed away, back in the direction we'd come from. We ended up staying in the same motel we'd left that morning, and I think that was the end of the trip. The car was a rental, so who knows what returning it was like. I can't remember that part at all.

'What I remember the most vividly is the ride in the tow truck, up in the front seat, all of us squished together and silent, except the driver speaking into his radio. We had to go past all the busted cars to get onto another highway. It went from bad to worse; the crash at the front was just twisted metal. It wasn't obvious what had caused the original collision, or even which cars were involved; they were so, so torn up.

'There was an ambulance that must have come from the other way, and it was just then lifting someone inside, and that's the part that horrified me, that I'd been trying to kill time, lying on a big rock in the shade, and meanwhile there was someone down the road maybe bleeding to death. Then I really thought I'd throw up. It made no sense, why our car got taken care of before that person was in a hospital. There must have been many, many serious injuries. Maybe deaths.

'I saw this big group of people – all ages, old, babies, everyone – some lying on blankets on the dirt, some sitting in strollers and wheelchairs. It was dark but I could see blood on clothes, makeshift bandages and slings. They were lit by our headlights. The red glow of the ambulance made everything look bloody. All the cars were bright colors – not like here. I was in a T-shirt and shorts, but everyone else was dressed for winter. It sounds bad, but I remember there were people dressed as clowns – some kind of traditional thing, I think. But in full costume, with makeup, noses, ruffled collars.'

Nance started to laugh. Heath caught Matt's eye, and they laughed too, looking over at Don, who was looking away, smiling. It was a long joke, Heath decided, having stopped listening halfway through. Clowns in Mexico.

'It sounds funny, but it wasn't funny at all,' said Leandra. 'It's a terrible memory I have.'

Everyone else was cracking up. Was there any more beer? No, but someone had seen a fifth of vodka in the back of a cabinet. They decided it would not be a bad idea to open it and replace it with a new bottle before leaving. Leandra was being gently hazed, but it would do her and her relationship good, Heath decided, to have something to recover from once they all went their separate ways. He took out his phone and texted the girl that he'd be back the day after next. They arranged to meet at a bar near his place that night.

'We almost died,' said Heath, handing the girl a drink, something she'd ordered off a cardstock menu. It came in a beveled glass, garnished with what looked like a pine-tree clipping. She sipped, let a smile start, then sucked the corners of her mouth in to show she was paying attention. Heath set his glass of beer on a paper coaster. 'Yeah. If there had been a car behind us, that would have been it. A huge pileup. Probably many deaths.'

'But you aren't hurt?' She looked at the door, then back at Heath, again smiling, then biting the insides of her cheeks, 'No one got hurt?'

'A total miracle.'

'How'd you get back?'

'I took a bus. They – my friends – were afraid of driving the whole way without getting the car looked at, so they went to a mechanic out there.'

He had vowed not to, but he ended up telling her everything: Don's ostensible indiscretion, Nance's overblown reaction, the fogginess of the ensuing trip. All reunions perspire with their own suppressed histories, but this was extreme: a suppression of the most recent of histories, an exaggeration of his own fifth-wheel status.

He told her about Matt's girlfriend, who was nice, and who had no idea. He told her that time had started to feel stretchy, every moment embedded in those before it, or wrapped around itself like a crescent roll, not flat and pointed like a triangle of dough.

The weekend had been an exercise in restraint. When they arrived, everyone claimed their rooms and then explored the house, hunting out their own corners. Heath sought out the grill, making sure it was dry and had enough propane. When he wandered back inside, he found Nance perched over a glass table covered in jigsaw pieces. On the box was a still life of a bird skull and a glass bell jar placed atop yellowing pages covered in scribbled non-words. She frowned, picking up one tiny piece and attempting to fit it into another. Over the following days, the puzzle took up hours of their time. Everyone, even Don, joined her in constructing the border, but by the end of the trip, it wasn't even half completed.

'I just went along with everything,' said Heath.

'What?' the girl asked.

'Not my place to intervene.'

'Why not?'

'It's awful, the way these people can't communicate correctly.'

'Correctly,' she repeated.

Heath watched her eyes narrow, saw female alliance express itself. 'It's sad,' he said.

'Are you going to vote?' she asked.

'I'm sorry, were we talking about politics?'

'No. I'm curious.'

'It's just crazy,' said Heath. 'I almost died.' That was the problem. That no one was ever really listening to what he was saying or trying to say. He drained the last of his beer, and without knowing if he would leave the bar altogether or simply detour to the men's room and come back to this table, new subject in mind, he stood up and wandered away. ■

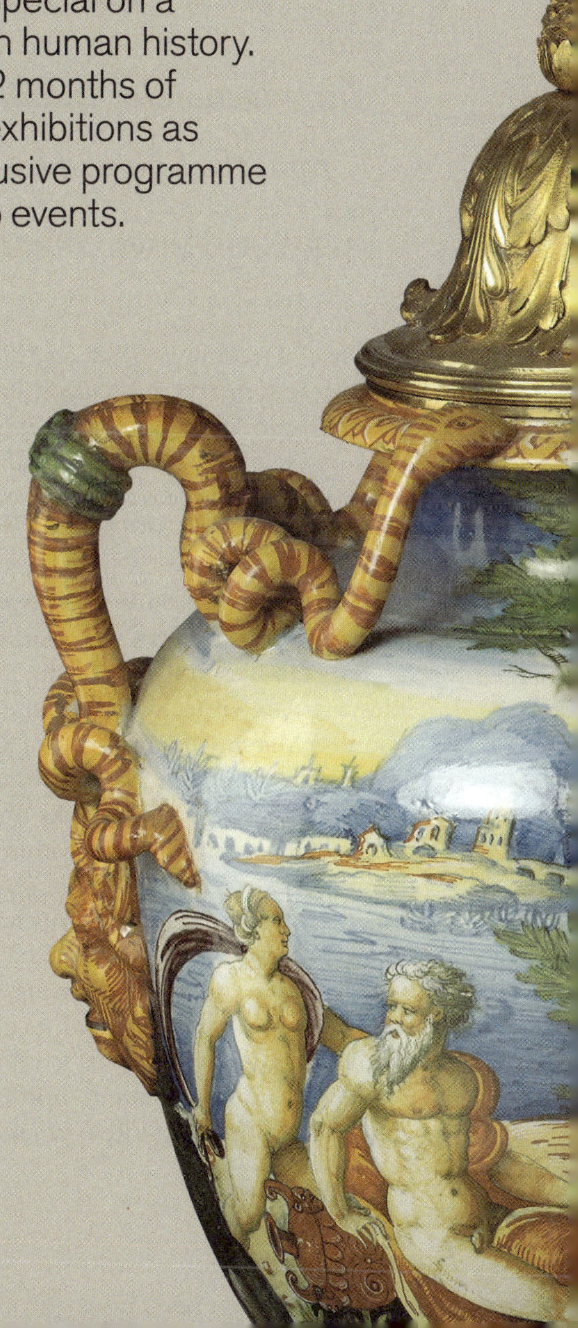

CONSTELLATIONS

Cian Oba-Smith

Introduction by Julián Herbert, translated from the Spanish by Rosalind Harvey

JERWOOD PHOTOGRAPHY COMMISSIONS

On 11 December 1988, an LP gas tank caught fire in the La Merced market in Mexico City. The fire spread to a warehouse storing fireworks, triggering an explosion that destroyed an entire block and left sixty people dead and sixty-five injured. From that day on, the wholesale trade and storage of rockets and firecrackers was banned in the capital. The community most affected by this decision was Tultepec, a municipality where people have worked with gunpowder since the seventeenth century and which produces around half the country's fireworks. To offset the economic losses faced by families in the trade, the local government established the International Pyrotechnic Festival in 1989, which is held every year around 8 March – the feast day of St John of God, the patron saint, among other things, of firework makers.

Although Mexican fireworks don't play a big role in the global market, they are used widely within the country. Most are made on the outskirts of Mexico City, in places where the old ways haven't disappeared so much as been layered over by global commerce and urban mobility. It is less an industry than an artisanal guild, marked by traces of its mestizaje heritage: the scale of its contraptions and the sarcastic virulence of its ceremonies suggest a hazy pre-Hispanic underlayer, but its key images – for instance, the bulls, which immediately bring to mind the Pamplona bull runs – are unmistakably Spanish. Fireworks are furious playthings: in Mexico, they are the second most common cause of accidents involving hazardous materials.

The *toritos* and *castillos* – the little bulls and castles that at the end of the festivities will burn amid the *cuetes*, *barrenos* and *buscapiés* (local names for rockets, squibs and other small fireworks) – date from the nineteenth century. But it was the Tultepec festival that turned them into an attraction for thousands of national and international tourists. Public attendance is crucial for this community of 150,000 inhabitants, beneath whose colourful euphoria lie two of the great problems of trade in the digital age: circulation and storage. The idea of setting fire to your product to achieve one iconic moment strikes me as a potent metaphor, both for living in a world that demands constant spectacle and consumes itself in the process, and for the joyous, loud and somewhat self-destructive Mexican popular tradition.

Oba-Smith first encountered his subject in 2023, by way of an old YouTube video that showed a man carrying a *torito* somewhere in Mexico. After months of research, he travelled to the country on his own in March 2025 to photograph the Tultepec festival and explore the relationship between community and craft. Crosses of fire suspended in the night sky; wooden mechanisms of interwoven straight lines and curved lights; luminous stars transformed by synaesthesia into sonorous controlled explosions. Each image hints at an elusive tapestry beneath the surface. Stars and animals. Constellations.

The idea that a photograph expresses a desire to consider the passing of time might seem self-evident, but when it comes to an art like Mexican pyrotechnics, it takes on a poetic weight. It is a contradictory craft: handmade objects, painted with meticulous care – like the blue *alebrije* bull captured on an urban roof ravaged by electric cables – require days of loving labour to manufacture, only to disappear in a few explosive seconds. Oba-Smith described it to me as an intriguing collision: a delicate, almost feminine process, ending in a macho spectacle.

On a rural wall in a local neighbourhood, outside a house made of concrete, tile and sheet metal, there is a mural dated 2020, which captures, in cartoonish strokes, the mythological solemnity and childish sentiment that run like a dual electric current through the ceremony of the *toritos* at the festival. The dark figures that appear at the foot of the beast – a Minoan echo, a bitter aftertaste of the conquest – are ambiguous: they might be priests, ancient warriors or boys wearing hoodies.

As well as being an explosive device, the *torito* is a disguise for the fragile human skin beneath it. In its basic form, it consists of a frame made of bamboo, cardboard and gunpowder, which a man straps to his shoulders to charge in jest at the crowd, all while the bull burns in a kaleidoscope of flashes. These one-person constructions are the most common, but in Tultepec the craftsmanship has become so remarkable that many pieces now reach the height of a house, and it is sometimes necessary to raise the electric cables between buildings to let them pass through the streets. Equipped with wheels so they can be more easily transported, these giants need several people to manoeuvre them, which for a brief time lends a solemn air to the danger and mischievous laughter that accompanies proceedings as they are lit.

Behind the spectacle, the ceremony and the labour, there is the body: the skin of every myth. And the body, besides biological, is historical. It is made up of generations – children, mothers, tools, techniques – but also of fashion, printed advertising, Mickey Mouse, the T-shirt of an English rock band, or the plaster cast model of the Virgen of Guadalupe.

There is nothing arbitrary about the correspondence between the lines traced by the stars and sparks in Tultepec, and the maps of scars that appear on the torsos and faces of the people photographed by Oba-Smith. The dark spots, scabs and keloid tissue appear as vibrant marks: a contrast agent that allows us to perceive the passing of time. This link between lights and burns seems to me to be a sort of mystical translation of the subject matter, because what remains of the gunpowder once it has burned away are dazzling scars. Once again: constellations. ■

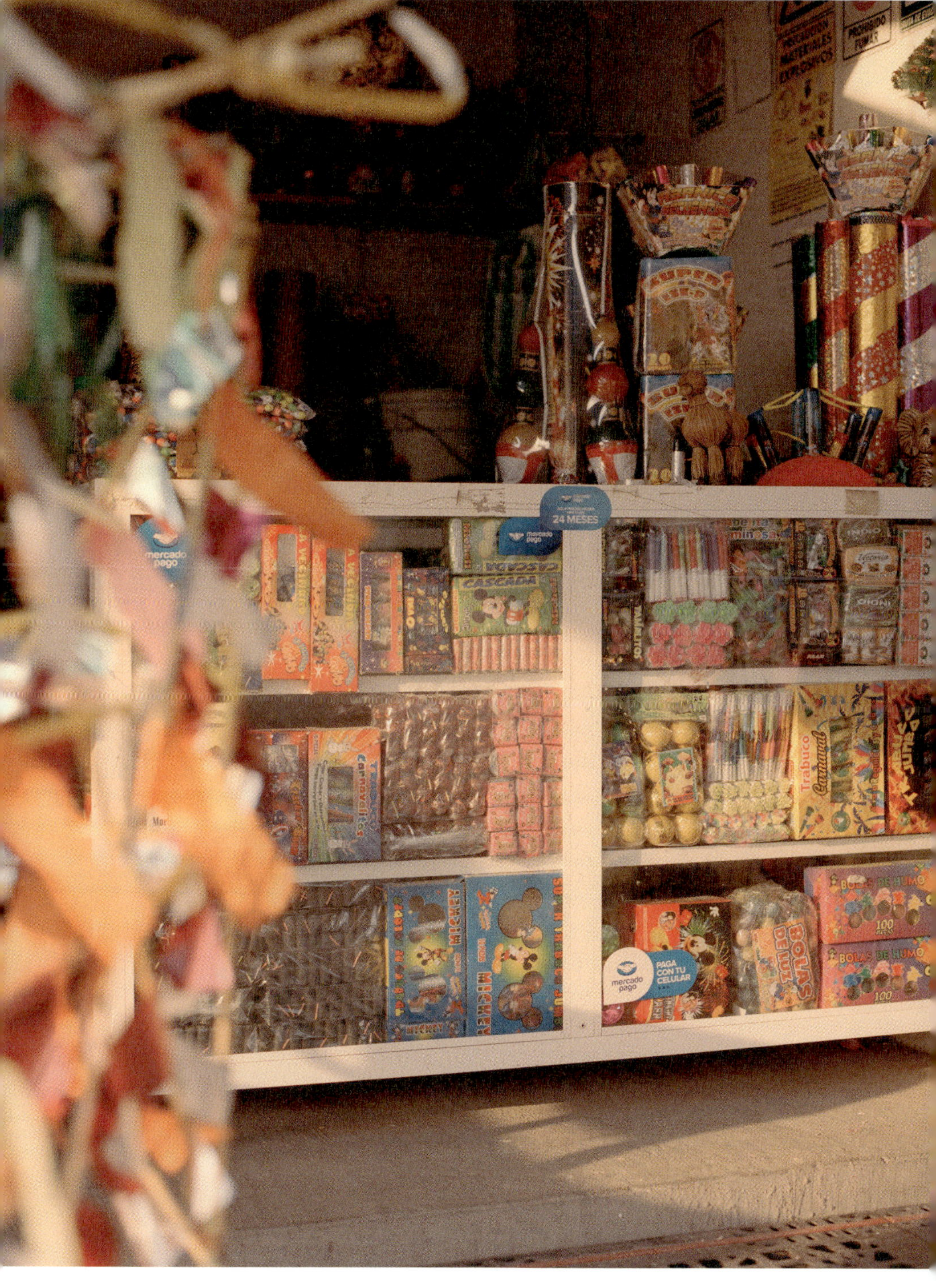
PROHIBIDO
FUMAR
24 MESES
mercado pago
mercado pago
CASCADA
SUPER
BOLAS DE HUMO
100 PIEZAS
BOLAS DELUX
BOLAS DE HUMO
100
Trabuco
Carnaval
Carnavalitos
MICKEY
PAGA CON TU CELULAR
mercado pago

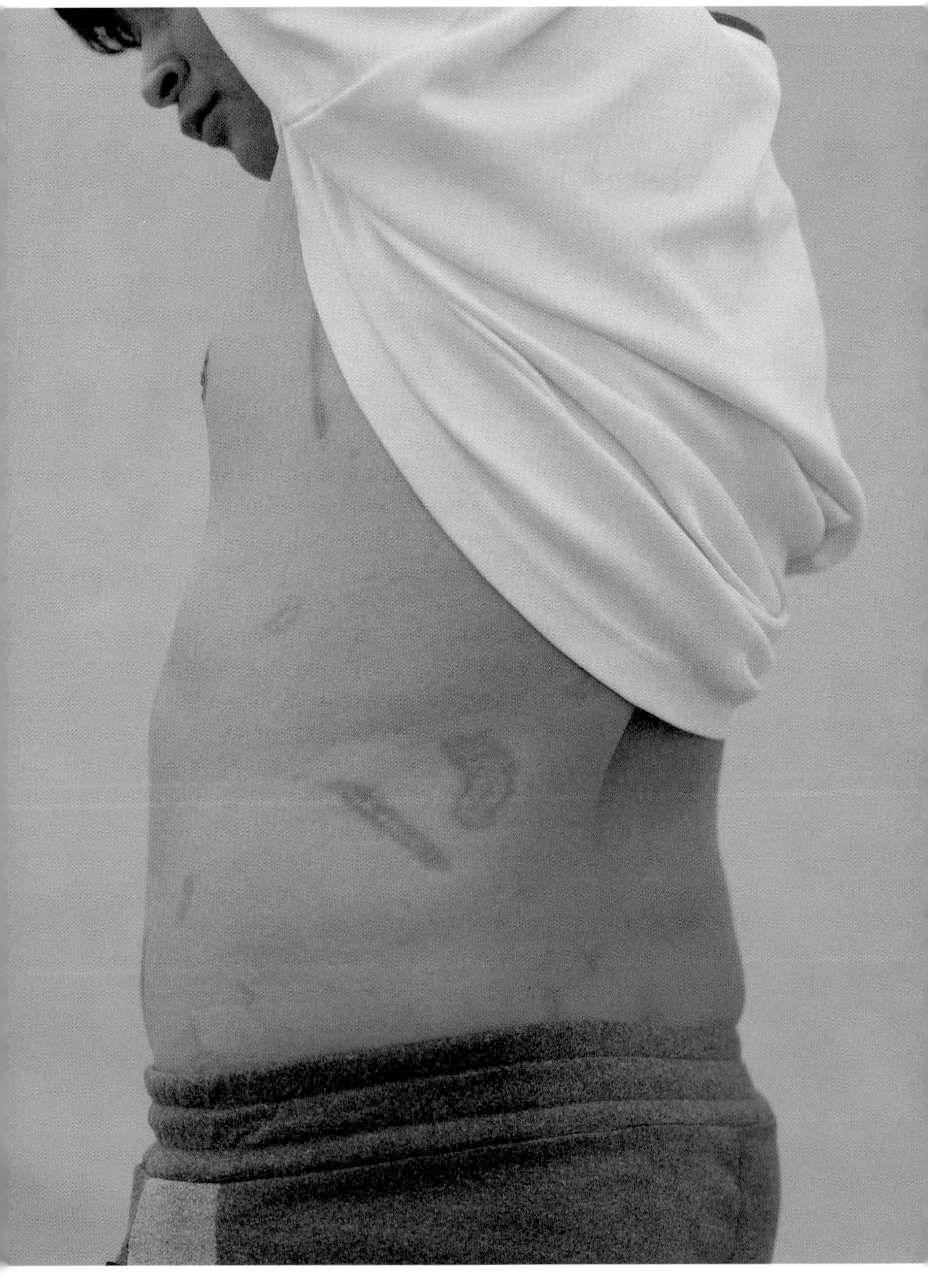

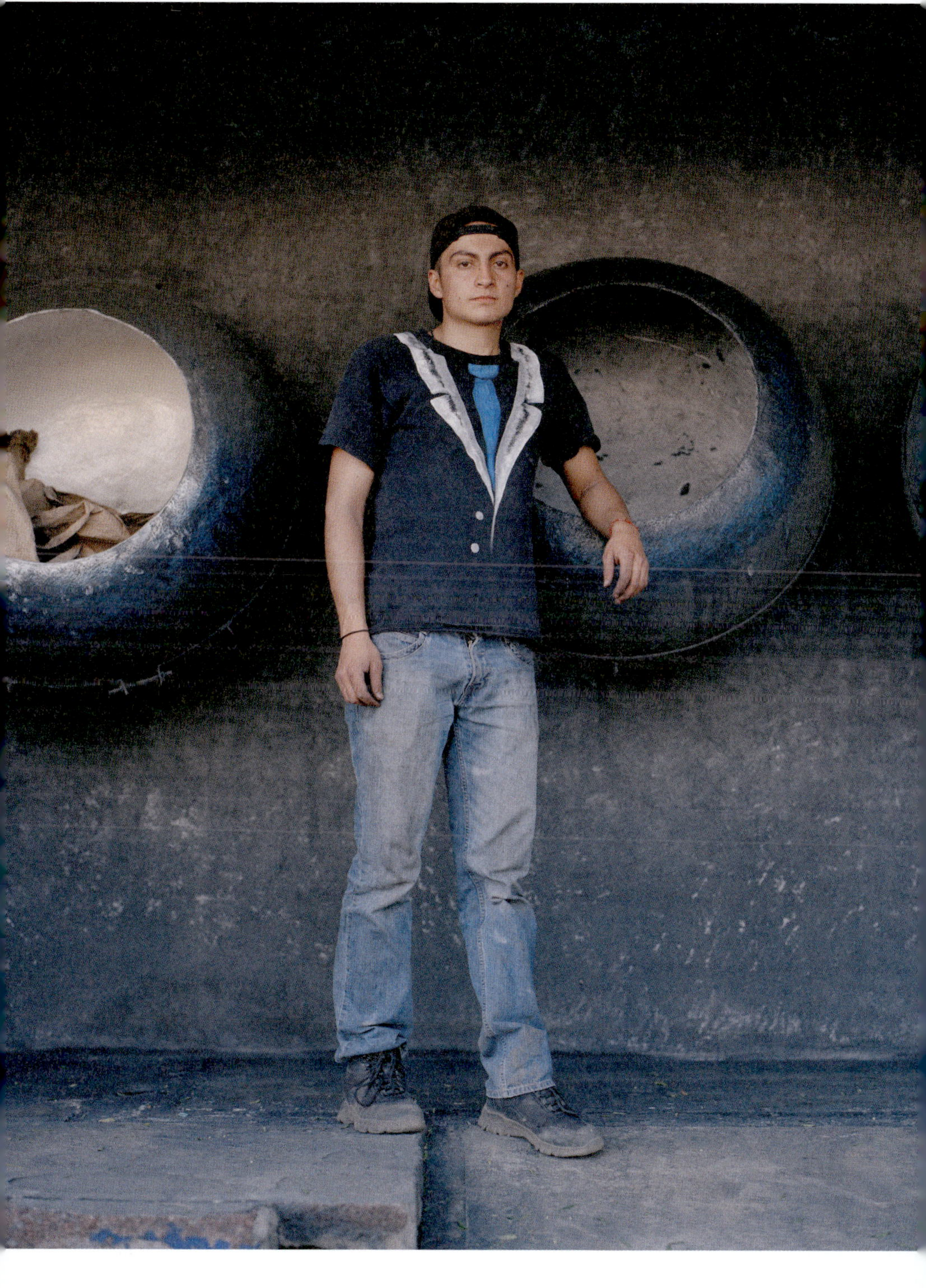

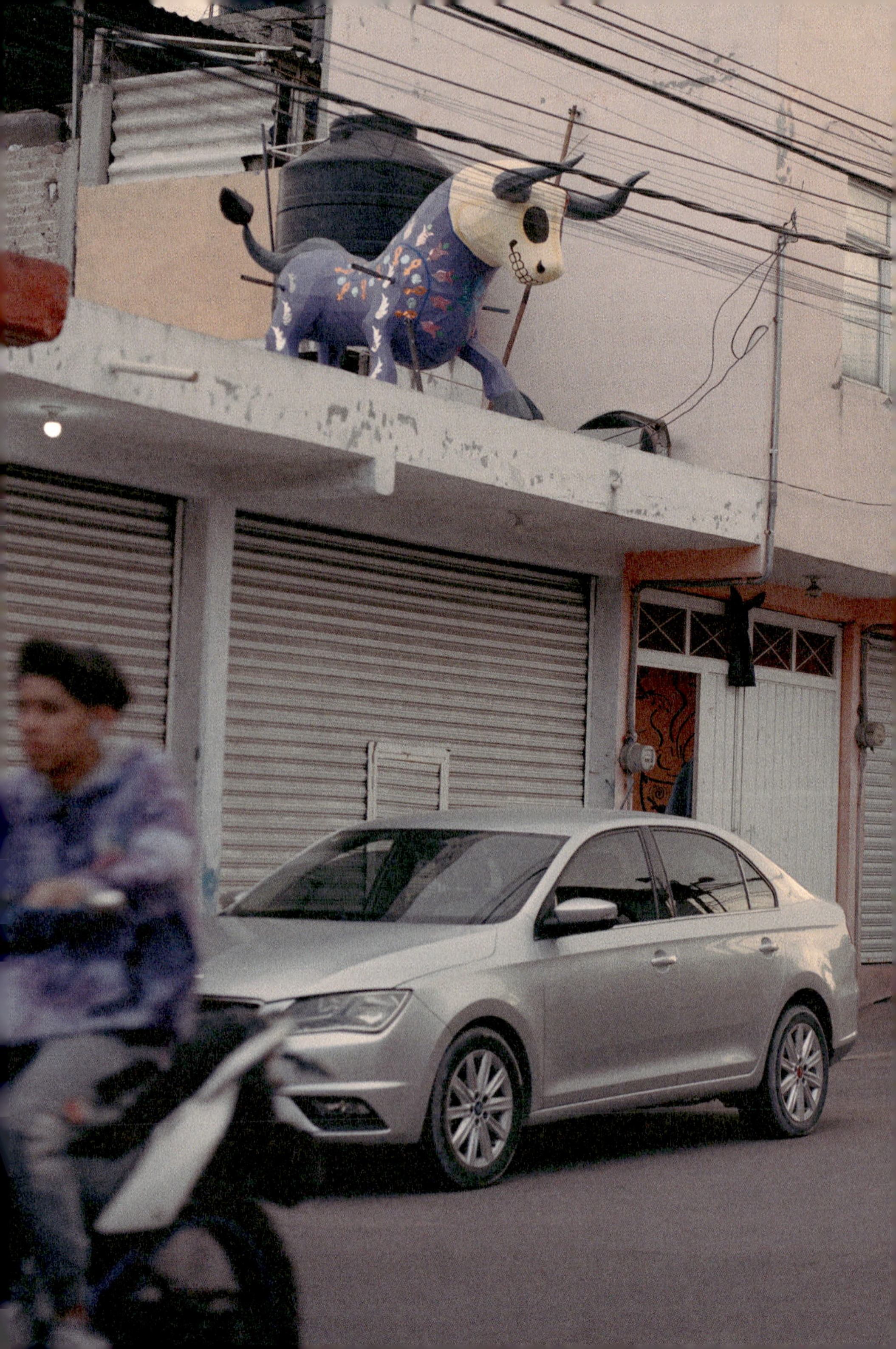

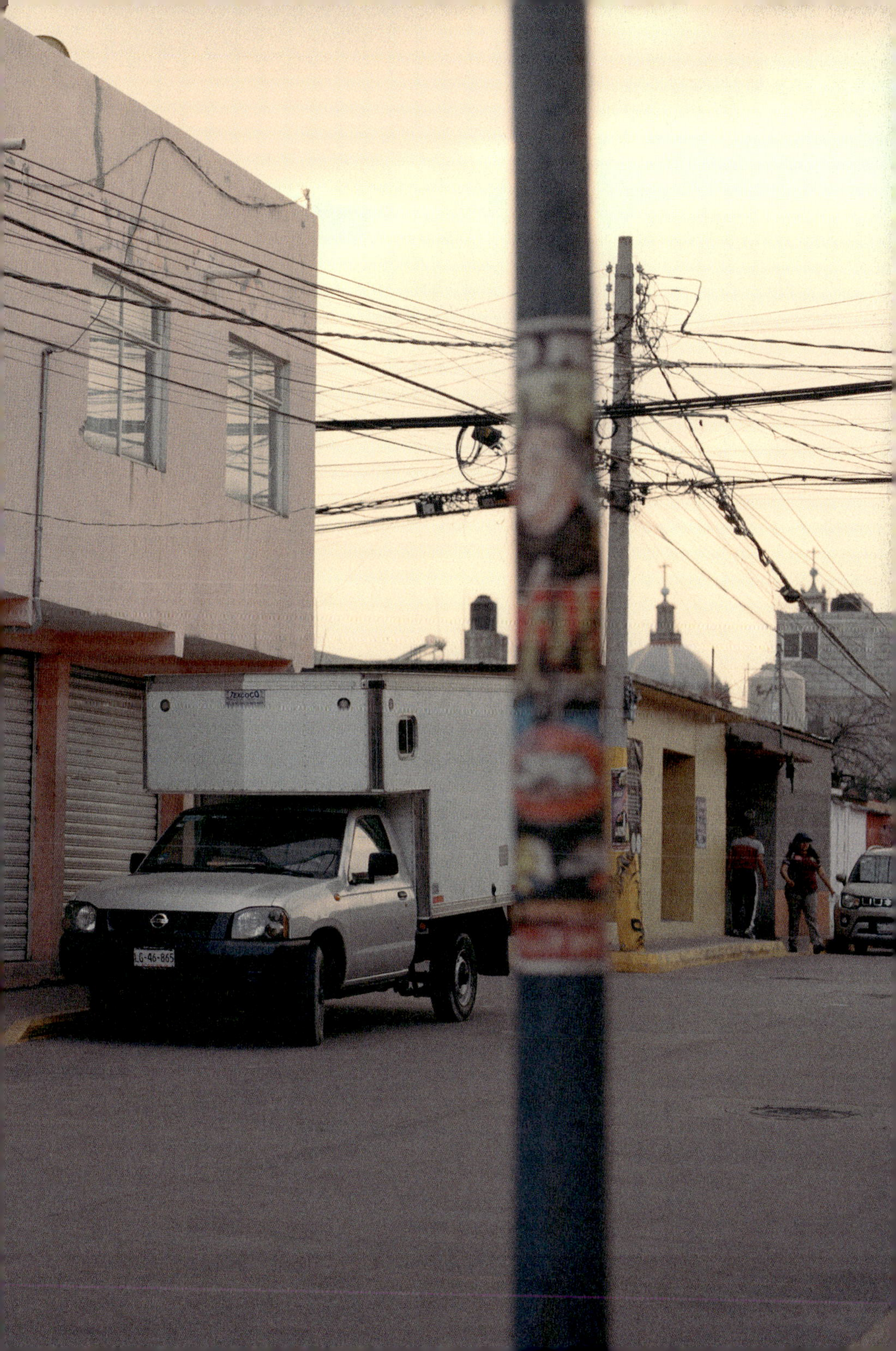

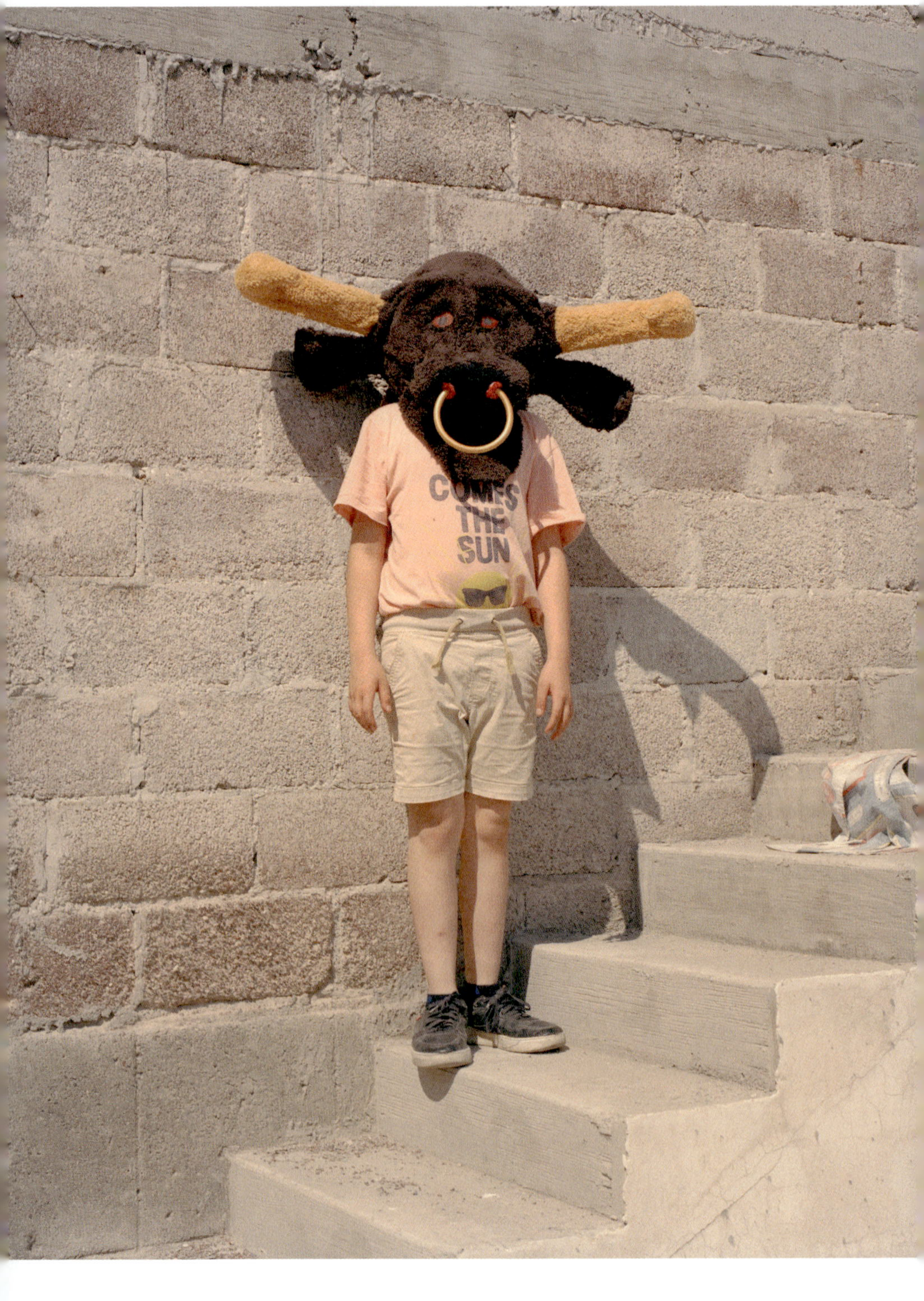

COMES
THE
SUN

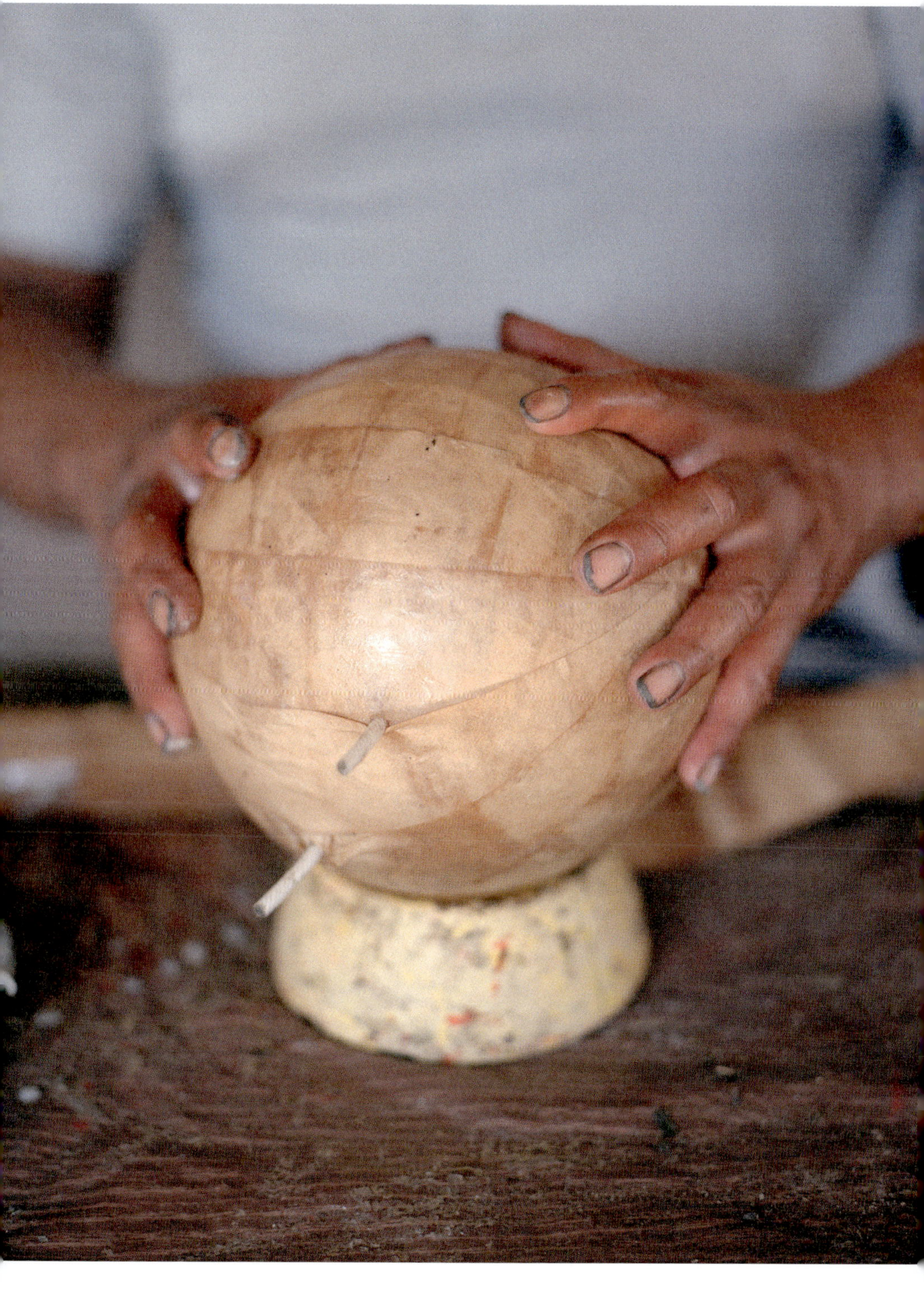

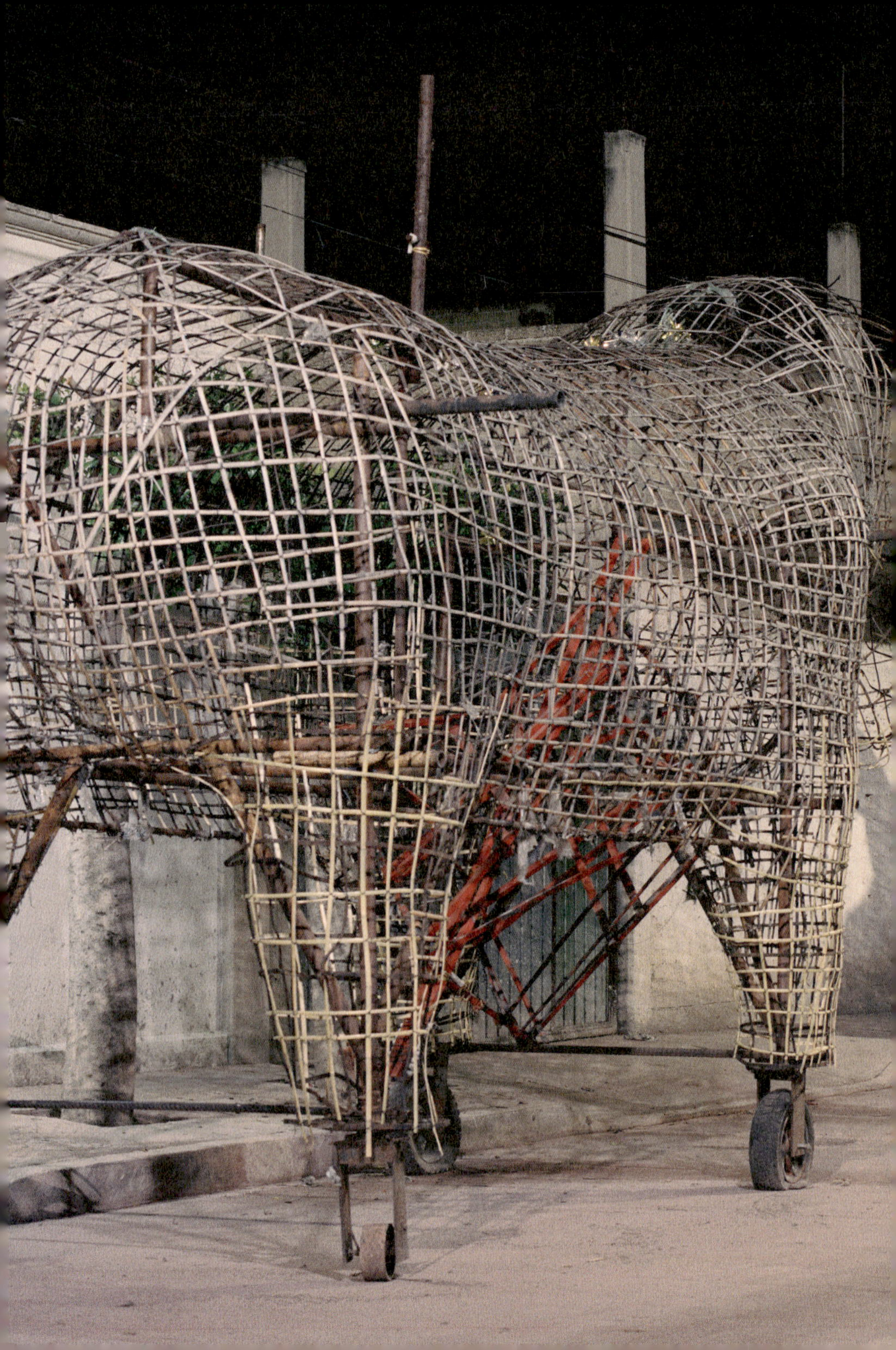

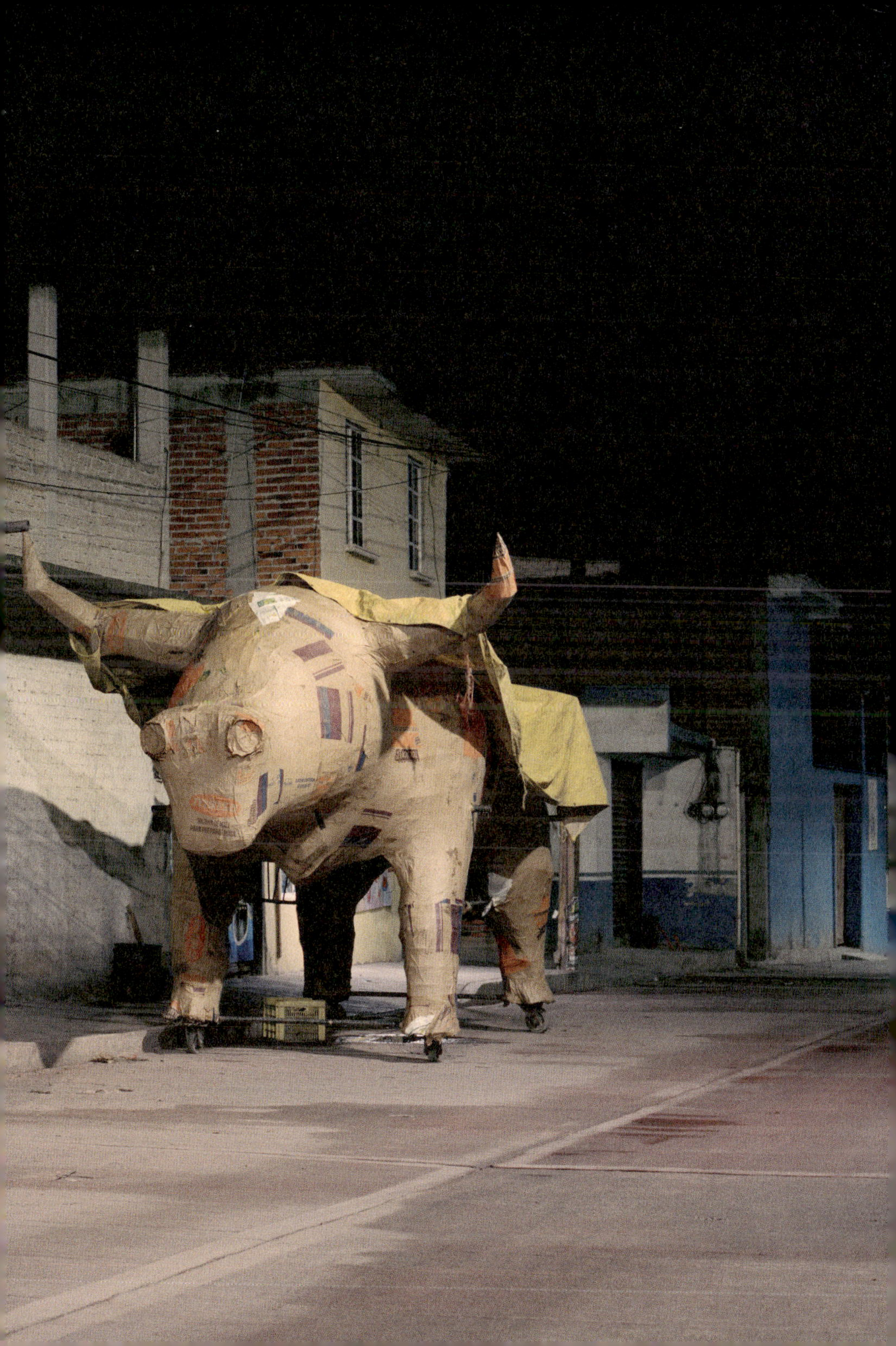

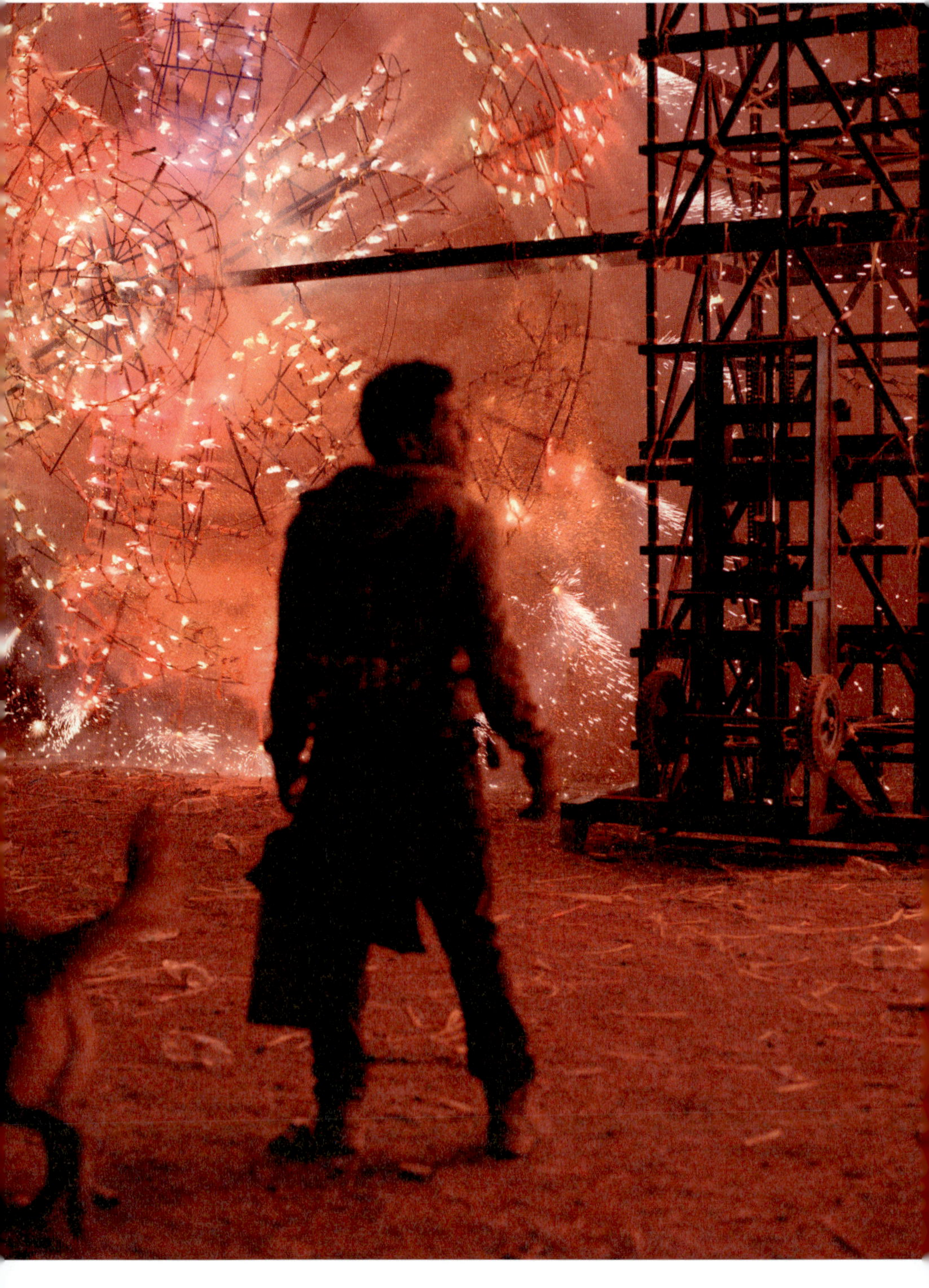

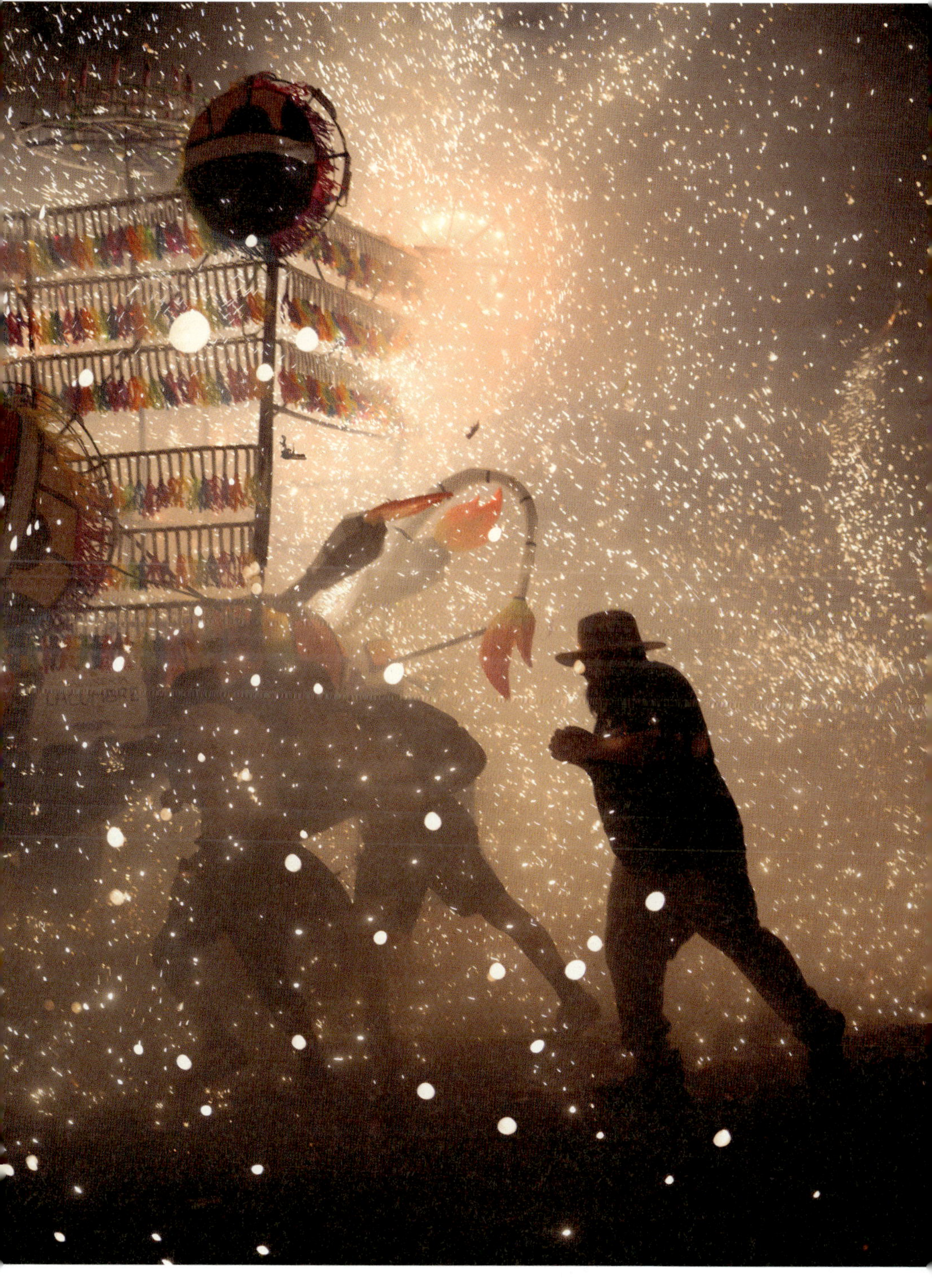

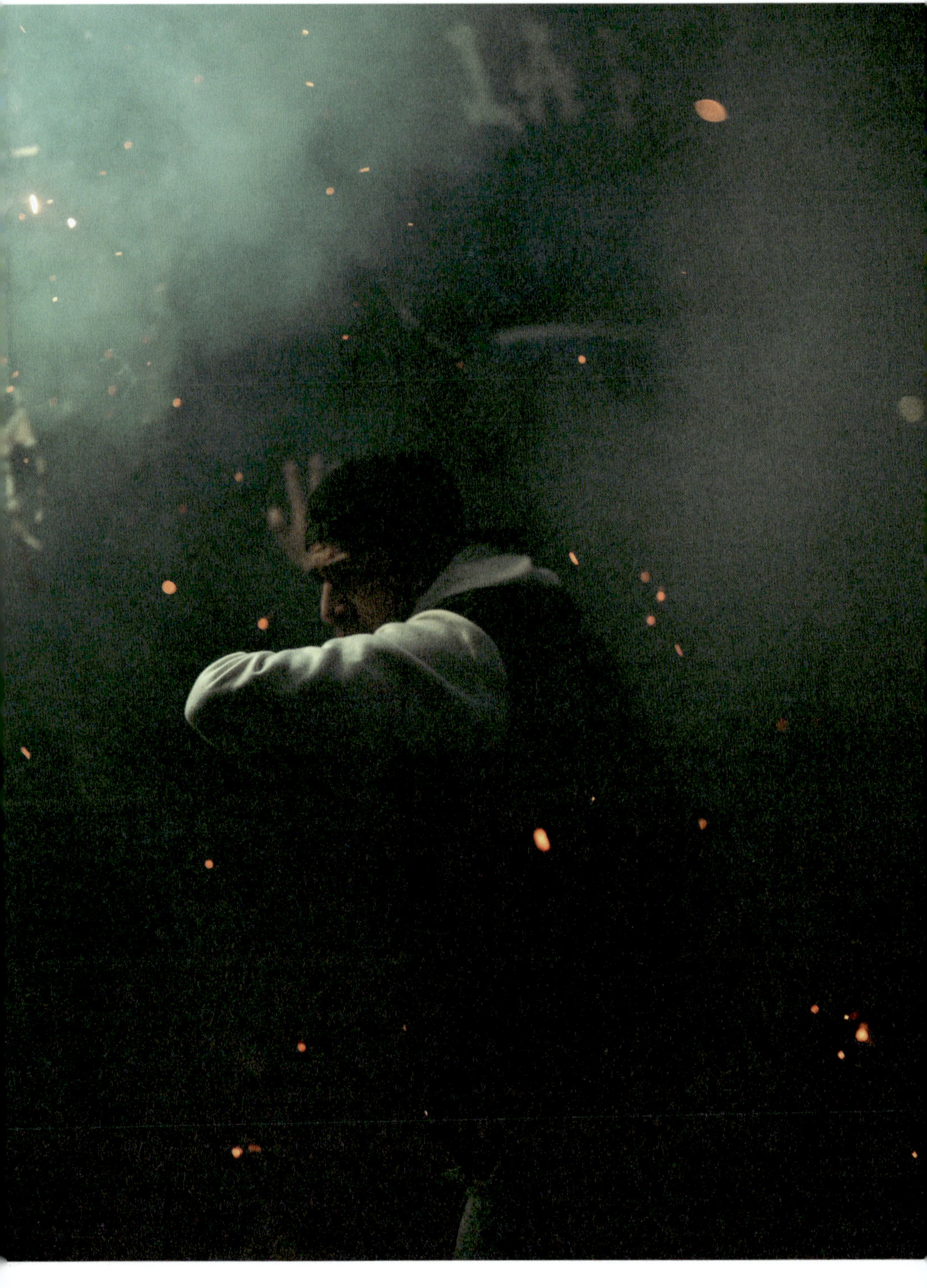

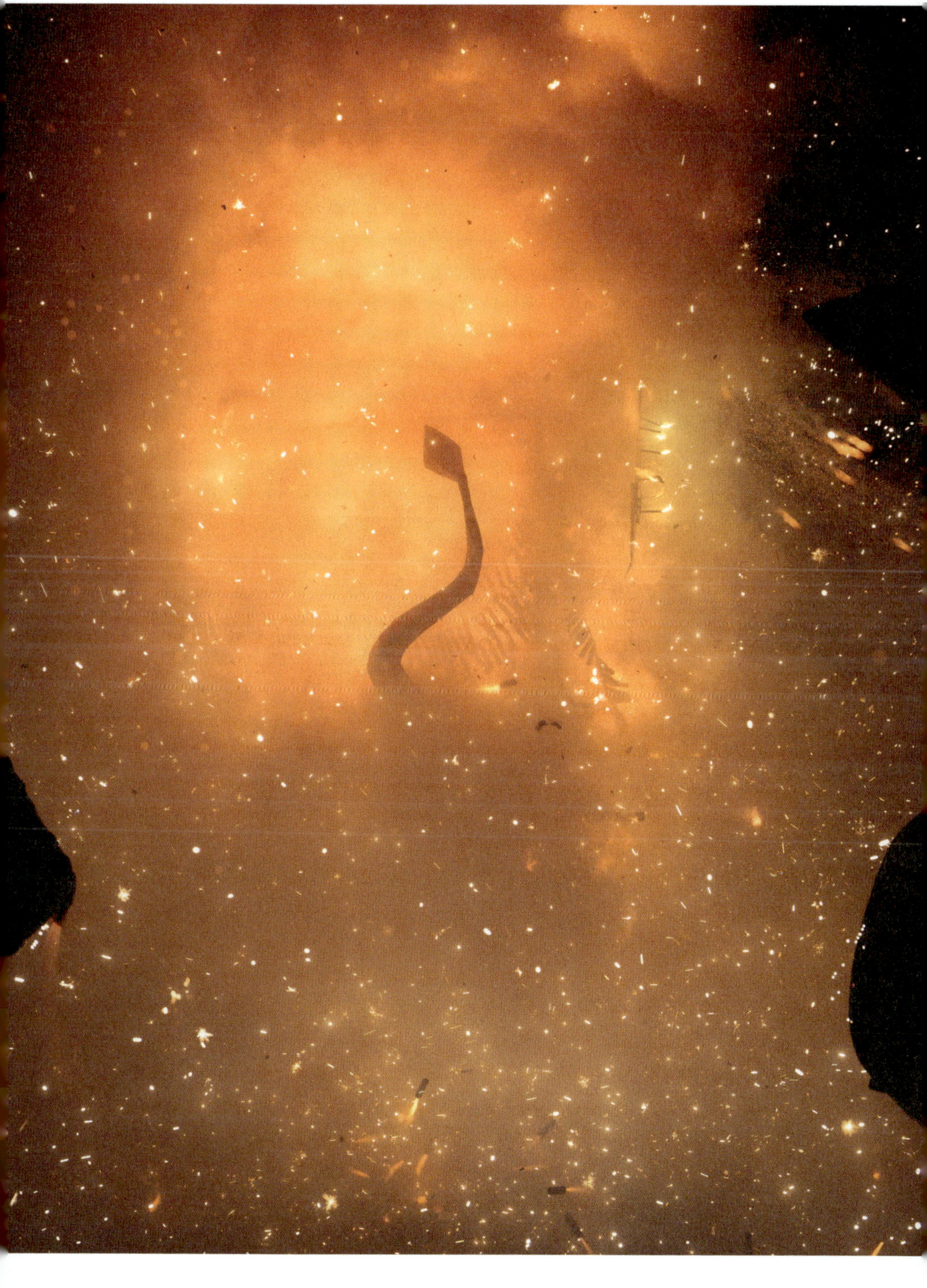

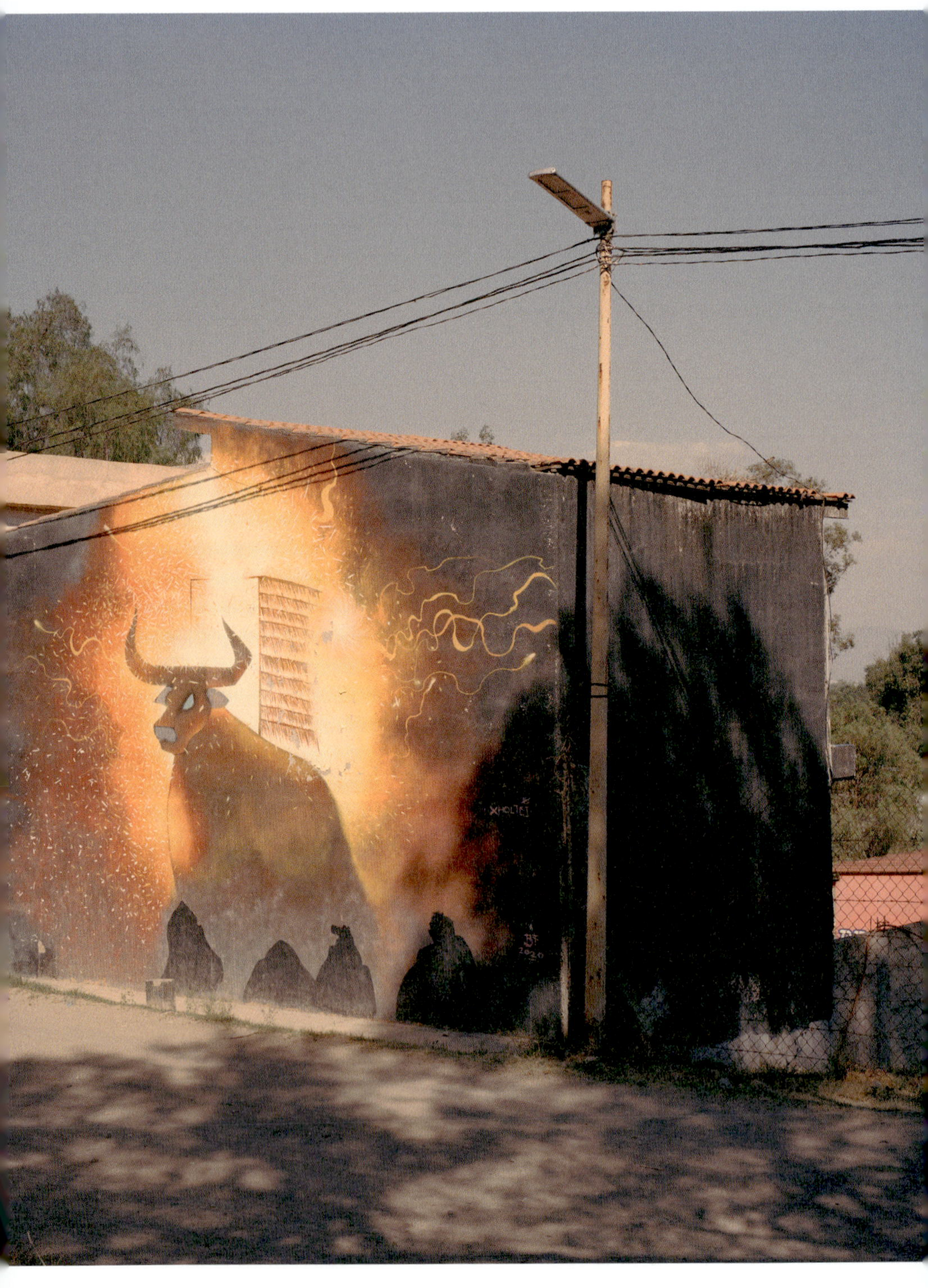
XHOLTEI
BF
2020

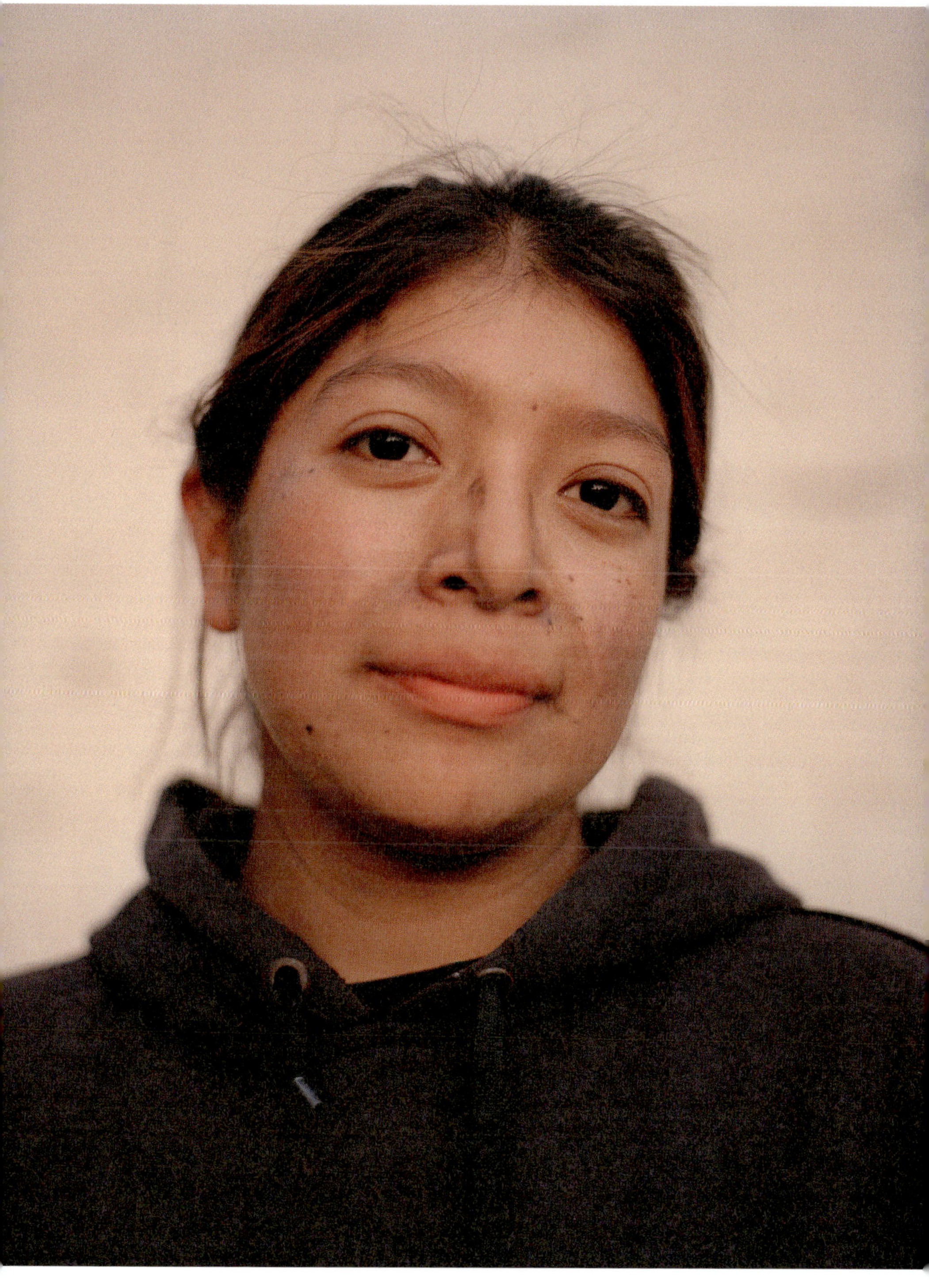

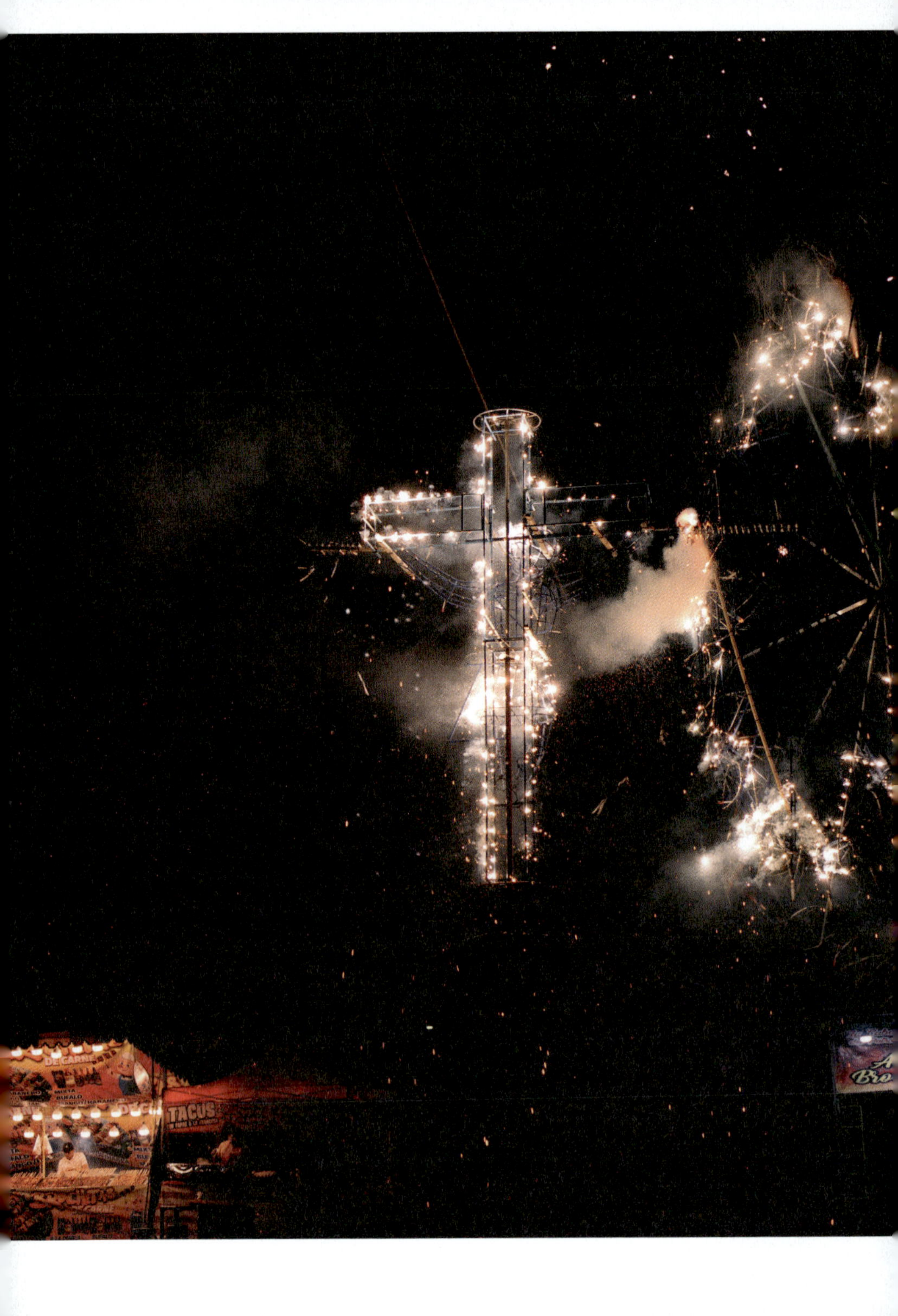

Nasim Luczaj

Drawing from life

Chagall is born
the night a great
fire breaks out
in the outskirts.

   A core shadow
  ought to be dark
      but soft.

Chagall's
grandfather slits a
cow's throat
in front of him.

   Careful to keep
those sharp edges.

Chagall's sister
dies of eating
charcoal.

     Follow the
  shadow shape.

Chagall's father
makes a living off
barrelling herring.

You want to keep
those highlights
loose.

Chagall can't visit
his mother's
grave; says his
talent was hidden
in hers.

If the eyes feel
too small, check
that the eye socket
isn't too big.

Black Hornet Nano

You can buy it
online, *smaller
than a sparrow*, weighing
less than a plum

(Which one?
Not Mirabelle, baby
fist a touch lighter
than the sun?),

Mac-grey to blend in
with the walls of Afghanistan,
where it first flew
under the name PD-100,

Personal Drone – skirted
through buildings
on black plastic wings, savvy
waitress dishing out sight.

If you can't afford
to eat out, a DJI Mavic
is a good start. It'll cost you less
than a phone. You will gain

situational awareness.
See how far
that takes you.
Charge.

longevity

we undress the tulips
cut their feet
barbie-diagonal

the florist's tip
is to make a hole
in the throat

but we can't bring
ourselves so we
let bodies soften

heads mop the table
rather than snap
grow bald mellow

yellow then green
receding feet first –
when we wake and go

to the living room
there are already petals
over our eyes

limp satin lids
over contaminants
over light

things we daren't
live with outright
or live without

we in our rear-
facing dream
who've never seen

our own faces
our own necks
air itself

the white stork

carnivore
serially monogamous

species of Least Concern
harbourer of parasites

like me
spends 25% of the time in Poland

the sexes are identical
though males a little bigger

she knows how to go far
and come back

how to plan for and manage
eternal summer

winter in the savannah
June centre-meadow

both journeys are the holiday
both homecoming

she lives on roofs
of ancient sites

builds nests on pylons
drops cute nuisance into gardens

slices frogs with her beak
curls her neck to sleep

as a tight question mark
to dream of answers

long-haul flights
inner magnet gone haywire

rocking up at the market
powdered or crucified

this happens in Morocco
not only in nightmares

still all I want is to travel
resort to soaring and gliding

look back at my still wings
rapeseed-tall legs

that thigh gap
child-wide

body backed
and forthed by sky

if I ask for directions
how will she laugh

pass a sentence
unincised

across her strait
of red lip

winged mascara
hidden skin

how do I tell her
my stork

bite's a map
I can't read

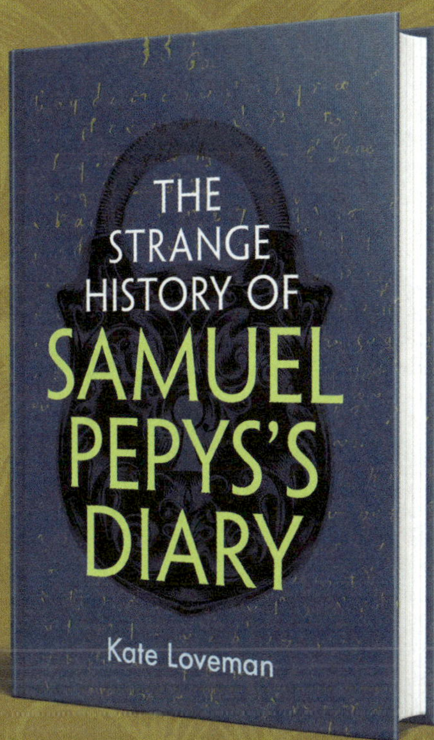

THE
STRANGE
HISTORY OF
SAMUEL
PEPYS'S
DIARY
Kate Loveman

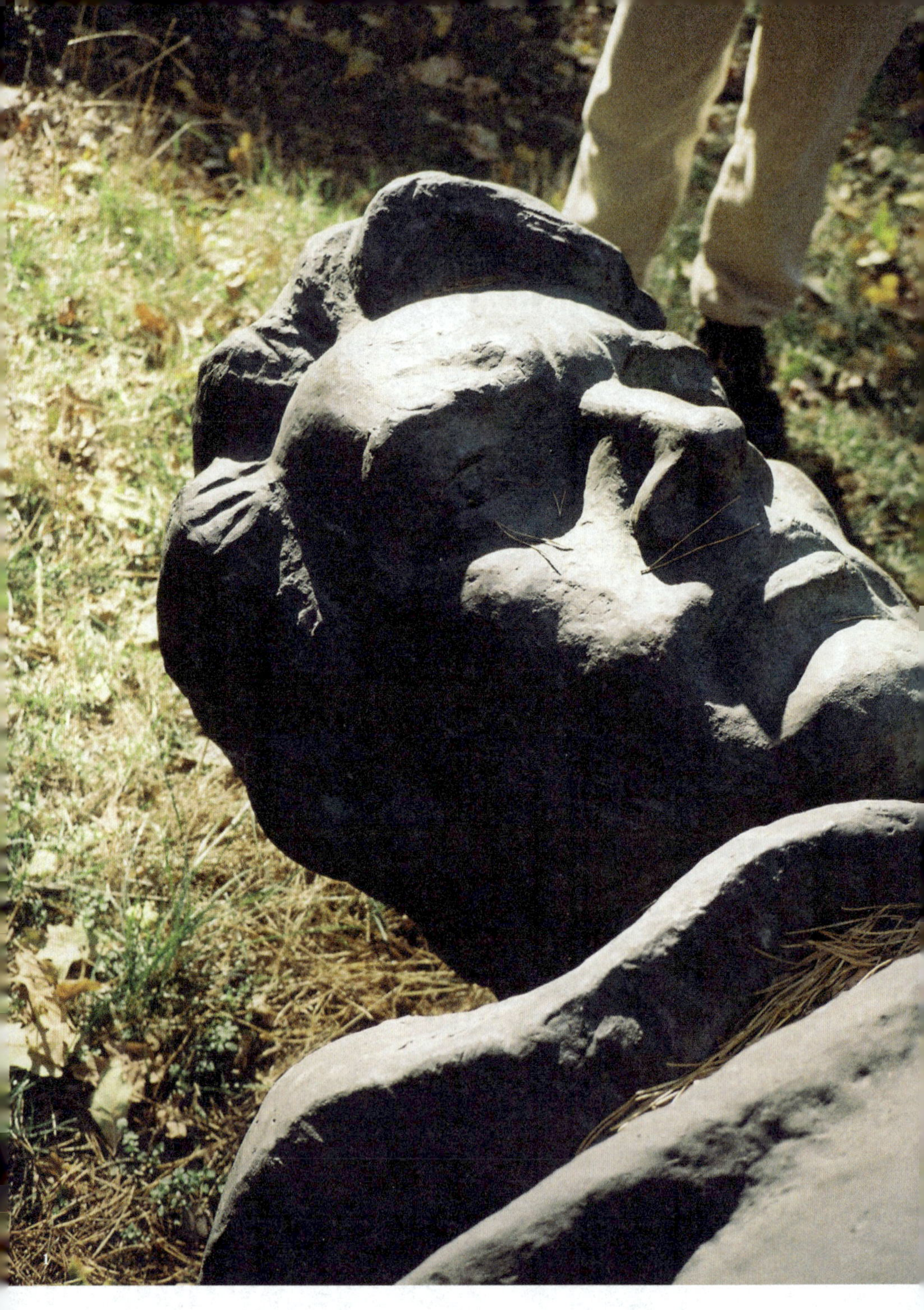

All photography by WILLIAM T. VOLLMANN for *Granta*

DRONES AND DECOLONIZATION

William T. Vollmann

'Regret for the passing of the old forms is like the grief of some
antediluvian creature for the disappearance of a prehistoric
habitat . . . The "landscape" will acquire a mask of iron.'
– Joseph Roth, 'Affirmation of the Triangular Railway Junction'
(1924)

'We have different heroes now.'
– Artak Hryhorian, Ukrainian decolonization activist (2024)

1

S ome of her was Austria once, and part of her had been Poland.
Starved and tortured by Stalinists into Soviet Republichood,
then raped by Hitler's Reich, she finally became some version of
herself, but then V. Putin thought to annex her back into another
empire: Re-Russify her! Give it to her good and hard, then beautify
the corpse with a mask of iron!

Her de-Russifiers fought back, and not only with drones and
artillery: Amputate the occupier's monuments! Ban his writers, no
matter how long ago they lived; rename his streets . . . 'Little Father
is no more,' cried that Ukrainian, Russian, Polish or maybe Austro-
Hungarian writer Joseph Roth. 'Where is the czar? . . . What sort of
world is this? A crooked world!'

I went to help her in my helpless way, with journalistic good intentions which sorrowed into love. From Berlin to Vienna I went, and then through the Czech Republic's golden-red forests, which here and there burst into ultra-yellow blazes beneath an ever-darkening silver sky. I glimpsed long, gentle slopes of well-mown or -grazed green grass and I saw decrepit towns; then it was afternoon among Poland's boarded-up brick buildings, with crew-cut young men lounging in packs while wearily beautiful old women dragged home heavy shopping bags. Passing through the town of Liszki I spied a church steeple graying in the twilight, and long after dark came the final border.

2

For the ninety kilometers between Lviv and Brody, towns stretched cool, bright and clean beneath the white-streaked sky. On either side of the road, a thin and intermittent wall of trees advanced toward a low bluish ridge-horizon. On the left, a cemetery's needle-sharp steles shone darkly behind a carefully plowed field of brown dirt; then on the right, beyond an emerald field, there crouched a castle upon a low wooded hill. Checking his phone, my fixer, Yurii, dated that structure at somewhere between the thirteenth and eighteenth centuries inclusive, then proposed that Ukraine's former masters had most likely trashed it because 'it's Soviet Russian to erase history, to create fake history'. Then we saw the road sign for Brody, which by some measure or other had come into existence in 1084.

3

BRODY

Joseph Roth grew up right here in Brody, which, eleven decades before my visit, had been almost incomprehensibly different: both Jewish and Austrian, to begin with, and meanwhile so close to the Russian border that in Roth's most famous novel, *The Radetzky*

March, where Brody, on the eve of the Great War, has been coyly fictionalized into B., Austrian Jaegers pay easy calls upon their tsarist military counterparts in order to drink up their schnapps and observe dreamy shows of Cossack horsemanship. The Russians pay equivalent visits to the Austrians, all parties unaware that 'over the glass bumpers from which they drank Death had already crossed his bony invisible hands'.

Having thought through how to most courteously ask Mr Vasyl Strilchuk, the director of the Brody History Museum – it was within his tiny office that we now sat – about certain local shifts of name, allegiance, et cetera, I remarked: 'I understand that Brody has changed hands many times.'

Jovial and stocky, with cropped and graying hair (he was born in 1975 but looked as old as I who had seen the light in 1959), he replied: 'Ninety-five percent of the people feel themselves Ukrainian. Maybe even a hundred percent, I don't know,' he added, laughing and spreading his hands.

'Brody before the Second World War and after were two different towns,' he said. 'Before 1939, the population was 17,000, of which a thousand were Jews. The rest were half Polish and half Ukrainian. According to the official statistics of Soviet times,' he continued, 'only seven hundred of the total population remained of those who used to live here before World War II, while the Ukrainian Partisan Army, which fought against Soviet rule, claimed that there were only three hundred.'

There had once been a railway station, which proved ever so convenient for receiving one's worried father or visiting one's mistress in Vienna; inevitably it was demolished. Between 1914 and 1920 alone (said Mr Strilchuk), Brody changed masters twelve times.

His grandfather had been conscripted into the Polish Army in good time to face Hitler; once the Soviets simultaneously invaded, he deserted and at a female relative's urging passed as a civilian, so he escaped the mass graves enacted by Stalin in Katyn Forest. When the Nazis took his horse, they said he could reclaim it; but when he took them at their word he saw them slaughtering Jews, for which they 'almost killed him'. How he got away Mr Strilchuk could not tell me, but his survival qualified him to be 'mobilized' by the Soviets, who marched him all the way to the horrendous Battle of Königsberg. There he got assigned to help evacuate his wounded commander, and became the only member of his unit left alive. They told him he was going back home, but 'Russians always lie', and packed him off to Manchuria, where Stalin now prepared to attack his Japanese frenemy. 'If Americans hadn't dropped the A-bomb,' Mr Strilchuk said, 'many more people would have fallen in battle.'

'And so,' he summed it up, 'my grandfather was conscripted three times, first by the Poles against the Nazis and Soviets, second by the Soviets against Nazi Germany, third by the Soviets against Japan. But when he went home, the local Soviets always required him to find the key to the church' – presumably because he was akin to the local sexton and they wanted to lock the place – 'but he said: "What do you want from me? I am a Hero of the Soviet Union, so why cannot I pray to my God?"'

The old Gymnasium building in Brody smelled sweet, clean and schoolish, maybe even blackboard-chalkish. The daylight's static diagonals on the stone-tiled floor and beneath the arched ceiling dwindled into a turquoise wall and door, which reminded me of Austro-Hungarian facades I had seen some years ago in Vienna and Sarajevo. I saw women cleaning, chairs and benches touched by sunlight, and heard the sound of a power tool. From this place, Joseph Roth graduated in 1913, with, said Mr Strilchuk, the highest marks ever received by anyone in the Austro-Hungarian Empire. (Mr Strilchuk appeared proud of that, and maybe in his shoes I also would have been. When the homeland's prospects are ominous, who wouldn't rather polish up old cultural furniture?)

Outside the Gymnasium was a bronze bust of Joseph Roth on a granite pedestal; on the wall were two Joseph Roth plaques, and below those a plaque for the fallen heroes in the Ukrainian–Russian war of 2014. Two old workers stood on a ladder just left of all those;

when I asked what they knew about Roth, one shouted out: 'I know when he was born and the dates of some of his works.' And just to prove it, he peeked at the dates on the plaques. That convinced me. It always saves time to be convinced. For example, I'm convinced Roth's Ukrainian, right down to his antecedents and works – all dead leaves on the wet and windblown grass of history, of course, but, well, the real truth is that I'm happy to call him Ukrainian if that preserves him from being purged from the national story, or 'decolonized'.

I never like it when authorities or committees of any nature, for any reason whatsoever, especially the noblest, officially expunge a writer's public presence. To ban implies to me that the censor harbors some discreditable motive, such as – this is the most excusable if also the most pathetic – fear that the writing might somehow be actively dangerous to the state. To which I demand: How could a dead writer's notions possibly threaten Ukraine, at least in comparison to a Russian drone? Or the censor might instead be impelled by outright hatred; not to mention the quotidian motive of self-advantage.

After we had dropped off Mr Strilchuk by his home, I started my practice of inspecting the commemoration parks for the Russian-killed soldiers in all the Ukrainian towns and cities I visited. In each of them, as at the New Jewish Cemetery, I could not help musing on Elias Canetti's aphorism that 'the slavery of death is the core of all slavery'.

Brody was rich in fresh flowers and fresh grief. Two young women stood with lowered faces by the glowingly washed-out likeness of a bearded man who grinned as if he had loved life. A middle-aged man puttered patiently by another display. When I asked if I could talk with him, he spread his hands and shrugged.

He said that this soldier had been a close friend of his own son, and had called him Father. The soldier had broken communication with his biological father for being pro-Russian. 'He was such a good guy,' the man kept saying, and all I could do was touch my heart and say I was sorry, while he wire-fastened to the dead man's portrait a little soft doll of a soldier-angel.

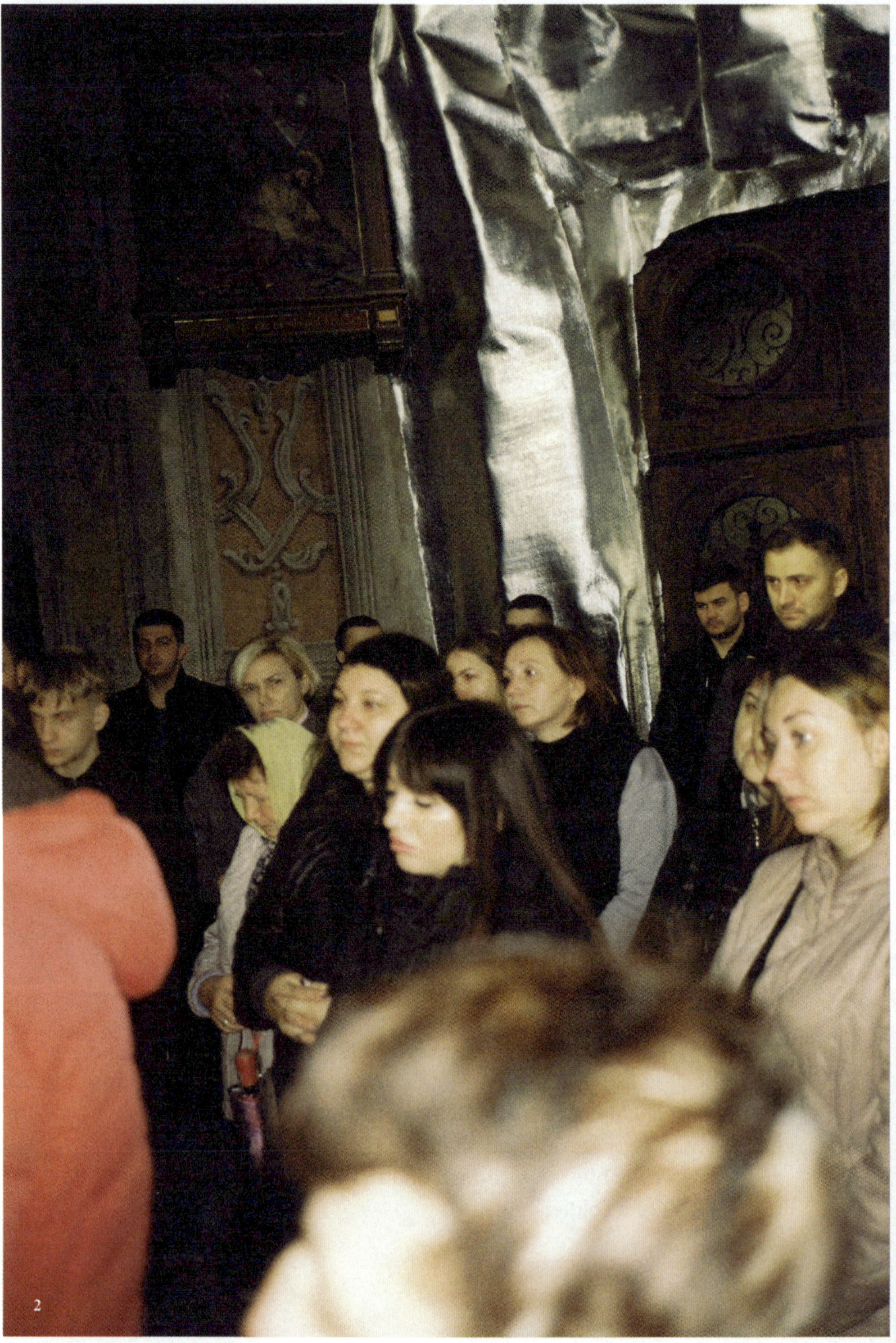

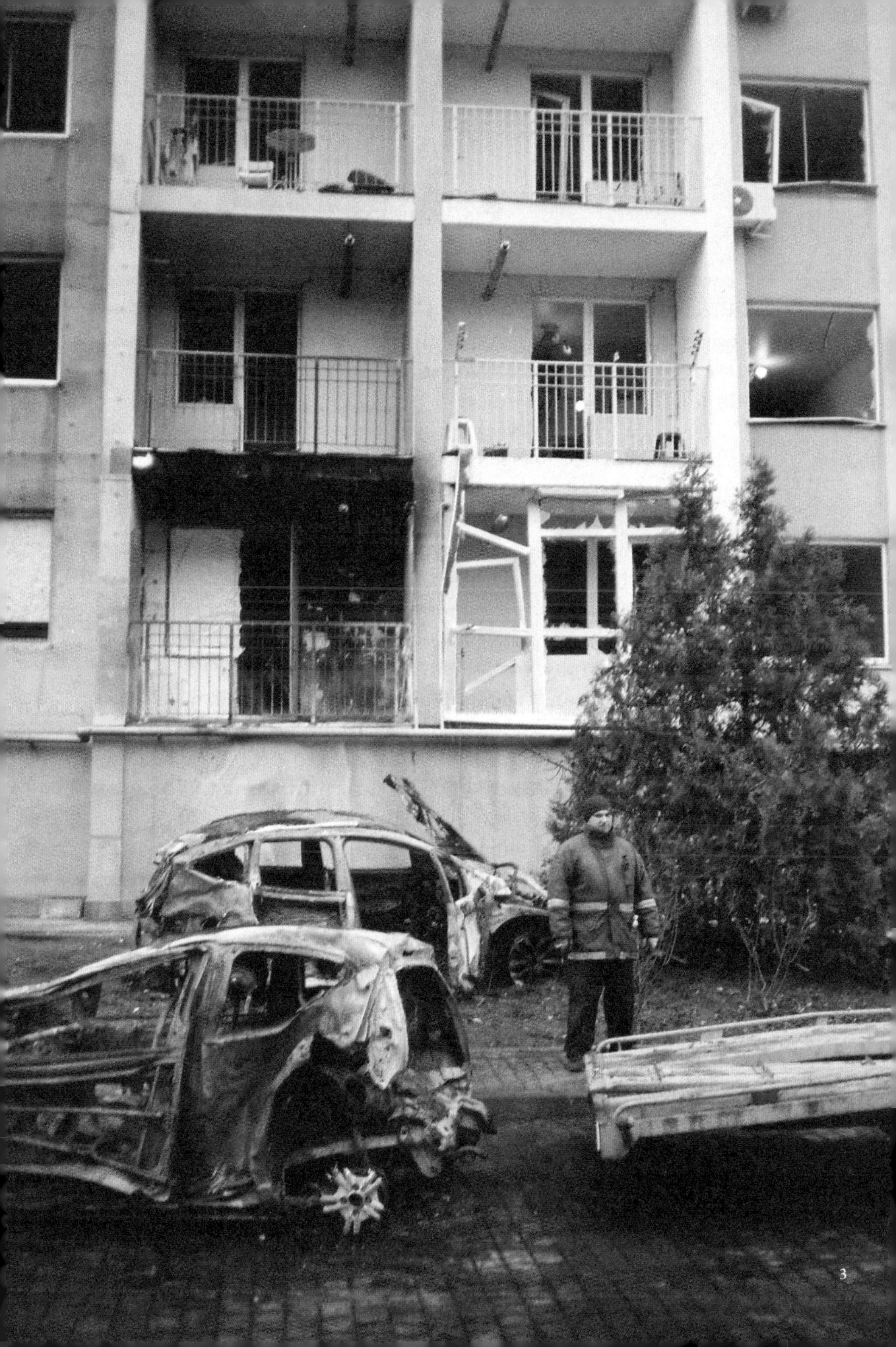

4

VINNYTSIA

It was a cloudless morning at freezing point when we reached Plzemohy (Victory) Square in Vinnytsia, 193 miles miles from Brody, where at 10.45 a.m. on a July morning in 2022, three Russian cruise missiles took care of twenty-nine Ukrainians, including a pretty little girl with Down syndrome.

The office center, 'Yuvileynyi', still looked rather shabby after its Russian makeover. A block away, the golden dome of an Orthodox church lorded it over the plastic sheeting in its windows, not to mention its scaffolding and blast-chipped walls. With only the basement now safe to occupy, we descended there, passing more beggars than I ever saw anywhere else in Ukraine – one of them was an amputee in a wheelchair – and entering into warmth and incense, we found the place packed with standing worshippers. The female choir sang beautifully. Yurii said that the ritual was in Old Church Slavonic, which meant that this denomination was linked to Moscow. 'They do say that they dropped all connection with Moscow,' he later remarked, 'but it may not be like that.' I asked Yurii if it would be appropriate to take one picture, and he consented, so I did, and a man whirled round to photograph me. Yurii said: 'They are so suspicious that even if you first obtained permission from the priest and they saw you get it, they would only be more suspicious.' Over and over the people crossed themselves and said their amens. When we were outside, I inquired whether they would now blame Russia for the war. 'Many of them, yes,' he said. 'But some of them might just blame the politicians. Many of them don't blame Moscow directly. They might say someone provoked the Russians. They don't say the Russians are good guys, but they don't put all responsibility on them. The Patriarch in Kyiv, they say, is false.'

There were now two denominations. The Ukrainian Orthodox Church was run by Moscow and the Orthodox Church of Ukraine was controlled by Kyiv. Some 700 out of 9,000 churches have shifted from Moscow to Kyiv – a small number, considering.

Courteously pausing in packaging her flowers, a florist in her little shop told me about the 2022 attack: 'It was an air raid and I didn't go to the shelter because the internet said the missile would fly over Vinnytsia . . . I was chatting with the money-change girl, and then suddenly there were loud explosions, one by one, and everything in flames! The market started to collapse. The bombs fell into the square, so our shop was not completely destroyed.'

'Did you have time to feel fear?'

'No, I was here on the corner, chatting with the girl at the currency exchange, and those three strikes seemed to happen all at the same moment. I was shocked. There was smoke and flame and I couldn't understand at first.'

'Why do the Russians act like this? How can it be in their military interest to kill a few civilians and increase hatred against them?'

With her hands on her hips, she said: 'They just hate Ukrainians. For me, I don't hate Russians.'

Of course, the 'house of soldiers' just behind the victory monument might have provided some military justification, but to me it was still a crime.

5

I had wished to visit Vinnytsia, because one of Putin's justifications for the invasion was that Ukraine was a nest of fascists, in which case the site of Hitler's former headquarters – *Führerhauptquartier Werwolf* – might be of interest. After that I thought to see Odesa, the city of Isaac Babel, and incidentally a current center of artillery drone manufacture.

My mother, who used to read to me when I was a child in her lap, and who taught me to cherish books, which have been the great love and consolation of my life, introduced me to Isaac Babel through his story 'Karl-Yankel'. In his concentrated passion, his sensuous lust for food and for women, justice, home, adventure, revolution and war, his bewildered fascination with cruelty, his self-hating attraction to antisemitic Cossacks and pitiless bureaucratic murderers, his horrifying gemlike plots and desperately resigned genius, I met something hauntingly new. Now I pity Babel's inability to turn away from pitilessness. His ideological confusions repulse me, but he paid full price for them: shot by his monstrous idol Beria, or, if you like, decolonized. The Stalinists might have thought of him the way Odesa's head Chekist thought of Froim Grach, the eponymous Jewish gangster who features in a Babel story first published twenty-three years after the author's execution: ('a first-rate fellow! . . . Odessa begins and ends with him!') Grach marches down to the Cheka office to straighten things out: he'll bribe them if they stop executing his thugs. What could be more reasonable than that? So they shoot him. 'Tell me one thing, as a Chekist, as a revolutionary . . . What use would that man have been in the society we are building?' The deputy, who knows Odesa, admits: 'I suppose no use at all.' And then he begins informing his Moscow colleagues about Froim Grach's adventures and triumphs: 'all the amazing tales which were now a thing of the past'. May Babel's tales never turn comparably, fabulously bygone! I will always love him for his genius – not for his political morals, but isn't genius enough? It is to me.

6

A few steps on in Vinnytsia, I met some good old titanic Soviet heroes. Having been 'decolonized' in 2011, they stood headless or lay on their backs, with autumn leaves clotted red and gold on their dead faces. There, for instance, lay Timchenko, Vinnytsia's one-time communist leader. The astronaut Yuri Gagarin remained standing – which is to say that his orphaned head and shoulders did. I have always admired his achievement, in which I take my human pride:

> First man to travel into space . . . son of a carpenter on
> a collective farm . . . launched at 9:07 am Moscow time

on April 12, 1961, orbited the earth once in 1 hour 29
minutes . . . immediate worldwide fame . . . made several
tours to other nations . . . killed with another pilot in the
crash of a two-seat jet aircraft . . . His ashes were placed
in a niche in the Kremlin wall.

Thus my 1976 *Britannica,* whose photo-portrait of that smiling young
cosmonaut (twenty-seven years old when he made his space voyage,
thirty-four at death) still coaxes forth my liking. Brave, intelligent,
handsome, cosmopolitan – what could the Ukrainians have against
him? Well, I would find out.

Mr Melnyk – the director of the 'Historical and Memorial
Complex in Memory of the Victims of Nazism' – said that in
Vinnytsia the 'decolonization process' had been in full throttle since
2015 (the year after Putin devoured Crimea), 'and at the beginning
of the full-scale invasion there was a decision to collect all monuments
here in preparation for a museum of the Soviet occupation'.

'Where was the Gagarin statue before?'

'This monument was in an education institution, inside of some
building, I don't know which. The decision to remove it was initiated
by the school's administration.'

'But why decolonize him? What did he do?'

Spreading his hands, Mr Melnyk said: 'It was a part of Soviet
propaganda to put up monuments to personalities who had nothing
to do with Ukraine.'

I thought about this. Wondering how far he would go in this
direction, I asked: 'Do you want to give the Red Army any credit for
liberating Ukraine from the Nazis, or given the circumstances would
you prefer to erase them?'

'We were just the land that was divided between the two empires,'
he answered coldly, 'so when one empire kicked out the other empire,
we were not exactly liberated.'

To me this was especially sad, because whatever happened
immediately afterward, Europe's deliverance from Hitler had been an

accomplishment of which all the participants deserved to be proud; as for the rest of us, I will remain grateful all my life that fighters from countries including my own defeated the 'Aryan' monsters with their mass graves and ovens. Of course I might feel more bitter if I wore a Ukrainian's shoes . . .

7

Between fixers in Vinnytsia (Yurii having turned me over to Yura in order to conduct emergency business in Kyiv), I de-lidded a Mexican beer on the knob of the medicine cabinet and peeled open a can of paprika-flavored Ukrainian potato chips.

While brushing my teeth, I re-admired the following bathroom notice:

> DEAR GUESTS! Due to military operations and possible damage to critical infrastructure, we ask you to be economical when using water and electricity. Thank you for understanding. Everything will be Ukraine!

In the morning, Yura drove me from Vinnytsia to Odesa: a good five hours through rolling cropland, with the latest memorials to fallen soldiers decorating every town. Each line of blue-and-yellow flags receded into yesterday's grief behind us, with tomorrow's horror being arranged right now in Moscow and Crimea. Underneath those flags stretched a wall of shoulder-to-shoulder portraits, dead men enlisted to stand living and vertical for their bereaved who must now make do with simulacra.

Three soldiers were standing in the road. Here came another billboard of a mother and children huddled in front of ruins, flames and smoke. Then beautiful yellow-leaved willows leaned toward each other on either side of the highway.

8
ODESA

Isaac Babel judged Odesa – or what quite a few of us, including Babel himself used to call 'Odessa' – 'the most charming city of the Russian Empire . . . a town where you can live free and easy'. Extra charm was furnished by the sunsets, whose lemony clouds reminded me of the rich soups served to Babel's gangster characters at their wedding banquets; nor should I skim over downtown's classical- and Renaissance-style architecture, which almost made for a miniature Paris or less sinister Saint Petersburg. Stately yellow edifices glowed in a dusk whose clouds were colored peach and gold. I remember one street corner where the sky, whose clouds resembled sandbars, was purple on one side and blue on the other of the plate-glassed sandstone edifice called KARDINHAL. One never knew what would get decolonized next, or for that matter become a Russian target. That latter issue might indicate why the nineteenth-century Hotel Londonskaya's first-floor windowpanes had all been replaced with fiberboard. (Both Chekhov and Putin stayed here. It was too expensive for me.) And there in the harbor, nicely sunset-gilded for my convenience, stood the shell of what Yura said was another hotel.

Enemy drones and cruise missiles certainly hindered me from pronouncing Odesa 'a town in which you can live free and easy', but the pro-army billboards did their best to brighten my expectations by showing soldiers as the rescuers of young women, little girls – yeah, you get it.

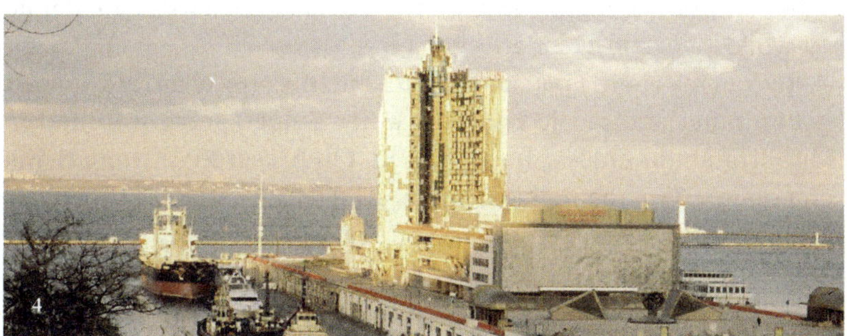

9

Passing the glowing store window, whose poster celebrated a pretty soldier who had made good by losing her leg to an artillery shell (she smiled out from behind the glass, looking very well put together, from her hair to her skirt to her long legs, the right one still made of flesh and the left one a black prosthesis), I followed Yura back to my cheap hotel (€40 a night, which made him feel sorry for me). Through him I asked the glum and nasal-voiced clerk, who never replied to whatever I said (which after all was in decayed pidgin Russian, the enemy language), what to do about air raids.

Yurii had said that most alarms were false because the drone or missile would probably pass by. The current Yura now remarked that in case of a missile a person would get only a one-minute warning, so what could I do about that anyway? But I owed my old body enough respect at least to learn the rules. The clerk told Yura that the desk would call me, which induced me to sleep in my clothes. I kept my daypack ready in case of the phone's late-night shrilling; whether or not I understood the words, I could run down the four flights of stairs to the lobby and out the front door to the sidewalk, then pull up the heavy vertical bar of the adjacent wrought-iron gate, hasten through the pitch-dark courtyard, turn right, descend a short flight of steps and turn right again into a bright-lit basement shelter crammed with rows of seats as in a bus-station waiting room. Yura assured me that it probably wouldn't happen although sometimes it did, multiple times in the same day or night. He had grown accustomed to the moderate risk while I was still a tenderfoot.

Back in my room I persuaded Yura into the only chair. He opened his computer and regaled me with a news video, fresh from today. 'Mobilization in Odesa,' he explained. On his screen a woman was screaming: 'Why the fuck are you beating him?' as they pushed her man into a yellow bus. The war, you see, was not going well – or as Yura expressed it: 'the Russians are making progress'. On the road from Vinnytsia, with waves of green fields filling our world-bowl and the horizon a ring of low blue ridges, he had told me the story of a 25-year-old medic he knew whose father was disabled, whose mother was a pensioner and whose sister had Down syndrome, making the medic his family's sole support and entitling him to an exemption. He volunteered in Kherson, bringing supplies to the infantry. To Yura he had said: 'I'm not afraid to die, but when I think about my poor sister, whom they won't take care of . . .' And he was brave; Yura saw the grade-A stomach wound he earned on the front line. When the conscription board seized him, they confiscated his phone, but his parents rushed to the office with documents while he hid in the lavatory as they pushed the others onto a bus whose destination would be less escapable. They freed him on condition that he return with more documents, then finally gave him his exemption. Of course the news video was horrible, and I said so; how would I have liked being frogmarched to Kherson or the Donetsk to die? Thank goodness I was a foreigner, with veal shashlik from a Tatar restaurant inside me and in my shirt pocket the passport that would get me out of here.

Then Yura clicked, tapped, whatever, until on his screen the jolly conscription scene gave way to Dmitry Zhdanov, the expert on Isaac Babel I was scheduled to interview. Round-faced, bald on top and gray at the sides, he wore circular spectacles, was patient, and truly did enthuse about Babel ever so sweetly. Mr Zhdanov and I agreed on loving Babel's sensibility, although he got crabby when I suggested that the writer had been allured by violence: 'Yes, in those memoirs he described all the massacres, all the terrible things that the cavalry was performing and all the most terrible things that Russians can do at war. The truth which he wrote, and of course he was hated for it by Budyënni. You can call him a mystificator.'

'So what does Babel mean to you and to Odesa?'

'He managed to show the Odesa of his time, to express its multiculturalism, to make clear that it was Ukrainian-speaking. His famous gangster Benya Krik uses Ukrainian phrases as well as Yiddish. The style is so original that sometimes you actually can't translate.'

When I inquired where I might be able to find an establishment that served meals such as Babel mentioned, Mr Zhdanov said that there was nothing left exactly, well, 'any restaurant that serves fish soup with lemon in it, and, as far as I know, typical Odesa dishes . . .' but he finally recommended the Tatar restaurant to which Yura had earlier steered me, an exotic place of filigreed lanterns whose ceiling shadows made interlocking gears whose teeth were as long and narrow as black dagger-blades; veal shashlik to be dipped in some kind of plum sauce (I remembered the haunting shashlik scene in Solzhenitsyn's *Cancer Ward*); mountainous green salads whose tomatoes were as immense as carnelians; whose Crimean onions could have been purpurite; and whose cucumbers, glistening with oil and speckled with dill, could have been beryls of gentle green.

I told him that it had saddened me the previous day when an interviewee had told me that Babel should be decolonized, but of course I was not Ukrainian, so maybe I did not understand.

'Renaming some streets is one thing, but nobody is going to delete him from our literature, our culture,' Mr Zhdanov said. 'There was even a street named after Babel, although there was a big renaming of streets and his street was renamed, but it was a small street to a burial office, located in such a quiet and remote place that his memory will not suffer much.'

At the end I asked him: 'Does the full-scale invasion turn people more against Babel?' 'It's not hate toward Babel himself,' he replied, 'but toward all Russian culture. Now we realize that there is no such thing as Russian culture! This horde has no culture.' He smiled out at me from Yura's screen. He was truly sweet, that mostly bald old egghead; he was an old egghead like me.

I thanked and embraced Yura, who was going home. Forty minutes later, as I was entering these notes, I heard the air-raid siren. It sounded neither near nor far. The telephone did not ring, so I waited for the siren to stop, but it did not. I heard nobody in the corridor. Since it persisted, I decided to shoulder my pack and trudge downstairs, just for practice. When I reached the lobby, the clerk looked at me and said in good and very kind English: 'That's the siren from the airport. This is the first alarm of the day. Yesterday there were two. You can go to the shelter if you want. I cannot go because if something happens I must stay here and warn all the guests.'

'Has anyone else gone there?'

'No one.'

'Well then I guess I won't either. Sorry to trouble you; I'm still learning my way here.'

He recommended that I take the elevator if something came, because it would be faster and was what everybody did. I decided in that eventuality to press the call button, and if the elevator did not come immediately, then I would take the stairs. It always did me good to make these little plans. I reascended to my room. There was now a sound like a rising wind. I thought it must indeed be the wind. For the first time I heard footsteps in the room above me, but they were buried and unhurried. By now the siren had ceased. I lay down on my single bed, and considered that the situation was scarcely much worse than being in remission from cancer, as I was. My armpits did stink a little from anxiety, and maybe my chest ached a trifle, so I had better toughen up if I expected to get any rest tonight and be of use tomorrow. Maybe I should take a pill. The phone would surely wake me up. And, yes, I would certainly sleep in my clothes.

10

Since I had stayed packed all night, it was little trouble to stroll out into that deep blue morning. The chilliness did not incommode any red, pink and yellow roses in front of the many-pillared Odesa Archaeological Museum (or did it still say Odessa? I forgot to check), most of whose many-arched windows had been fiberboarded over in, I hoped, anticipation rather than reaction to the Russian onslaught. Around the corner stood the equally grand workplace of the definitely single-s'd ODESA CITY COUNCIL (EXECUTIVE COMMITTEE), whose right-hand niche lodged a white bust of what, from his serpentine accoutrement, must have been the god Aesculapius, while in the left stood a pleasant-breasted young lady whose sickle (unaccompanied by the hammer which would have Sovietized her and therefore required decolonization) presumably made her Ceres, a likely goddess for the immense granary called Ukraine. Next I revisited the Crimean War cannon facing the harbor, with that war-damaged hotel tower not far left of its aiming point. Its plinth wore many plaques, one of which, GLORY TO RUSSIAN WEAPONS, had of course been decolonized. Pushkin still remained on his pedestal, facing perpendicularly to the Black Sea, with that pentuple-sidewalked boulevard of empty benches and lofty trees, many of which grew out of square wooden-walled boxes with a bench on each of their four sides, receding below him into the peaceful air. Wasn't Odesa the so-called 'city of Pushkin'?

My budget hotel still purveyed an ODESSA CENTRE MAP, whose double 's' likewise survived as a double Cyrillic 'c'. With its aid I reached the Opera Theater (which, according to Yura, had ceased performing Tchaikovsky). On a bench I watched pigeons fly over a ring of bright rose bushes as easily as would a flock of murder drones.

In the afternoon I was strolling through Babelonia again when the siren went off. My stomach clenched, probably a learned habit from the bombardments in Sarajevo thirty-two years ago, so maybe I should get over it, and all the people I saw began staring down at their little phones. Was anybody walking more quickly than before? An old lady gazed anxiously up at the sky; an optician advanced to the window of his shop and stared out grimly, but those cell phones must not have conveyed any frightful news because nobody was hurrying, let alone dodging into basements. I kept about my business like a good junior Ukrainian. ('Odesa is slightly closer to Crimea,' Yura had said, 'so it seems that they target Odesa more than Vinnytsia. In Vinnytsia it will take three minutes by missile, and here maybe two. In general, Odesa is not hit every single day. The last incident I can remember was maybe four or five days ago.')

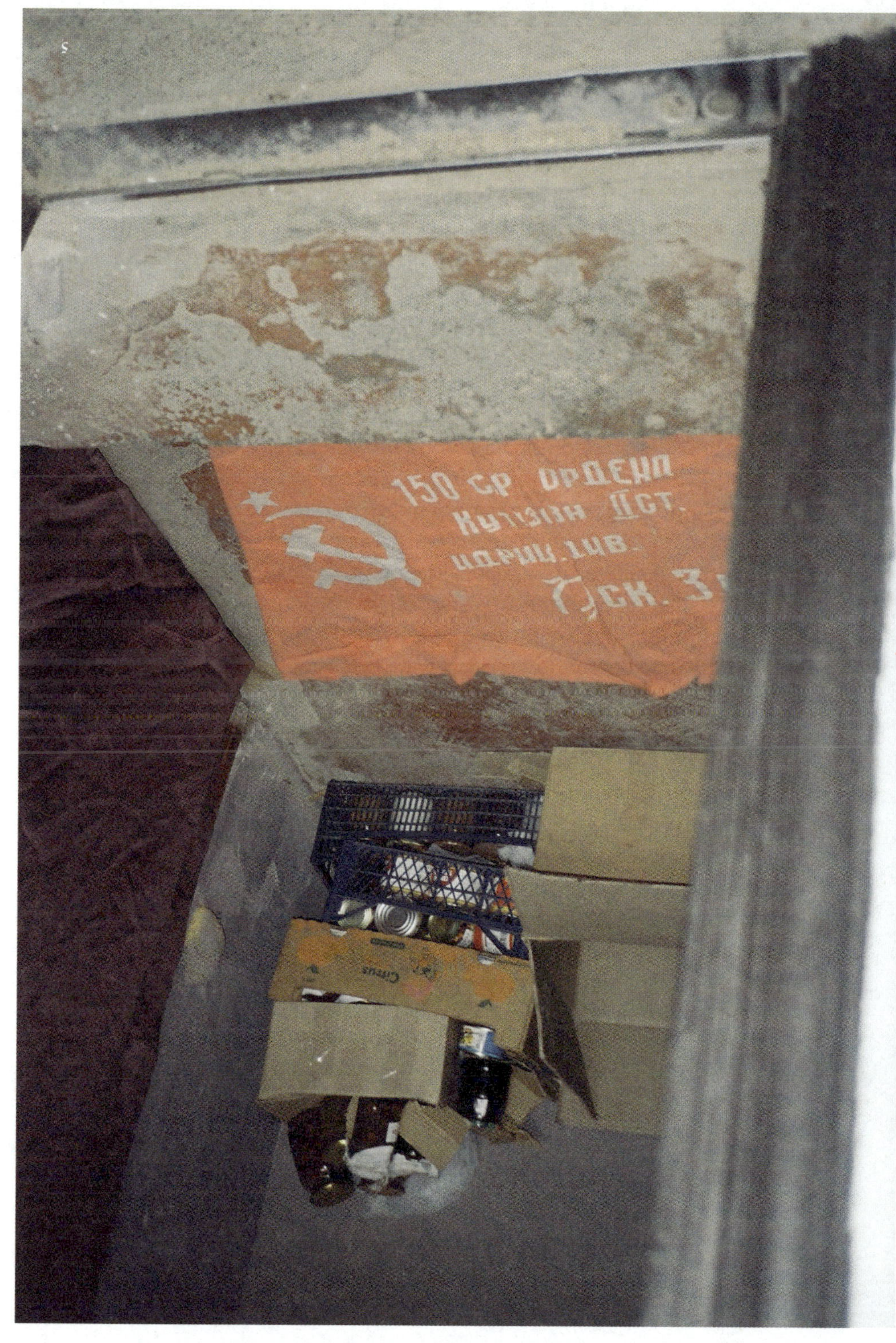
150 СР ОРДЕНА
Кутузн IIСТ.
идриц.див.
Уск.3

11

Yura's neighbor Lesha suffered post-traumatic stress disorder from a drone that 'came buzzing straight toward my forehead'. He was born in 1988, a year before the Berlin Wall came down. Slow and slender, shadow-eyed, with his brown hair parted, he sat across the kitchen table from me, both of us comparably outfitted in overjackets and undershirts, while his felines padded around – for he was most definitely a cat-lover, as will become clear. I never saw such kindness to animals as I did in Ukraine. Yura, who specialized in dogs, and inflicted on me several cell-phone videos of his creature's poses and performances, would carry on our drives a small bag of canine food from which to feed the hopeful salivations of that tribe on streets and at petrol stations.

'At first I felt quite secure,' he began. 'My niece, my sister's daughter, she lived quite close to the Shkolniy's military airport, which was even more dangerous than here, so she came to my place because at hers there were missiles.'

'We were then at quite high spirits,' continued Lesha. 'My friends and I decided to join the Territorial Defense to see what it was like. They turned us away and said they had enough manpower. My inner circle, they're quite creative people. If there was a need, we could do it. The common atmosphere was high morale. At that time we watched plenty of videos on TikTok showing how well equipped Ukrainian soldiers were. So we decided to devote ourselves to volunteering. We created a chat we called "The Headquarters". There were eight of us, including one girl who worked at a local IT company. Through the company we raised money for different defense needs. There was one guy in our inner circle who, I won't say he reported to Russia, but he would tell us: "Not everything is so simple." He didn't want us to help with territorial defense, even though we were only getting things like wet wipes for soldiers. Then there was this ad from a maternity house asking for help. We brought them a few boxes of medicine. It was quite an emotional moment. All those girls, those nurses, they were almost crying and hugging us.'

Lesha resumed: 'I kept up these volunteer activities even when my sister and her daughter fled to Germany; they have been there ever since. It is curious that during the first eight months of the war, everything was fine and we smiled at the military and had the experience of being some kind of united society.'

Scratching at the glass table with his ringed hand, while one cat or the other leaped onto his lap (he'd pet them, then fling them off), he continued: 'Then there were the first cases of conscription officers pushing people forcibly onto the buses, which we call "basification". At first we didn't believe it; maybe they were giving Russians targeting information and that was why they were arrested. Now we know it was conscription. There is no reasonably intelligent person who would like to be forcibly pushed into the back of a bus, treated like a goat. Maybe for a year, a year and a half, people's attitude toward the president was still very good; he was a hero in a way, with maybe ninety-five percent ratings. We had a feeling that all our officials stopped doing their regular activity, which was stealing. Then we saw that they had gone back to doing as they used to do. There are still many good people who are willing to make sacrifices, and we still respect the military, but everyone had begun to hate the president and the politicians.'

Clearing his throat and clasping his wrists in his lap, Lesha said: 'I experienced how our government takes care of our people when on January the 15th the first Shahed drone hit the opposite apartment block. I lost some windows, some window frames, the roof was damaged, and the feeling was not good, of course. My friend helped me to repair windows three days later – Get away from here,' he told the cat. 'I won't pet you.' The cat stayed, so he petted her. 'On the night of the twenty-fourth, a Shahed [Iranian-made kamikaze] drone hit the roof of my building. It was maybe ten meters away from my flat. I was inside at that moment. It was terribly unpleasant. I had that feeling that it was flying directly into my forehead. It became louder and louder. It was making that sound *bzzzzzzzz*. The area was targeted multiple times.'

'Why?'

'I don't know for sure. People were saying that they were targeting our DBR [the State Bureau of Investigation], which is an FBI replica. But DBR isn't military. I don't know for sure, but that facility used to be a bank . . .'

I supposed that was as good a reason as any for getting droned.

'Electricity was cut off, and plaster was pouring from the wall. I would say that the building shook and moved twenty centimeters. Everyone survived. There had been an explosion just before and everyone had run into the common corridor; until then everybody had ignored all the alarms, and so had I. One girl came running, asking for help because her door had jammed. I managed to open it, and the flat inside was completely ruined. Her cat was killed. When we were evacuated, the common entrance area had lost its roof, and the next three or four rooms not only had no ceilings but not even walls . . .'

His face became blank; the Russians might have fitted him with Joseph Roth's iron mask.

'How do you feel now when you hear the sirens?' I asked him.

'If there is a warning I go to the corridor, and if I hear their buzzing I have a panic attack. Sometimes I crouch down right there in the street . . .'

12

To all parties who might have wondered who bears the credit for removing Catherine the Great (or Catherina as he called her) from her Odesa pedestal, let me tell you: 'I did it,' said the activist Artak Hryhorian.

He was born in 1997. 'My parents are from Armenia but I was born in Odesa,' he said in simple English, which was considerably superior to my Ukrainian. 'After Maidan, from the beginning of 2014, I was talking revolution. We were planning a response to Russia's major occupation of Ukraine, and after sitting in a cafe we saw Catherina the Great's statue and discussed what to do about it.

There are a lot of similar issues here in Odesa, and many people have an opinion. We knew then that if we did something like bring down Catherina the Great there would be a lot of talk, a lot of passion. But after the full-scale invasion, everybody understood how important it was to be Ukrainian. Things change when Russian missiles break on your head. We needed to emphasize the differences between Ukrainians and Russians, because in the UK, in the US, people were thinking that we were like a part of Russia.'

Artak's generation was not the first to dislike Catherina, whose 'Greek Plan' gave Odesa her name in 1795. Robert Conquest reports that in 1966 the first secretary of the Ukranian Communist Party 'departed from the traditional line so far as to describe Catherine the Great's annexation of the Ukraine in hostile terms'. And, reader, if upon you had been inflicted some grand public monument to the robber of your nation's independence, why, then, you just might feel the same.

'Where is she now?'

'She's in a museum, in some box.'

'What about Tolstoy and Tchaikovsky?' I asked. 'Should they be decolonized?'

'My personal position, about Tolstoy first, is that we don't need him. He's not Ukrainian at all. We don't have a Walt Whitman Street! Tchaikovsky is different; Ukrainians know him from school, we study him. Tchaikovsky was not a martyr for the Russians. But Putin started making Russian propaganda about Tchaikovsky, so maybe we need to refute him there, too. That's why we have a special committee where we discuss this kind of thing.'

'What about Isaac Babel?'

'We've already resolved Isaac Babel. He's brought a lot of fame to Odesa, but most people know about Odesa not because of Babel but because of the port and swimming and so forth. If we join the EU, why should Europeans only know about Babel and Pushkin and Dostoevsky? Some pro-Russian Armenians or Latvians might say "I read Babel when I was eight years old; he was good," but when you speak with our children, at eight or nine, they won't have read this Soviet writer. We have different heroes now. So he should be decolonized.'

I remembered a line from Joseph Roth: 'Children need examples that they can understand and will remember. They can learn the truth later!'

I also remembered something from that already mentioned gangster story 'Froim Grach': 'He walked up Ekaterininskaya Street, made a turn by the statue of the Empress, and went inside the building of the Cheka.' No Cheka anymore, no Empress, no Babel: It would all be perfect.

(The translator Peter Constantine writes that following his arrest in 1939, Isaac Babel 'became a nonperson in the Soviet Union. His name was blotted out, removed from literary dictionaries and encyclopedias, and taken off school and university syllabi. He became unmentionable in any public venue.' We all get decolonized sooner or later, if not by drones or executioners, then by time's piling of forgetfulnesses upon death. If Babel grew unmentionable here, well, wouldn't that be ordinary? Antique survivals bloom and then die. After powerless grieving they will be replaced by the latest grand equivalent of Catherine the Great.)

'What about decolonizing the Orthodox Church?'

'In Odesa, if you see a rich church, it's a hundred percent Russian.'

'Red paint?'

He laughed. 'We talk about that, but it's for our state security service to act. The solution will be found in Kyiv, not in Odesa.'

Artak was likeable, cheerful, brave and willing to explain his position instead of simply imposing it. Perhaps that would change. I wondered how far he would go.

I shook his hand and he embraced me. Whenever he was not decolonizing, he was on the front line with his military unit: 'I do small drones.'

13

O n the wall of the coffee shop, across the street from the Odesa
Academic Ukrainian Music and Drama Theatre, some patriot
had magic markered: FREE AZOV! Azov being the right-wing, Russian-
speaking, hard-enduring volunteer unit (created in 2014) whose
yellow patch bore something like a compressed and tilted swastika.
In 2016, Amnesty International publicized allegations of pillage
and torture by Azov. For a good month in 2022, Azov stymied the
Russian besiegers (who designated them terrorists) in the supposedly
nuclear-proof tunnels and cellars of the Azovstal Iron and Steel
Works in Mariupol. Once Azov finally surrendered, the victors began
putting them on trial, which would arguably be a war crime because
international humanitarian law prohibits convicting soldiers for
participating in hostilities. Other Azov formations remained. In 2024,
America's State Department, which had previously agreed with the
Russians, decided that Azov was not a terrorist group after all, and
hence could receive US weapons.

Another sign of the times was a little red novelty paperback
whose title and densely printed contents consisted exclusively of the
Ukrainian version of FUCK THE RUSSIANS!

14

<h2>TOWARD THE FRONT: MYKOLAIV</h2>

A s in typical European bye-bye style, there was a sign for Odesa
with a slash through it, immediately followed by a military
checkpoint conveniently situated between two automobile accidents
decorated with broken glass, skewed cars, police and grim drivers
exchanging information (there were no conscription officers, and
the baby-faced soldier with the big rifle waved us wearily through);
and for an encore a band of reeking, brown diesel smoke stung our
faces while visibly occluding the nearest field. I asked Yura how much
riskier Mykolaiv might be than Vinnytsia or Odesa. 'Well, of course

we are closer to Crimea,' he said. 'With a missile in Vinnytsia we might have three minutes, in Odesa two minutes and now maybe ninety seconds.'

Despite the traffic, we reached Mykolaiv in less than three hours, stopping once at a petrol station where Yura fed a skinny, hungry dog from his small bag of dog food. We rolled past more grain fields. Yura had once raised chickens, which he said were lucrative. He had tried to grow mushrooms in one of the sandstone catacombs beneath Odesa, but when the crop gave off spores, he and his partners almost died. I suggested that he try to to sell Ukrainian cereals to some middleman. It might be a way to help him get out of the country when (I did not say this) the Russians came in. I quite loved him for being a wheeler-dealer who was also compassionate and honest. I trusted him with my life and promised not to jump out of the car and leave him to be droned alone.

We passed over the estuary bridge which the enemy hit in 2022, greatly hindering Yura and his journalist clients. It was rebuilt, and I wondered why the Russians did not destroy it again. Then came dark fields behind a long wall of trees, and Neskuchne's greenish-looking Orthodox dome. Mykolaiv was so close to Crimea that I often heard people thank each other with the Russian *ochen spasibo* instead of the Ukrainian *dyakuyu*. Rows of white birch trees shone on certain streets. And there were so many Soviet monuments, ever so many chiseled stars! 'We need to call Artak,' I said, and Yura liked that jest; until returning to Odesa we would invoke that likeable zealot anytime we discovered something especially egregious to the decolonizers (who, I gathered, had already blown up a monument to the KGB).

At the coffee shop Yura texted the military again because our permission to visit Kherson still had not come through. I asked whether we could go without permission, but he was reluctant, and I have never been a go-getter boss when it comes to pushing others into danger. Yurii's car in Lviv had been barbecued, and in the unlikely event that we survived a drone strike Yura would need a new car and both of us would have medical bills to pay, so we contacted the military again that evening. He checked the news: 'Kyiv was significantly attacked by drones last night,' he told me. 'And the Metro partially collapsed. But I think it will be fine.' There went forty minutes. Yura wanted sushi for lunch, so I said why not? Each roll was well padded with cream cheese. Yura worried about me when I drank orange juice, because he thought it would give me diabetes. He preferred healthy foods, such as gas-station wraps packed with cheese and mayonnaise. Strolling past an apartment building from whose roof the enemy had taken a hemispherical bite, leaving behind some scorched dangling stuff, we found his restaurant and ordered sushi to go. That spent half an hour. I wanted a new daypack for my cameras and film because the old one's zipper was going; that cost me the equivalent of €17 and expended another twenty minutes. We had dithered and delayed as long as we could. Yura looked at me, and I said: 'Well, how safe is it to roll toward the next town on the Kherson road?' – 'Well, not extremely safe, but fuck it; let's go.' Was I coaxing him to his death? In 1994, two colleagues and I had jointly decided to drive to Sarajevo after our United Nations flight was canceled. One was a high-school classmate and our interpreter. Either the Spanish UN battalion gave him bad directions or else he misunderstood them, because he and the other man ended up dead.

Of course to his family and several of his friends I was the murderer. Well, Yura was a professional; this was his job; he had showed me cell-phone videos of situations more terrifying than any I had survived, so fuck it; let's go. It was half an hour to Posad-Pokrovske, halfway to Kherson.

15

POSAD-POKROVSKE

From the beginning, I had assumed that America's involvement in Ukraine, as was the case in Vietnam and Angola, was intended less to save our ally than to bleed the Russians.

Off to the right of the road to Posad-Pokrovske was a wrecked gas station. Over the years I have gotten pretty sick of wreckage, but maybe a photograph of this might convince somebody of something, never mind that the war was almost certainly lost.

'Is it mined here?' I asked Yura. 'I mean, it is concrete and asphalt…'

'It should be okay,' he said a trifle dubiously.

Yura had seen someone walking on the side road into town. Since he said that people were rare here, I sent him off in case he could catch the man, so I could speak to him. I gingerly proceeded across the cracked pavement, step by step. I do not mind telling you that I inserted neither toe nor finger into the rectangular hole in the gas-pump island, whose war-typical scorched smell was sweet-tinctured from leaking residual fuel, while on the bright highway, which my shaded vantage point beneath a skeletonized awning made brighter still, a lime-green tank sped by.

By then Yura, bless his heart, had found some villagers gardening. He said a few of them might tolerate being interviewed. I spoke to a strong-looking lady named Oksana, who obliged, smiling and

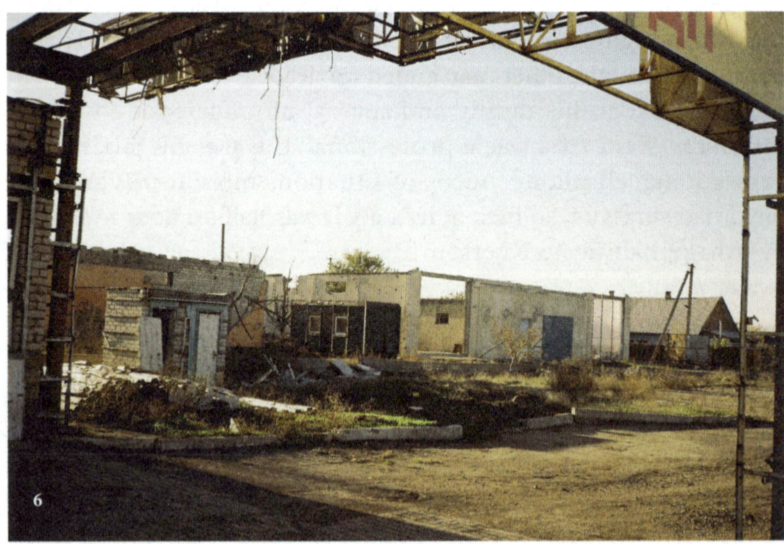

shrugging. She was born in 1977, in Kherson, where her mother still lived.

'I will never forget how it happened,' she began. 'Chornobaivka Airport, where Russian soldiers were located, was hit with missiles and bombs. At 6 a.m. my husband went to work in Kherson as usual. There weren't many jobs here; that's why he worked there. A bit later we found out that their so-called "special military operation" had started. We saw helicopters and jets from Russia flying over Kherson, but even then we thought it would not go that far; how could it? This is the twenty-first century . . .' She spread her hands, narrowed her eyes and stared into space.

'On the twenty-fourth we were still planning how we would pick up our daughter from her school, a science lyceum in Kherson, and we still had the impression that the governments would somehow negotiate and it would not be a real war. But then on the night of the 25th of February a Russian military column entered our village.' She sighed.

'The air forces from both sides, they started to destroy this village. For two weeks we were in the basement. With me were my husband, my son, daughter and grandson. My daughter-in-law's father was killed in Chornobaivka on the first day of war. He was shot dead; that's why I took the rest of their family to our place. I had a very nice basement, so we gave shelter to four families and some children, and it was a good place, very warm. We all sat there back to back. There was a four-month-old baby with us. We made beds on two levels, and a furnace because it was cold. There was already no electricity, gas or water supply . . .'

'And food?'

'We kept pigs, and we had some pickled onions in storage, and actually we kept on working. On the edge of the village is a food-canning factory where I worked as an accountant, and since not everyone had stocks of food, we produced some cans and pickles to supply people with. We would wait until there was no shelling, and quickly load the car with whatever we had produced. The factory operated until the 14th of March. On that day we loaded the last car with what we had made.'

She was a leader all right, this woman with the blond hair, green parka and bass voice. She was the only kind of leader worth anything, the kind who cares for others.

'*Da, da*, we departed one night toward Odesa. Locals provided us with shelter, and police helped as well. Then we went our separate ways. I came back here on the 14th of November 2022. Kherson had been liberated on the 11th of November. My mother lived through the whole occupation – eight and a half months. There was no water, no gas, no electricity. She told me that there were a lot of Chechens, and in the last stage they would capture people and put them into basements . . . We took her to our place after liberation. My husband and son, they joined the army one month after it started, and they are still serving. My son is thirty and my husband is fifty. Often I go to them, since they only have leave every three months.'

'That's permitted?'

'Try to refuse our women from visiting loved ones!'

I grinned back at her. 'Do you think the war has gone well?'

'No.'

'Is anyone here pro-Russian?'

She laughed. 'Of course. Nearly all of them fled to the Russian side. Try to imagine us before, living together and looking into each other's eyes! I actually want to suffocate them.'

By her estimate, the population of Posad-Pokrovske approximated 3,000 before Putin's little operation began. Now it was around 800.

'If you go to Kherson,' she said, 'you will see the water canal, which UNICEF recently repaired. It was a border between our troops and theirs. Now we find a lot of so-called presents in it – hardware, weapons, corpses of soldiers – theirs and ours. We call different NGOs to take them away.'

'Was Posad-Pokrovske mined?'

'Not much. It was mostly shelled.'

'So it's safe for you to walk around?'

'Without de-mining I wouldn't dare to enter my house. I knew that *Katsapy* [an offensive word for Russians, implying goatishness] had gone inside, because my laptop was stolen and then I electronically located it in Russia. They would often set up booby traps and mines . . .'

'And what do you do now when you hear a drone?'

'We hear drones here almost every night, at least five or six. They produce this buzzing noise. We call them mopeds . . .'

'How far down the road toward Kherson would you advise us to continue?'

She smiled and shook her head. 'Mm, mm,' she said. 'With such a car you're super noticeable. I wouldn't advise you to go there. Even Chornobaivka was hit yesterday with drones. You could go to Chornobaivka, but don't go too close to the airport.'

'If we're on the road and some drone comes, what should we do?'

'Speed up,' she replied, without much certainty.

16

Stopping at a petrol station to gas up and then snack, Yura on a cheese wrap, which they happened to burn, while I had better luck with my veal kebab wrap, we continued our separate labors. He hounded the military for me yet again while I, in my high-powered journalist fashion, watched the muted flatness of the fields darken into something that might be superficially construed as green, above which lay a narrow band of orangish-purple, a slightly wider one of purplish-red above it, and on top a wide vague streak of orange gave way (as in some past master's Japanese block print) to a whiteness and ultimately to blueness, with a sly crescent moon on top.

It was definitely getting on to the witching hour, when the drones would come hunting. We agreed to hustle back to Mykolaiv. By then it was awfully dark. Yura would rather have returned to Odesa and resumed work here in the morning, but since we had not reached Posad-Pokrovske until nearly four, I thought it better to book some cheap hotel. In response to this proposal, Yura cited the case of a journalistic team who had stayed in a Mykolaiv hotel. When their foreign car gave them away to Russian dronesters, in buzzed one of those 'moped' horrors and killed them. For this reason he persuaded me that we should rent an apartment. That was how we came to meet Olga, a youngish woman, standing in the courtyard of a Soviet-era apartment block named after Comrade Lyaginva, Hero of the Soviet Union. When Yura looked him up for me on his phone he turned out to be, as Yura put it, 'a Soviet spy'. (Where oh where was Artak? The egregious monument still even bore a star.) Olga led us up three flights of dark stairs that stank of cockroach poison. It was not easy to get in or out of our flat, there being several locks and keys, each conjugation of which required its own trick.

After Olga departed, we descended to inspect the so-called shelter: a series of dirt-floored cellar crypts reached by untrustworthy stairs with wobbly railings. The entire building felt unsound. I told Yura I would rather be killed in our apartment than rush down into one of these dark and grubby graves to be crushed when the low ceiling collapsed. So that made it easy; I would meet all perils in my bed, perhaps even with Ukrainian junk food in my hand. When we went out to move the car and buy bottled water (Yura had warned me that Ukraine's filtration system had grown inadequate), we walked past Lyaginva's monument again.

How much dynamite would be needed to decolonize this city in which nice old ladies greeted me in Russian?

Then our permission came through. We were to drive two and a half hours each way to meet somebody or other in the early afternoon, and then we would see what we would see. The military asked for my blood type; I vaguely thought it was the most common one, group B, so that was what I said. I thanked Yura, who went off to work out at the gym, and then lay down in my bed.

Shortly before midnight I was awakened by the air-raid siren. Of course I was half-dressed anyway, but it was a comfort to hear Yura puttering about in the living room. After a while the whining stopped.

17

MYKOLAIV (AGAIN)

In a coffee shop in Mykolaiv, we debated what gift to bring the soldiers. I voted for vodka, but Yura thought cigarettes would be more divisible and maybe even fungible, so I spent around €50 for I don't know how many packs of smokes. 'So Mykolaiv was fine but Odesa was hit last night,' he told me. 'It was like when they hit Kyiv. Multiple drones from different directions. They launched ninety-two drones and our anti-aircraft only managed to hit sixty-two. A man in a car got killed because he was unlucky enough to be there the moment it exploded. It was a terrible attack. A school was hit. Nine were wounded.' He showed me a video of people screaming: 'Fuck! Shit! Run, you faggot!' (His translation.)

He looked at more news on his phone and said: 'I think we're soon going to lose the rest of Donetsk. That will be terrible for our metal production.'

At mid-morning we set out for our rendezvous, following the Kherson road. I remember a Soviet tank on a pedestal, with its red star painted out with blue paint. Brick houses watched me from behind ornate picket fences, modestly hiding their smashed windows and sheared-off walls behind amputated trees. A sandbagged bunker guarded someone's semi-skeletonized home. There were houses with chips cut out of them, and houses stripped down to the rafters. Beside the road grew fields of white-eared wheat; I supposed they would not be harvested this year.

On a wide blue-brown river, men were rebuilding a bridge, working from a wooden span that sagged beneath the weight of their truck. 'I remember when this bridge was destroyed,' Yura said.

Then we saw two cows and a green-gray field-horizon. Some houses looked good from a distance. There were even goats; they reminded Yura of his granny, who had kept one. A painted red star glowed out from the ruins. In the next settlement, a sign read: PRAY FOR UKRAINE. 'Oh, I remember this village,' said my friend. 'It's dangerous. I knew one of the deminers who got exploded here . . .'

Here came a monument from 1944–94; poor Artak could not be everywhere, so it still retained its star.

18

VELYKA OLEKSANDRIVKA

In the village of Velyka Oleksandrivka, close to the front, soldiers and civilians hobnobbed in quiet streets, broken walls and open rafters for their backdrop. Two young women strolled past a brick building with gnawed-off corners. I saw children playing.

But poor *Granta*, as it now appeared, must have lacked clout with the Ukrainian military. When we showed up at the rendezvous with helmets and bulletproof vests at the ready, it turned out that we would not be allowed to visit any forward positions. Yura was disgusted, and I a trifle annoyed, but I consoled myself that this would be better for our health. Besides, all *Granta* had commissioned was 5,000 words, and I would exceed expectations by submitting 40,000 words, which they would only be able to cut down so much. No doubt we could have gotten into trouble on our own, at modest personal expense and considerable risk, but why take the trouble? At the instructions of a ponytailed press officer named Sasha, we stationed ourselves in a coffee shop whose annex had a tree growing out of it. Since the place stank of cigarette smoke, I offered our bag of cigarettes to our soldier interviewees, who rebuffed the present, at which I thought, oh well.

Group interviews are best conducted with low expectations. The talkers talk; the rest keep quiet. When there is a party line, it is silently enforced. Yura simply could not interpret more than one sentence out of every ten, so all I could do was ask my questions and hope some day to get rough transcriptions of the answers, which I did. It was a sunny day and I got to learn about drones.

'My call sign is Smile. My name is Oleksandr. I won't tell you my surname.'

'Would you say that the other side is out-producing you in drones thanks to Iran?'

'Iran doesn't help Russia with FPV [First Person View] drones. All spare parts for FPV drones they get from China, and they also have some of their own production. Let's say China supplies them with some unique spare parts. The rest can be assembled in a kitchen.'

'If it is not classified to tell me, would you say that Russians have three times more than you do, or ten times more, or what?'

'They do have more,' Smile answered. 'I would say they have approximately twice as many FPV drones.'

'Do you have glide bombs?'

'Yes we do, but that is not our domain.'

'Could you tell me what you do in the course of a drone operation? How do you know that you have succeeded?'

He spread his hands and smiled. He had wide, blue-green eyes, a red beard and a bright, young face. 'It begins with preparation,' he said. 'We need to set up our drones to make them ready. Then we assemble the ammunition, and watch the video broadcasting from other reconnaissance units. When we see a target, we report to our commanders and if they approve, we launch our drones. Usually it's a Mavic drone that confirms that we've managed to hit the target.'

'How often would you say a mission is successful? It must be pretty difficult to escape from a drone . . .'

'I would say the success rate of our flights is around sixty to seventy percent. Of course it depends on the training level of their troops. They're also preparing for battle. They scrutinize the battlefield and the frequencies we use, and depending on this data they can dial in on electronic warfare targeting their vehicles.'

'Is it more important to target Russian soldiers or infrastructure, such as supply depots or fuel tanks and so on?'

'It depends on the infrastructure. Their antennas and means of surveillance are definitely more important than infantry, because infantry without these facilities is useless.'

'How near are we now to the enemy?'

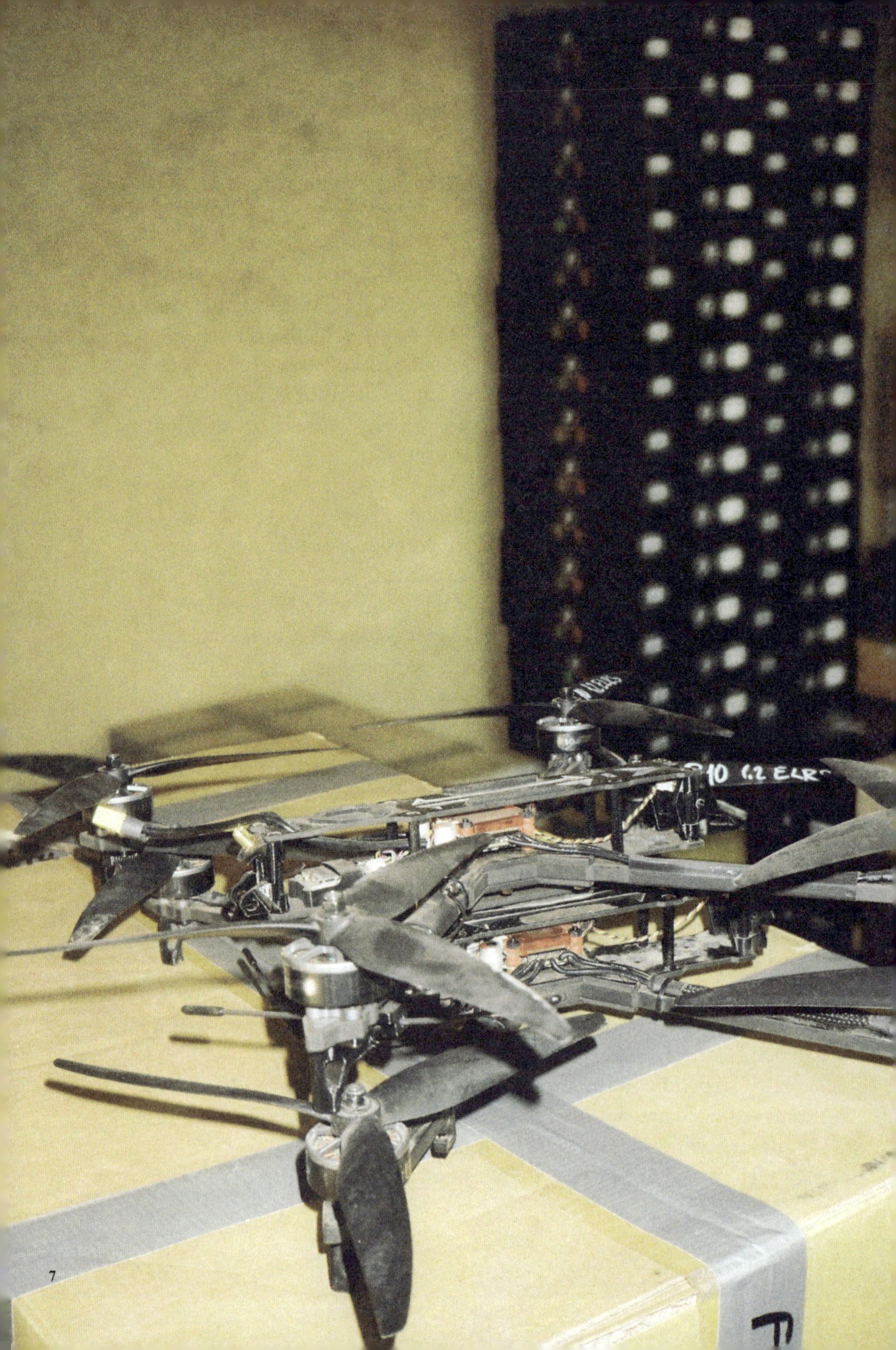

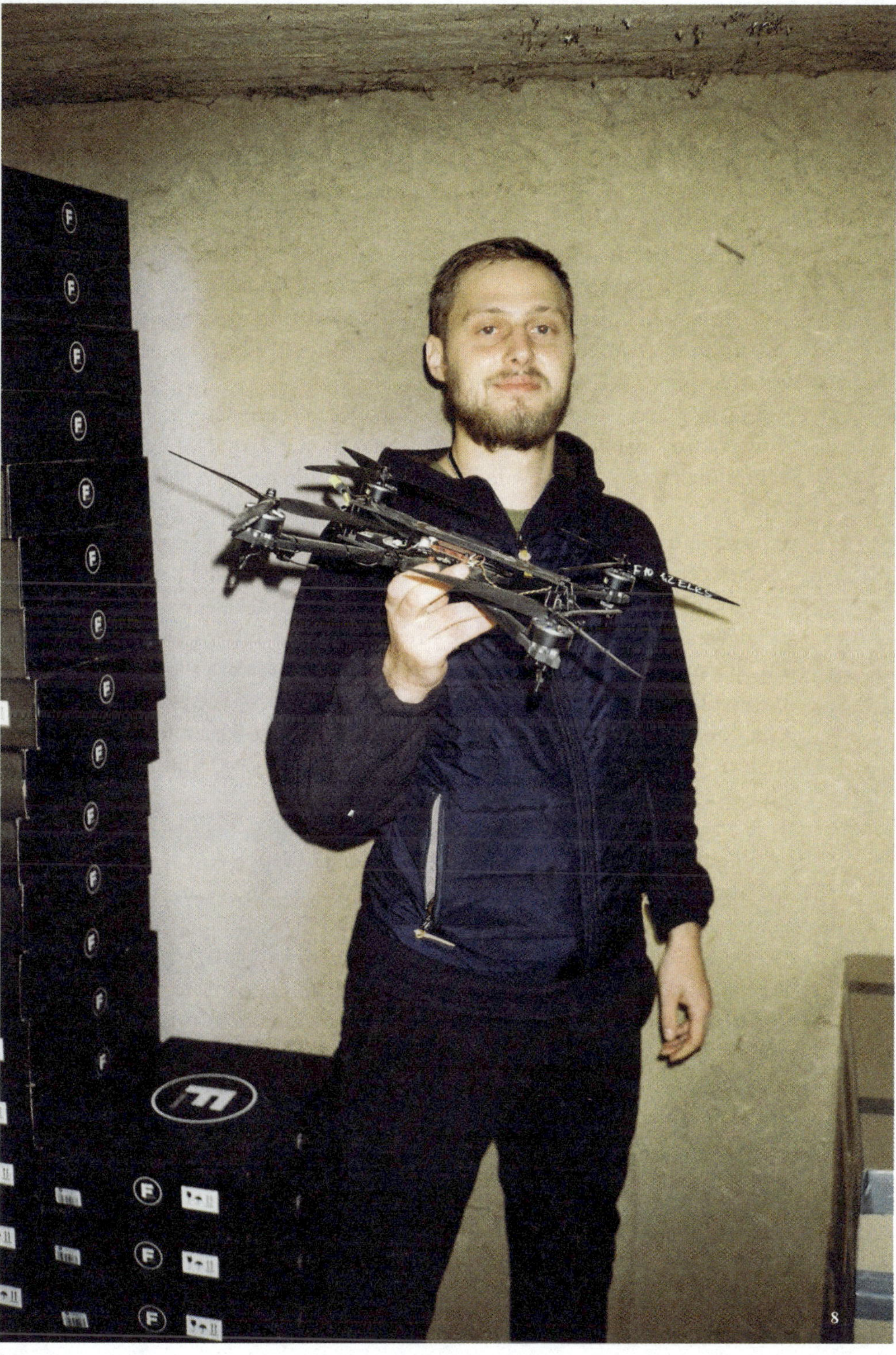

Smile clasped his hands in his hooded sweatshirt: 'From here to the battle line? Must be twenty something –'

Another soldier interrupted: 'No, it's more like sixty kilometers.'

'What is the most typical threat to you here from the Russians? What do they usually use?'

'Their KAB glide bombs [500-kilogram finned projectiles] and Shahed drones manage to reach us here. They also have reconnaissance drones with them.'

Smile's crop-haired commander Oper then put in: 'And "Supercams", their wing-type reconnaissance drones, because without them they can't locate the precise coordinates of a target.'

'If they see you with a reconnaissance drone, how quickly can they respond and attack?'

'It depends on the type of weapon they use,' Oper said. 'They need to find a target. To do reconnaissance and then confirm everything and request their aviation to attack – realistically that takes a few days. But let's not hide the fact that among the locals there are those who support them. If they want to inform, and the enemy are provided with coordinates from those collaborators, it isn't a problem for them to prepare some missile launcher like the S-300 and hit us quite fast.'

'Can you tell me what your typical day looks like?'

'I get up at four or five, when it is still dark,' Oper said. 'I check the live streams and connect our communication system with headquarters. Then I prepare drones, upload drivers and set them. After that I renew information on my laptop 24/7 and just wait for a target to appear. Once there is an order to launch, my armorer brings a drone loaded with ammunition. I fly it toward the target. This repeats again and again. When the front is active, I can fly around forty to sixty missions. It's calmer here at the moment, so we have more free time.'

'What is the typical range of your drones?'

Smile answered: 'They can go up to thirty-five kilometers within the enemy's rear. But on average it's fifteen kilometers. I'm talking about small FPV drones. We also have FPV kamikaze wing-type drones, with ranges up to sixty kilometers, but they are used only against very important targets.'

'Yura tells me that this front is getting more active, and there are more drones than before.'

'They have many more drones,' Oper said, 'and the density is getting higher. The thing is they produce them on the state level. But we have the advantage of being more mobile and flexible. We are mostly supplied by private organizations or individual donors. But on account of our smaller quantity of drones, we can alter them more quickly.'

'In general,' Oper said, 'our smaller number of pilots complete missions more efficiently than theirs. We analyze the air space and watch how they fly. Many of our guys use the same frequencies that they use. So we can see when they launch their drones and if they are managing to hit targets. Their typical practice is to launch a drone and then find out if there's a target. Quite often there is no target, and they just lose the drone somewhere. So it seems they just launch them for the sake of some quota.'

'So last night in Odesa, for instance, would you say that was mostly from the incompetence of their drone operators that they couldn't hit any military targets, or you think they hit civilians on purpose?'

'They just use all the weapons they have,' Smile said, 'and they don't care what they hit. Also of course they can lose their route, which often happens because of our electronic warfare. But I still think they target populated areas on purpose to spread panic.'

'Do you think the front line situation here is stable? Or are you losing ground?'

Oper answered: 'When we were defending positions in Donetsk, they threw an enormous amount of force to assault our positions. They never lacked manpower. We managed to destroy a lot of their machinery. During our last days there, they ended up assaulting our positions with old civilian cars, "GAZ-66s" and "Bukhankas" simply covered with rubber. They ran out of resources. But once again it came down to the amount of manpower. They had a huge amount. Before their assaults they performed "preparation activities" – covering our position with dense artillery fire.'

I tried to imagine that nightmare.

'What can you do,' he asked me bitterly, 'if you have four people in your own position, and even if you hit the enemy's armored vehicles they hit your position with glide bombs and then assault you with maybe forty men, along with artillery, FPVs, Mavics and other drones that drop explosives and gas . . . which is prohibited by the Geneva Conventions? I don't even know what kind of aid we need in such a situation. You can't do much against artillery and KAB glide bombs. Here in the Kherson region, the direction is different. The enemy aren't prioritizing it. We all understand that in order to cross the river they will need certain big resources. And they are using their main resources in Donetsk right now. In the future it's likely that they will make an assault in this direction. I wouldn't be surprised if they sent soldiers swimming across the river. I remember how we watched them at dawn heading toward us: a column of thirty people simply walking toward us in an open field . . .'

In *The Radetzky March,* a rich and amoral alchemist named Chojnicki (destined to go mad in the Great War) tells one of Joseph Roth's protagonists what hardly anyone else can see: 'The Fatherland no longer exists . . . The fact is we're all dead!' That was the thought that crawled out of my head and down my neck as I listened to Oper. That was the thought I did not wish to think.

'What if you could inflict more damage on Moscow so that they start to feel what you are feeling?'

'Do you mean hitting civilian infrastructure or what?' Oper asked.

'Yes, maybe damage their infrastructure, to make people afraid . . .'

'Definitely, in my own opinion, it should be done,' Oper said. 'I wouldn't hit civilian infrastructure, but their people should see us hitting their production lines and refineries. When I say production I mean military production, their warehouses. That is actually already happening. But if we could do it with missiles, it would be great. They learn from us and we don't learn from them. That's our problem. They needed a few months to adapt to the new reality of drones, but then they did. They tried to assault the town of Vuhledar directly and then they just took it with a flanking movement. Look at Kurakhovo. They encircled it. So they've found their tactics. What's the point in attacking directly if you can go round the flanks where there are fewer forces?'

19

In the village, Sasha escorted us to a house that had been commandeered by a drone unit. I inferred that the previous owner, who was 'a former Soviet soldier', had fled to Russia, unless something else had happened to him. On the doormat was a hammer-and-sickle communist flag.

When Putin pressed the START button on what became the Great Game of Drones, Zhenya 'Patifon', aka 'Party Fun', evinced the same patriotic spirit as Yura's neighbor Lesha and ever so many of their countrymen. He incarnated what one of Odesa's military billboards called *stav plus*, something like 'check, plus!', meaning: 'Yessir, I got this, and will not only get it done but exceed your expectations.' He was someone who had not given up.

'Have you always been good with electronics and engines?' I asked him.

'Before the full-scale invasion, I headed the production department of a furniture enterprise. This all started when I disassembled my first Orlan drone. We'd seized three of them from the enemy, and I removed their thermal vision devices, trying to figure out how we could use them. It was my first experience with electronics, actually.'

'How soon after the invasion did this happen?'

'I joined the army on the third day of invasion,' he told me, not without pride. 'And I made those devices six weeks later. In the beginning of the war I was serving in the Bakhmut area, in an anti-aircraft regiment. We managed to hit thirty-six targets in the course of six months.'

'This is probably an ignorant question, but would it be possible to emit some kind of frequency to make all enemy drones in one area fall out of the sky?'

'Only nuclear weapons could do that, because such a wave doesn't exist.'

'Yura told me that when the sound of the drone stops, that's when it's falling and is about to detonate. So when it falls, has the enemy turned off the motor?'

'They actually often fly along motorways so that their engines won't be heard. Usually when they start to attack, they ramp up the engine to maximum, so really the drones should be even louder. If you switched off the engine, you would slow it down.'

'Then how come it gets silent?'

'That might be the case with a drone that drops something. Or it could possibly be the effect of distance. An explosion one kilometer away will reach your ears in three seconds. If it takes ten seconds for the sound to come, that makes it approximately three kilometers away. You won't hear it immediately.'

'Is it true that Russian drone production centers are centralized? In that case, if you knew where they were, you could do more damage to them than they could do to you . . .'

'I think they spread out production just as we do. Our private producers [not the state ones] use five or six locations to make even a simple drone. Let's say that in one place they produce batteries, in another they produce bodies, in one more they'll solder everything and in still another assemble them. So such a strike wouldn't achieve anything. It would just temporarily damage the enemy's logistics.'

I wished my father were still alive. That gadget-loving efficiency expert would have loved learning about drones. He would have had practical advice for the dronesters. Maybe he could have made a difference, unlike his dreamy son.

'Do most drones still require humans to actually launch them? Could you be a hundred kilometers away and have some robot send up the drone so that you are completely out of range?'

'One pilot wearing his flip-flops and drinking tea in Kyiv can fly a drone somewhere in Donbas. In five minutes he has bombed something and his drone can automatically return to preset coordinates. At the same moment this guy connects to a drone somewhere in Kherson or Kharkiv. There he hits some targets and again uses the automatic home-in. This way one pilot can use around ten drones per day.'

Holding up a fat cable, Patifon said: 'This thing will allow you to operate a drone here even as far away as the USA. You have a LAN [local area network] connection and a transmitter located here. Another one we connect in the USA. We need good internet and that is it. This transforms protocols.'

He got up and led me to another part of the room. 'Let me show you the bomb we use for our land drone. It is seventy-eight kilograms of cumulative explosive. If it goes off at a distance of eight meters from a tank, the tank completely loses its engine.'

'This is something you made?'

'Yes. But the bomb is a separate, standard device; I just attached it to a land drone. It was originally designed to explode bridges and concrete constructions.'

'Suppose you stay in this house for a little while and Russians start to suspect something? You must be moving from place to place every week.'

'We used to move more often in Donbas. Here we do it less. If you want, I can give you my phone number and you can be the first to shoot my machine-gun drone from the USA.'

That was my conversation with Zhenya 'Patifon', aka 'Party Fun', of the 72nd Brigade.

20

MYKOLAIV

In the WOG Cafe of the WOG petrol station just outside of Mykolaiv, I sat entering my first notes on a drizzly morning while Yura ordered a cheese and chicken wrap, in whose salubriousness he devoutly believed. The night before, the enemy had struck Odesa again, this time in six locations: buildings flaming, wrecked cars, no casualty numbers released. Yura reminded me: 'Of course our government will not say if military targets were hit, but with an attack this big something was hit.'

To illustrate what a glide bomb could do, he showed me photos of a multistory apartment building after the Russians had brought it up to date: whereas a drone or even a missile might merely punch a hole in three or four floors (when the enemy hit Mykolaiv's blocky Regional State Administration Building in 2022, the cruise missile created an ovoid patch of sky in the middle), a glide bomb could smash a wide channel from roof to basement and below – leaving the end pieces standing, maybe, but if there was a shelter, logically located in the subterranean center of the building, its occupants would be crushed or incinerated. The range of these weapons remained only twenty or thirty kilometers. Since they had to be launched in clusters from jet fighters, which as the Russians had been surprised to discover were vulnerable to Ukrainian anti-aircraft defenses, their evil power rapidly weakened beyond the front line – 'Making it very dangerous,' Yura cheerfully remarked, 'for places such as you and I have been to.' (All the same, I had to force him to accept an extra €200 for the two days we had rolled the dice. He felt he was taking advantage, since not even one drone had hunted us.)

In Lviv, Vinnytsia and Odesa, I had been practically invulnerable to glide bombs. But the history of humanity is the history of benevolent progress, so the enemy's big brains were doing their patriotic best (wouldn't you?) to extend those weapons' reach. 'Putin is dreaming of Odesa,' Yura said. 'Maybe he will be satisfied to annex from Kherson and Donetsk, west past Odesa, and then give what's left of Ukraine to Poland.' As it was, the Odesa situation was already – as one might sloganize – NOT BAD FOR VLAD, as I verified for myself by visiting one of the previous night's impact points.

21

BACK IN ODESA

We reached Odesa at about one o'clock. The strike site was in the northern outskirts, 7 kilometers past the formal city line. We rode the old Soviet dam road along the *limon* (a not concisely translatable word that referred to something like an estuary or a lake) where Yura's grandmother used to take cold mud baths. Yura told me that the *limon* was 'going extinct', but what wasn't nowadays, excepting violence, despair and authoritarianism? The black shore was clotted with salt. We were negotiating the traffic circle where 'many men don't like to drive, because these conscription bastards often lie in wait'. Gas stations and dormant fields made their usual inspiring impression. Ahead of us, gray road met gray sky. 'This area is often attacked, because, you see, there are all these warehouses.' At the next checkpoint a young soldier stood looking cold, with his machine gun aiming down his belly; I waved at him and with an absolute minimum of effort he motioned us through. Across a field rose a horizon of bright-painted post-Soviet apartments, collectively named Seventh Heaven ('7 Nebo'), because they had been built for the mutual mercantile benefit of their occupants and the mega-market Seventh-Kilometer, which was now inevitably declining thanks to the internet. Apartment towers rambled bewilderingly on. A few caltrops (far too few) remained in helter-skelter huddles in case the Russian tanks should come. For now they served the convenience of scrawny pissing dogs.

This was the place. Yura checked the news. A mother had been killed, and her husband and son lay in the hospital. Eleven others had been wounded. But Yura had gotten ahead of himself; those were the

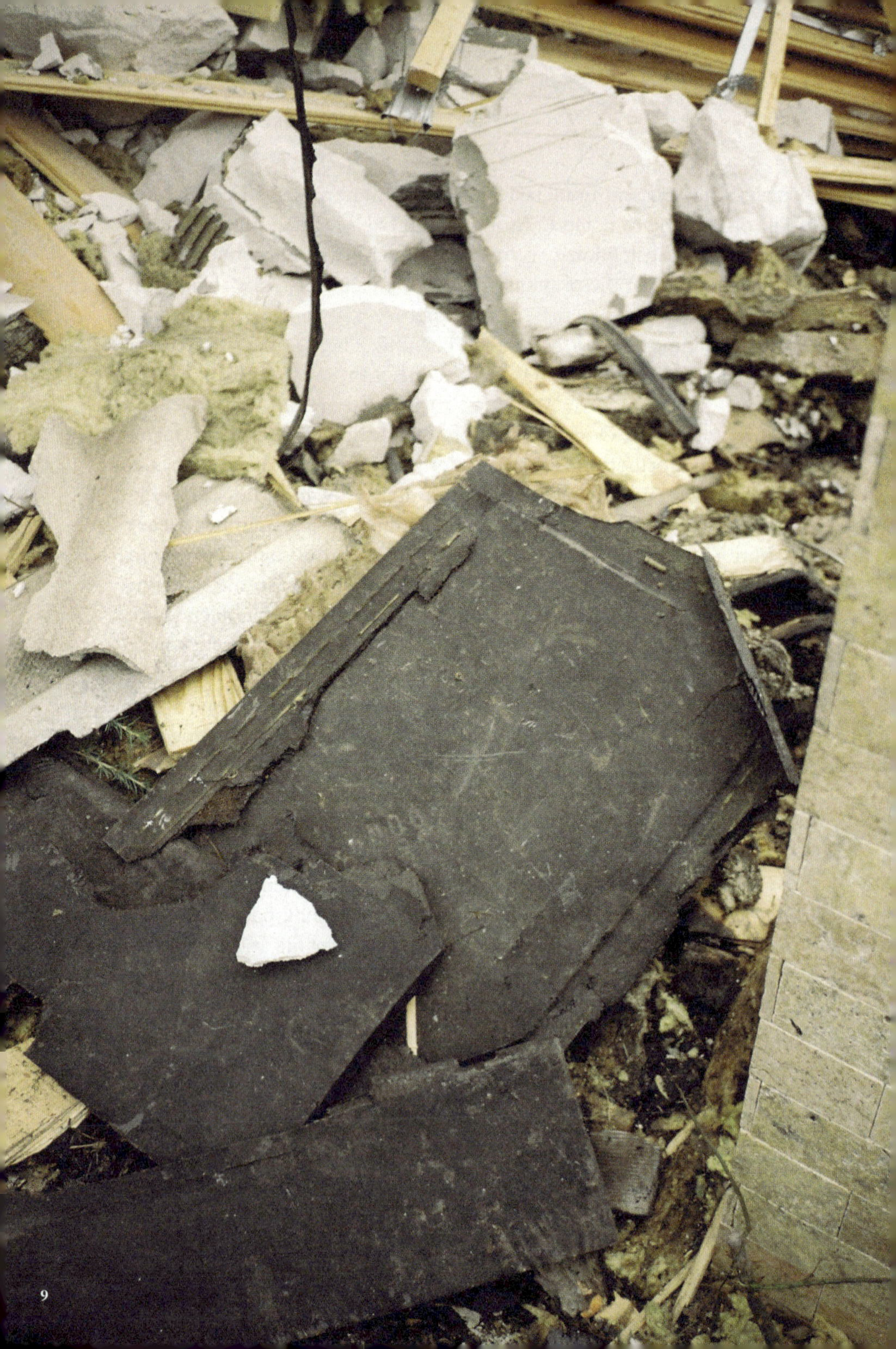

previous night's figures: last night one unknown person had been killed here and nine were wounded. On his phone he played for me some bystander's video of the hissing flame-wind and the musical shattering of window-glass. I walked up and down the canyon between apartment-cliffs, taking pictures. It was surprising how many buildings on both sides had been hit. There was a pretty good crater. 'You see,' my friend said, 'it is one of those big Iranian drones, maybe the size of a car.' As men winched a scorched vehicle onto a flatbed truck, children watched happily. A boy took pictures. Grief ached in my breastbone.

Why was Putin doing this? Shall we do him the credit of supposing him to be as good an egg as Hitler or Stalin, who accomplished their wonders in a spirit uncontaminated by selfishness? Joseph Roth summed up the type in a little screed from 1921: 'He is strict with himself in order to be violent with others . . . He fries that others may broil. He wants war so that others may die.'

22

At the opera house in Odesa the frieze stood defiantly pale and static against the night. In the doorway of a girlie bar, a man showed off two empresses in astonishing, glittering metal dresses. When I asked if I could take a photo-portrait, he sent me about my business. A girl who held the reins of two ponies, hoping to earn money from little children, allowed me to take her picture. I had wandered into what might have been the brightest Saturday street-night of downtown Odesa, where there were families, lone men and kissing couples living how and when they could under a small but significant risk of getting murdered. A stately couple promenaded down the leaf-spotted, black cobblestones, museum windows fiberboarded up behind them.

Entering a bar whose upside-down glasses glowed gold above the counter's candle lanterns, I found myself forbidden to sit here or there. I was only allowed a seat at the bar, but on sufferance. Instead of mating my non-existent phone to some vile grid of bars and pixels as the bouncer instructed me to, I ordered a shot of Havana Club, trusting that I could afford it, as indeed I could; it cost maybe €5. I admired the weird old brick ceiling, whose large-squared wrought-iron lattice might make it less of a death trap if a drone came. I listened to the sounds of ice cubes in the bartender's cocktail shaker and watched the flame pull its glowing orange dodges within the nearest candle-lantern. I wondered at the shiny lines of light in the long hair of the two rapid-speaking young women at the bar beside me. This was a professional machine of a place where I, a shabby foreigner, was hardly welcome. The bouncer sneeringly inquired if I supported Trump, and when I said that I did not, he disliked me slightly less.

23

The next day Yura and I went to see the cake artist Alla Belousova. Her home, from which she ran her business, had been struck on Friday night. But how would we find her? Yura checked his GPS and it did not know, so he rang her up. 'Oh, it must be this damn renaming of Kyiv streets,' she told him. Yura said the activists ('sometimes they're really stupid') had objected to the name of her street. At the beginning it was First Street; then (well before decolonization) some committee changed it to the problematic Stikolova, whose original was 'just some guy with a Russian surname, so what are they going to do? A lot of Ukrainians have surnames like Ivanov. Will they decolonize our names?' I asked what he would do if they demanded that he change his name, and he said: 'I'd tell them, fuck you! Stikolova, it means glass, actually. So then they changed it to Tomato Street.'

Alla Belousova and her husband Petya were Odesans, married for twenty years, and they had two children. Creeping cautiously through the wreckage in their backyard, trying not to slip and cut myself on wet, broken glass or sharp-snapped rebar (Petya tried to take my arm, but I waved him off because I was a big-shot journalist; I even had a press pass), we reached Exhibit A. 'Here it is,' he said in Ukrainian, and showed me a shiny hinge and a blackened wing from the drone that had done this: an Iranian 'Shahed', whose name was appropriate, for it means 'witness' and the thing had definitely seen what it was doing to Ukrainians. In the photograph I took it does not look like much in its undistinguished blackness against the miscellaneous white shards; maybe it could pass as a scrap of roofing material.

'This is where it landed,' Alla said. 'We had a nice garden, and before this no one would look at it! And now that it's ruined they all come to look . . .'

And there was the carp pond. Were its inmates still alive? The husband grinned at me and said: 'Sure. You can go fishing if you want.'

Alla Belousova had a delicate face. She was wincing, perhaps trying not to cry. Her open vulnerability further grieved me. Perhaps she had not yet begun to hate. Her kitchen was warm and electrically lit. It still smelled of fresh cake frosting. I wanted to buy a cake to help her, but there were none available. She offered to make coffee, but I would have been ashamed to take it.

'We live on the second floor with our children,' she said, 'and when the siren sounds we normally stay in the basement for two or three hours.'

'Does anti-aircraft defense make a drone strike less harmful, or does it make it worse?' I asked Petya.

'If it hits the fuel tank or the wing,' he said, 'it unbalances the drone.'

I nodded. I liked the wry and gentle way in which Petya smiled at Alla. It was sweet to see them link hands.

'I hope there will be peace for all the world,' she said.

'I wish the same, but I don't think there will be,' I said.

'In the years before the Great War . . .' wrote poor, wise Joseph Roth, 'it was not yet a matter of indifference whether a man lived or died. When someone was expunged . . . someone else did not immediately step up to take his place, but a gap was left . . .'

24

ODESA, ODESSA

In Lviv there had been the restaurant 'Baczewski'; open for only ten years so far, but serving old-style Jewish cooking: rice with sheep's milk, rabbit in truffle sauce with horseradish on the side, and creamed spinach, walnut brandy, yeah, yeah! Now, that would have fit right in with Babel's Odesa stories! What reader could resist a little lip-licking at the wedding of Benya Krik's sister, where the guests scored 'fish soup in which lakes of lemons shimmered like mother-of-pearl'?

For Odesa, the local Babel expert Mr Zhdanov had suggested the Tartar restaurant to make me feel Babelish; after Yura brought me there I returned twice on my own, delighting in the Eastern opulence of those emerald salads and that shashlik ever so tender, not to mention the tiny white bowls of yellow-tan hummus redly frosted with paprika; of course I washed all that down with beer. Sitting on cushions whose red, white and black stripes held patterns at first sight almost as ornate as oriental rugs, although they in fact repeated, I admired all the wall-hung plates I could see; each was crowded with its own world of birds, flower-studded stems, leaf clusters like hands of curling, tapering, pointed-nailed fingers. And as night came, the sweet pale-orange reflections of the lanterns hovered in the sky as patiently as the enemy's reconnaissance drones (again I remembered Yura telling me about the time that one of them hovered over the car, buzzing, while the colleague whom he was escorting 'bulged out his eyes with fear, and then that bastard jumped out and left me to die, so I thought, aha, that's how he is'). Now the sky was indigo, and no one sat outside under the awning. It was after five. Couples passed wearing heavy jackets, almost all of them hooded. I left a good tip and went out. On the corner, a blond flower girl stood encircled by plastic buckets of wares. Inside a bar whose neon-orange appellation made the dark sidewalk even darker, a lonely barmaid waited for something good to happen while her own client, an older, grizzled type, bent over his cell phone. Almost adjacent was a brow and nail

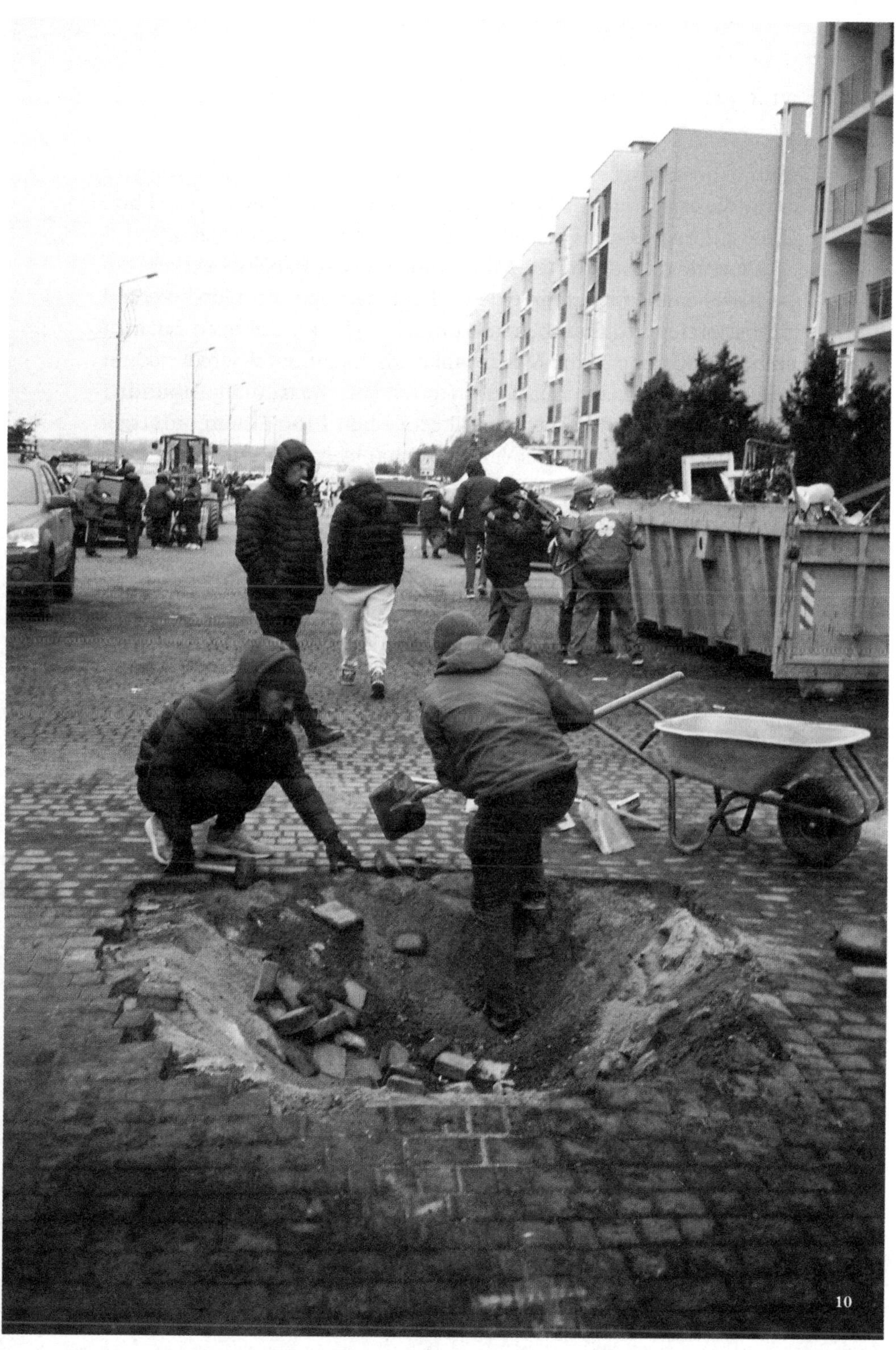

establishment, where women groomed women at little tables, and a middle-aged man pedicured a girl who curated her phone. Then came a florist's shop, white-floored and glowing like heaven.

Doubtless in its way the Moldavanka was as Babelish as ever.

Babel and Roth, and maybe brilliant, decadent Pushkin – I could almost pretend to find them all down in the high-ceilinged cellar of arched sandstone of the Moldavanka-ish restaurant where we could feast in antediluvian abundance (to tell you the truth, it astounded me how well the Ukrainians still ate; when I took them out, they never finished their plates; Yura wouldn't even take leftovers to the dog because it was 'on a diet'; maybe once the Russians finished swallowing Donetsk, metal production would decline, and then maybe electricity, which might affect food production). Who were the true antediluvians, who belonged in double-s'd Odessa? Well, Yura shared some of my hesitations about decolonization. He even spelled an awful lot of place names in the old Russian way. As for me, I was a Joseph Roth character. I knew that the American Empire in which I lived was approaching its imminent end, but I could not quite believe it. All those drones our corporations pimped out, when would they come to us to spread terror, agony and grief? I could have been the footman in *The Radetzky March*: 'It seemed to him that the hour was finally come when the supernatural forces of the world would appear in their full viciousness and unmistakableness.' ∎

Photography:

1. Vinnytsia
2. Lviv
3. Odesa
4. The Russian-struck hotel, Odesa
5. Velyka Oleksandrivka
6. Posad-Pokrovske, occupied February–March, 2022
7. Velyka Oleksandrivka
8. Velyka Oleksandrivka
9. Odesa
10. Odesa

This article was supported by funding from Open Society Foundations.

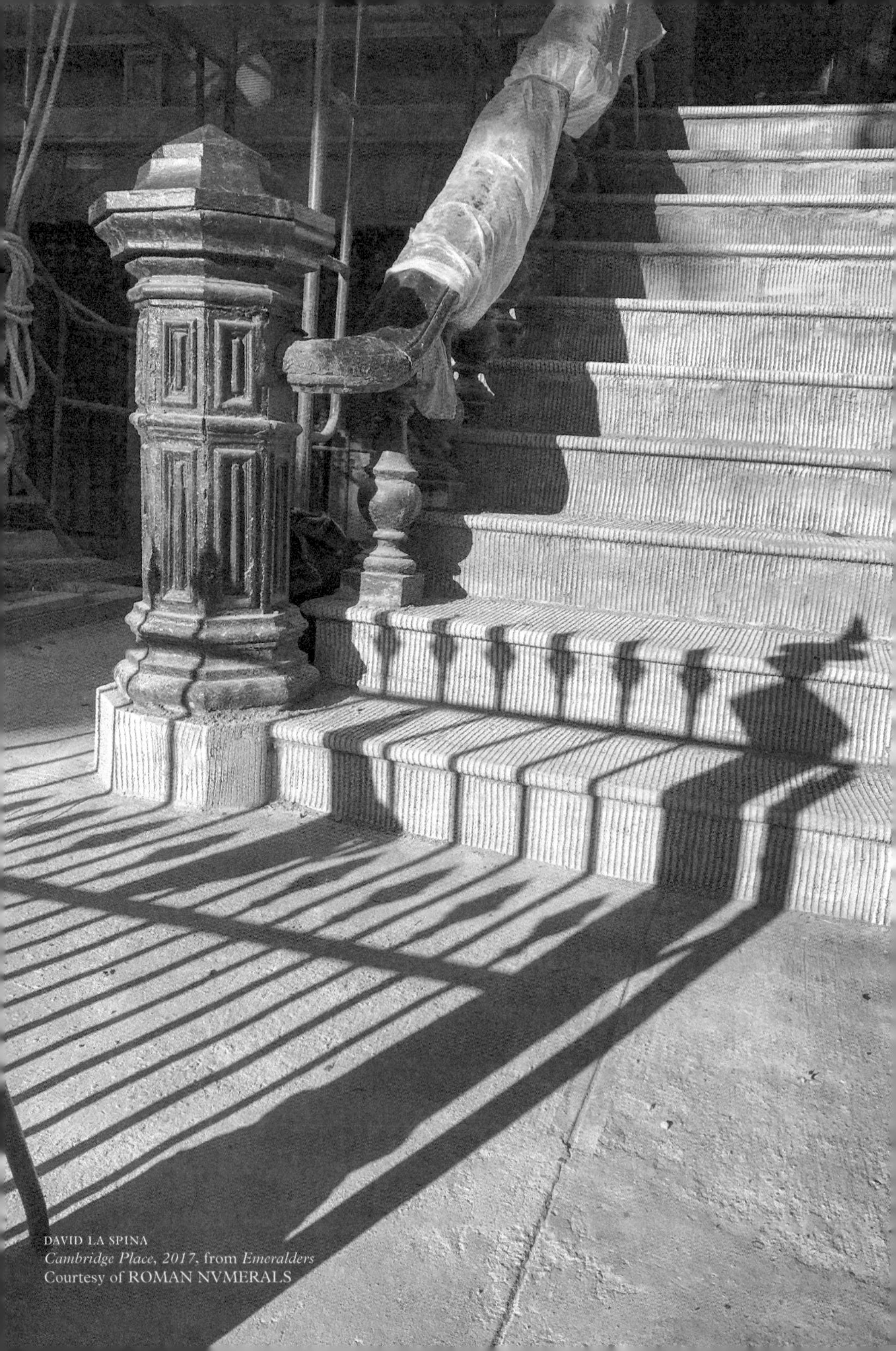

DAVID LA SPINA
Cambridge Place, 2017, from Emeralders
Courtesy of ROMAN NVMERALS

MY FIRST HUSBAND

Stephanie Wambugu

When I got home I set my purse and a bag of Vidalia onions down on the counter. Then I took off my Chanel flats. I'd paid too much for them and they pinched my feet, particularly after walking many city blocks, as I had that day. I wasn't alone in the apartment. The lights were all on. Plus, the television hadn't been turned off. Then I heard footsteps coming from the next room and they were my husband's. He came up behind me and put his large hands on my shoulders and guided me to the armchair. Then he bent down and kissed me on the crown of my head and asked me what I'd done that day. We had been having some marital problems, despite having been married for only eight months. The wedding had been a big ceremony in Newport, Rhode Island, and throughout it I remembered feeling like an imposter, like I'd somehow snuck in. Just after the wedding, I told my mother that I didn't think I was cut out to be a wife and she explained that women who believe themselves too unconventional for marriage are only flattering themselves with ideas about their own peculiarity when in truth they're just as boring as everyone else. The therapist we started seeing for forty-five minutes once a week suggested we try to foster a sense of connection in our marriage by asking one another each evening: what did you do today? And then answering honestly.

We had managed, for the previous three weeks, to pose the question, but I never could tell if he was answering honestly. I myself often answered vaguely, and more than once I had lied about who I'd seen or how much money I'd spent, so I could only assume he was lying too. My husband wasn't a stupid man. He was capable of secrecy and evasion too, and adept at getting what he wanted by omitting the things that might make the other person unhappy. That was why I had married him, because he was my equal. But I was beginning to understand that equality wasn't enough. In any case, considering the day I'd had, I felt I shouldn't lie because what my lies obscured for a short time would invariably come to the surface later in more disruptive ways – ways that made it difficult to be a wife and a person.

'Sit down,' I told him. He sat and turned off the television which had been playing a commercial for diabetes medication. I began to explain what had happened to me that afternoon, starting with the fact that I'd gone very far Uptown for a sandwich. I was eating my hero in the park by the river, I told him, and drinking a Coke, when a woman walked up to me. The woman was wearing large sunglasses which covered most of her face. She looked a bit haggard, sort of eccentric, and she stood so close to me that I thought she might become violent. Not being able to see her eyes made it hard to understand what she was after. I didn't know what she wanted: food, or money, or my purse. So I offered her half of my sandwich. She said that she wasn't hungry and took off her glasses. She had very dark green eyes and I saw that she was really beautiful with her face uncovered. I thought then, she's probably just an artist and she looks disheveled on purpose. The woman sat down on the bench next to me and the afternoon sun caught her face in the most arresting way. It was all a bit dramatic, I told my husband, and I was pretty turned on. He nodded. Our therapist had told us to validate each other's honest answers, even when they made us uncomfortable. That was how trust was built.

Then, I said, the woman leaned over and outstretched her hand.

'Can I touch you please?' she asked. I nodded. She put her hand on my face. Her palm was coarse. She held my cheek in her left hand, and then brought her right hand up to my face as well. Her expression betrayed real sadness, but it couldn't have had anything to do with me since I had just met the woman, I told my husband.

'You look just like my daughter-in-law,' she said. 'I thought I'd seen a ghost. I come out here walking each morning. My apartment is just up there.'

She pointed up at Riverside Drive. I looked in that direction and nodded. Then we looked ahead silently as joggers and dog-walkers passed us by.

'My son's wife, Sarah. She was so bright. So pretty. Had everything going for her. Then she killed herself. I never understood why.'

I told her that was terrible and put my hand on her knee to comfort her. Any sexual feeling I had was gone. The woman told me her name and asked me to join her upstairs for a cup of tea; she wanted to look at me a bit longer. For whatever reason I agreed. I put the remainder of the sandwich in my purse and walked with her up the sloping path, out of the park and into the street.

'I won't keep you long,' the woman said. 'Are you on your lunch break?'

'No,' I told her. 'I'm between jobs. I used to work as a reporter.'

'Sarah was a writer too. She wrote novels. She was editing the third one just before she died.'

The woman told me she was sure I'd find more work soon since it was New York, and there were always opportunities for those who wanted them. If you were bright, attractive, took initiative and truly wanted to work, you could have anything you wanted in New York. That was why it was the greatest city in the world. Then she said her building was just up the next block. Once there, we got into an elevator lined with brass and rode up a few floors, where she let me into her kitchen which was full of masks and pieces of folk art she must have collected in Mexico and the American Southwest. She let down her hair and took down a photograph from the refrigerator and set it down in front of me. And as I looked at the picture – and I looked at it for a very long time – I truly believed I was looking at a photograph of myself. This dead woman, Sarah, looked more like me than my own mother, than my sister and cousins. Down to the way she wore her hair, we looked just alike.

'Now you see what I mean,' the woman said.

'It's unsettling,' I told her.

'It is, it is,' she said and produced another picture from the fridge where Sarah looked even more like me than she did in the first. It was a wedding photo taken by the beach. Not unlike the New England beach where we were married, I told my husband. Sarah was smiling with her bridesmaids, all of whom wore black cocktail dresses and looked ahead, unaware of their futures. I didn't tell the woman about my wedding; the other coincidences were enough. To share more would be pointless and cruel.

The woman went into the next room and came back with a black garment bag. She set it down on the long dining table and unzipped it: an ivory dress with white rosettes embroidered along the neckline.

'I designed this dress,' she said. 'I'm an artist. I make watercolors. The roses on the neckline, those were my idea.'

'It's beautiful,' I said. I looked down at my watch. I should be going, I said. I had been with the woman for more than an hour. I wasn't sure how it was possible – time was moving in such an odd way.

'Will you put it on? I'm sure it'll fit. You're the same size as Sarah. The size Sarah was. Kill to be that small again,' the woman said, pulling a veil out of its garment bag, smoothing it out in the mirror. 'Go ahead, try it on.'

'I couldn't,' I said. I thought that to try on that dress would have been too much, but I was so suggestible in that woman's apartment, surrounded by photographs of her dead daughter-in-law. I stripped down to my panties and let the woman help me into the dress.

She buttoned me up and placed a veil over my head. Then she

looked at me with the expression prisoners sometimes have when they've just been released and can't believe the world is still the world and they're in it, or something. Do you know what I mean? I asked my husband. He said that he thought he understood, but I wasn't sure if he did.

I kept talking anyway. I told him that the woman had to hold on to the table for support, that she was shocked. At the same time she looked happy to see this doppelgänger in the old dress.

'I kept all her clothes. My son can't stand to have them in his apartment. Too traumatic, he says. But I don't think remembering is traumatic,' she said. 'Must be a generational thing.'

I looked at myself in the mirror in the hall. I could see the Hudson River through a window. I looked down at the river and up at myself in that wedding gown, back and forth, and thought I had better stop coming Uptown.

I was startled when the woman came up behind me. I was even more surprised when she told me that she had texted her son, that he was a few minutes away.

'He needs to see you for himself.'

I didn't think that it was a very good idea. But somehow, I told my husband, I felt that I was completely at this woman's mercy. The idea of walking outside and getting on the M11 bus home without seeing it all through was unthinkable. I didn't know if they were just grief-stricken, or just crazy, or what.

'When did she die?' I asked.

'Two years next week,' the woman said.

Then, 'She was like my own daughter.'

'Must be a real loss,' I said, staring down at the wedding band on my left hand.

We sat for a while at the table drinking Chardonnay and waited for her son to arrive. I asked for some ice cubes for my wine and she said she would have some too. I wouldn't ordinarily drink so early in the day; I found it impossible to stop once I started, but it would have been rude to refuse the woman's generosity, I told my husband.

I made a point to be explicit about this with him because he had been concerned that I had been drinking too heavily since I lost my job and because it was yet another thing I lied about, how much I drank. She moved to top up my glass and I told her I was alright. The doorbell rang and we both stood up. She pressed the buzzer, and some moments later a short man with dark hair appeared in the doorway. I noticed this only because I towered over him, as you tower over me, I told my husband. He was dressed in business casual and looked pretty sharp, though it wasn't my style, or yours, I said. He didn't seem alarmed by the scene – his mother drinking wine with a woman who looked just like his dead wife, but then he was a man who had likely found the lifeless body of his own spouse.

He seemed neutral about all of it when he pulled up a chair at the head of the table beside us, and that made me feel at ease. He looked at me for a long while without saying anything, and then slipped onto the floor. I was worried that he had fainted. But he got up onto his knees, reached out, and began to kiss my hands. I didn't pull away. I wanted him to have whatever little comfort I could give him – what did it matter? It wasn't real. It was just a fantasy. A fantasy I felt he deserved.

'Mom, can I be alone with her for a moment?' he asked.

'It's up to her,' the woman said. I told them it was fine. The woman drank what was left of her wine and then said she was going out for a walk. She told me that if I got tired of wearing the dress, I should just take it off and put it on her bed. Her son could show me where the bedroom was. The door shut behind her and we were alone. I asked him to get off the floor. Sitting across from him again, I asked him his name and he said that it was Matthew. I told him a bit about my life, how I lost my job, where I grew up. I was candid about our marriage, I hope that's alright, I told my husband. My husband said that it was fine.

'Sarah and I had a very difficult marriage too,' Matthew said. 'She was a deeply unhappy person. And I always thought that it was because she was a writer and writers were temperamental, that maybe she would mellow out with age, but she never did.'

'Are you a writer too?' I asked.

'No,' he said, 'I teach engineering at Columbia.'

'Do you enjoy the work you do?'

'No,' he said, 'I grew tired of it years ago. The students are the worst part, though my colleagues are awful too.'

He helped himself to the wine on the table.

'On the night of our wedding she confessed there was someone else, had been for two years, a lover Upstate. She didn't even know how to drive, I don't know how she managed it.'

'Trains,' I said. 'Why didn't you annul the marriage?'

'Probably for the same reasons you don't divorce your husband,' he said. He explained that he had loved her a lot, hadn't wanted to change her nature, which he had understood as soon as he'd met her and continued to understand up until the day she died. He asked me to take off the dress. He said he couldn't stand to look at it anymore. I couldn't unfasten the buttons on my own and I asked him to help me.

'It isn't just the way you look,' he said, standing behind me. 'It's your mannerisms too. The way you talk. It's surprising you haven't run into anyone else in the city who knew her.'

'Well, I don't really come Uptown unless I want a sandwich,' I said. I covered my breasts with one hand and asked him where his mother's bedroom was. I placed the dress back in the garment bag and followed him down the hall and set it on her bed. We stood at the foot of the bed and when he asked me to lie down, my initial thought was to say no out of loyalty to you, I told my husband, but when I thought about it, I realized it wouldn't be a violation of anything – it wasn't real, only a consolation. And, I asked my husband, how often do these things happen?

I agreed and sat down on the bed. He pulled down my stockings and put his right hand between my legs. Then he continued to do the things he presumably used to do with his wife. He didn't ask for my input. He seemed to be following a progression that had little to do with me in particular. And despite that, or maybe because of that, I had an orgasm even though, as you know, I told my husband, it's been very hard for me to finish since I lost my job. When he came, he cried, which felt appropriate. I mean, who knew what was appropriate in a situation like that? We held one another in his mother's bed, and he stroked my forehead with the back of his hand and asked if it would be alright to spit in my mouth, Sarah had always liked it and asked for it. I told him it was fine.

'Can I see you again?' he asked afterward.

'I'll have to ask my husband,' I told him, ' And of course we'll have to mention it to our marriage counselor.'

He told me he understood, but that should I change my mind I could find his name on the faculty directory for Columbia University's Engineering Department. Then he told me that when he looked at me he felt glad, that it wasn't logical but it made him feel like there were many Sarahs in the world and that some of them had survived, were surviving. He hugged me. There wasn't anything sensual about it. It felt like pure gratitude. Like the time we took LSD together in school, I told my husband, and we kept saying we felt one hundred percent thankful to be alive. My husband didn't say anything, but I knew he remembered.

Then Matthew got up and dressed himself. Back in his plain shirt and pants, he went into the next room and came back with the clothes I'd been wearing. I put them all back on. I slipped into my uncomfortable shoes and headed toward the door. When I kissed Matthew goodbye, he handed me a photograph of Sarah. He kept several in his wallet and wanted me to have the one where he felt I looked especially like her. The one where she was wearing black and sitting in a park, just as I had done earlier that day. Outside, I saw Matthew's mother walking up the stone steps a little ways ahead. Her head was bowed and she didn't see me. I went in the other direction toward the grocery store crowded with people just getting off work. I bought a bag of Vidalia onions and stood in line with all of the other living people who needed whatever they needed. They all seemed to wait with impatience, but I was glad the line moved slowly because I wasn't yet ready to go home and resume my ordinary life. Holding the onions, I sat down at the student bar on the corner and drank one beer, then another. I burped as I watched undergrads flirt badly, binge drink and make out with one another and I was relieved to see this because all the articles I had read lately insisted young people weren't sleeping with one another anymore. Risk and lust are not over, I thought, as I stumbled to the bus stop. I boarded the M11 and stood up front, as close as the bus driver would let me. I watched the bright road up ahead punctuated by the wipers moving across the glass, slowly pushing away the spring rain. I came to our street and saw that the lights were on and I was glad because I knew I'd see you and could tell you what had happened to me, I told my husband.

When I stopped speaking, he stood up and paced the length of the living room many times. He held his face in his hand and opened his mouth as if he might speak, but didn't say anything at all. Because I thought it might clarify things and might explain the inevitability of what had happened, I handed him the photograph I'd been given. He folded it once, then again without seeming to look at it. When he left the room and shut the door behind him, I sat for a long while in the armchair without feeling any remorse. ∎

Paul Muldoon

The Prisoners on Alcatraz

1

As if shackled to it like a galley-slave to his oar,
a prisoner on Alcatraz repeated that line from Pope
about how to err
is human . . . Who knew the blue-footed booby
has rarely made it ashore
and only with difficulty has a saber-toothed salmon
been restrained in an electric chair?
To repurpose G.B. Shaw on Hearst's San Simeon,
this was the kind of penitentiary God might aspire
to build had He the money.
A prisoner on Alcatraz might well have enough spare
time to mull over aspects of The One and the Many
Plato and Plotinus had simply never considered,
such as may be seen when a sea wave finds its stride.

2

Thus the prisoners on Alcatraz developed a real flair
for rendering their own heads in toothpaste,
soap, scraps of toilet roll, hair collected from the floor
of the barber shop. The Warden might boast
said prisoners must pay a dear
price for such crimes as still pressed on their chests
but to a guard glancing through their cell door

they would seem to be sleeping the sleep of the just.
The prisoners on Alcatraz were granted hot showers
mostly to deter them from taking the plunge
and striking out for that not-too-distant shore.
They would now give themselves carte blanche
to contend with their fellow Argonauts
as to whether Alcatraz refers to a pelican or a gannet.

3

Until Capone tried to cut the line for the barber shop
and was met by a blade held to his throat
and a merry jape
from a kid who didn't hold him in sufficient dread,
he might have thought to skip
The Rock as a dime-a-dozen gangster skips bail.
Until now, no one had ever made good their escape
mostly on account of the push and pull
of those icy currents. But the prisoners who met throb
with throb now painstakingly cast a pall
over themselves just as the fogs might drape
a standard-issue sheet over a buoy-bell,
the idea they might guide themselves by its clang
being one to which they had long since clung.

4

Keeping nothing back but the bearings of the island
was Jim Hawkins' main aim
given the pirates' propensity to sing like Jenny Lind.
As for Long John Silver, his face big as a ham,
he spent long periods licking his wounds
in solitary. A keg. A veritable powder keg.
The fact that he was mostly three sheets to the wind
may have explained his going off at half-cock.
The fact that when the guards who scanned
the corridor called out and no one answered
should have had them keep their eyes skinned.
Meanwhile there was Samson the Nazirite,
ever savvy, ever astute,
taking hold of the pillars on which the house stood.

5

The pillar perished was whereto the prisoners leant
and hoped to find some brief succor
even as the librarian loaned
them a book on the death of Socrates. The cigar
Capone had favored was the Arturo Fuente. To paint
flesh tones, that's the biggie. Long before he was shorn
of his locks, Samson had jawboned

his enemies, heaps upon heaps. He'd then adjourn
to the Admiral Benbow or similar haunt.
It was in just such a handy cove D.H. Lawrence
had himself painstakingly honed
his skills, several prisoners developing a tolerance
for the confined space
in which they might yet happen on the Isles of Spice.

6

In the world of trolleys and cable cars
for which the prisoners had long since sighed
but for which they were only now plotting a course
they expected to meet Ben Gunn in a three-piece suit
of dressed goatskin. There were widespread rumors
Ben would occasionally hot-wire
a goat but refused to show the slightest remorse
for his actions. The same Ben would have been aware
a goatskin coracle almost inevitably veers
away from more than toward
its objective. He would have known a centrifugal force
was what had him sprawled on the thwarts,
known the great artist entrusts himself to the Muse
because great art is less methodical than hit-and-miss.

7

Scanning the tree nymphs, dryads and hamadryads
who slipped among the birches and silver firs
were the reporters digging for dirt
on William-Adolphe Bouguereau and his affair
with a nineteen-year-old model. An occupational hazard,
some say, when the light is from the north.
The great artist will reassert
his claim art must always touch a raw nerve.
It's a borrowing from French, the word 'deflowered'.
Another of those flowery French terms.
A band is always more likely to flirt
with disaster when Machine Gun Kelly plays drums
and the banjo player, seemingly all over the map,
is the undisputed leader of the Chicago mob.

8

Whether it refers to pelicans or gannets or the riffraff
to which Alcatraz was now prone
was a speculation that had become increasingly rife.
Since syphilis had gnawed away at his brain,
Capone held the gannet to be not only a knave
but the Knave of Hearts.
Pelicans and gannets are both known to jackknife

into the boundless waste of a recreation yard.
Pelicans and gannets are both known to remain aloof
even as they 'recreate'
the illusion of being true to life,
much as those prisoners would hoodwink their guards
by summoning Zurich or Zacatecas or Zagreb
from heads of toothpaste, soap, and toilet roll scraps.

9

As the undisputed leader of the Chicago mob,
Capone was naturally disinclined
to entertain the ghost of a 'maybe' never mind mope
about his cell. Now there was a glint
in the eye of every cub reporter sensing a scoop.
Not only had the prisoners on Alcatraz done a switch
but constructed a makeshift periscope
with which to keep watch
on the utility corridor. If Bouguereau had lost his grip
on reality it was because he'd pooh-pooh
the idea an artist may do more than grope.
The prisoners' pressing raincoats against steam pipes
went unremarked by the guards in their turrets
who scanned for tree nymphs, dryads, hamadryads.

10

Though great art is less methodical than hit-and-miss
the prisoners on Alcatraz wouldn't roll the dice
merely to muss
Capone's hair any more than they'd toss
a quarter. A squeeze
from a concertina. The basket in which Saint Paul
was lowered over the wall of Damascus
was no more than a wicker pail.
The raincoats held in a makeshift vise
itself held by two galley-slaves.
The prisoners would be aiming not to create a fuss
or draw too much attention to themselves,
hoping against hope they'd make themselves scarce
in the world of trolleys and high-strung cable cars.

11

Taking hold of the pillars on which the house stood,
Samson had the cut
of a trusty who was less a trusty steed
than a stoolie with an extra gait
somewhere between a canter and a fancy foot.
'I mean garboard,' he'd said, 'as in garboard strake.'
The tube used to force-feed

a prisoner who went on hunger strike
was also made of rubber and might or might not
be of use in caulking a coracle. The pirogue
Robinson Crusoe had hollowed out in his hour of need
was much on Jim's mind as he embarked
on this tale of unvarnished viciousness and violence,
keeping nothing back but the bearings of the island.

12

That they might yet happen on the Isles of Spice
was neither part of the grand design
nor a function of free will if, as some suppose,
it is impossible for mankind not to sin
after the fall. The hiss
at the end of the utility corridor
was the hiss of a fire hose.
Silver. A quartermaster who gave no quarter.
They can rig the gallows, they can tie the noose.
Maybe Saint Augustine's *non posse non peccare*
was a dictum that was completely on the nose.
Not only would that nineteen-year-old marry Bouguereau
but bear him five children before she reached dry land
and the pillar perished was whereto he leant.

13

An idea to which these prisoners had long since clung
was that each might read one hundred books
a year. A far cry from The Clink
in which the ghost of Sir Thomas Wyatt still unpicks
one of his father's sonnets. The Hospital Wing
had seen Capone stretched on a rack
of his own making. If they did indeed hoodwink
their guards by dint of their artwork,
the prisoners on Alcatraz, unlike those in Sing Sing
or Atlanta, knew most art-making won't wreak
havoc with the system but merely sink
without trace, be it in La Rochelle or on The Rock,
where things had been more or less shipshape
until Capone tried to cut that line for the barber shop.

14

Their heads of toothpaste, soap, scraps of toilet roll
would offer some measure by which to gauge
how resolutely each now lay, albeit thin as a rail,
under a drift a guard was meant to catch.
Their sculpted heads may have offered a false
sense of security to all ambassadors in chains
but were indicative of how the artist necessarily fails

if he lacks the courage to take a chance.
Their heads of toothpaste and soap imbued their cells
with a scent that would linger over their cots
long after they themselves had set sail
in that raft conjured from vulcanized raincoats.
Not only in their visions, therefore, but in their valor
would the prisoners on Alcatraz develop a real flair.

15

Such as may be seen when a sea wave finds its stride
and rocks a massive construction barge
from across the narrow strait
spanned by the Golden Gate Bridge.
It was only by acknowledging the San Andreas fault
the prisoners might stand a chance of reaching port.
It must have taken them forever to inflate
the raft before they clambered aboard
and rowed with all their might,
their inflation device being the bellows of a concertina
borrowed from an inmate
who himself borrowed Lawrence's *Sea and Sardinia*
a good ten times in the course of one year
as if shackled to it like that galley-slave to his oar.

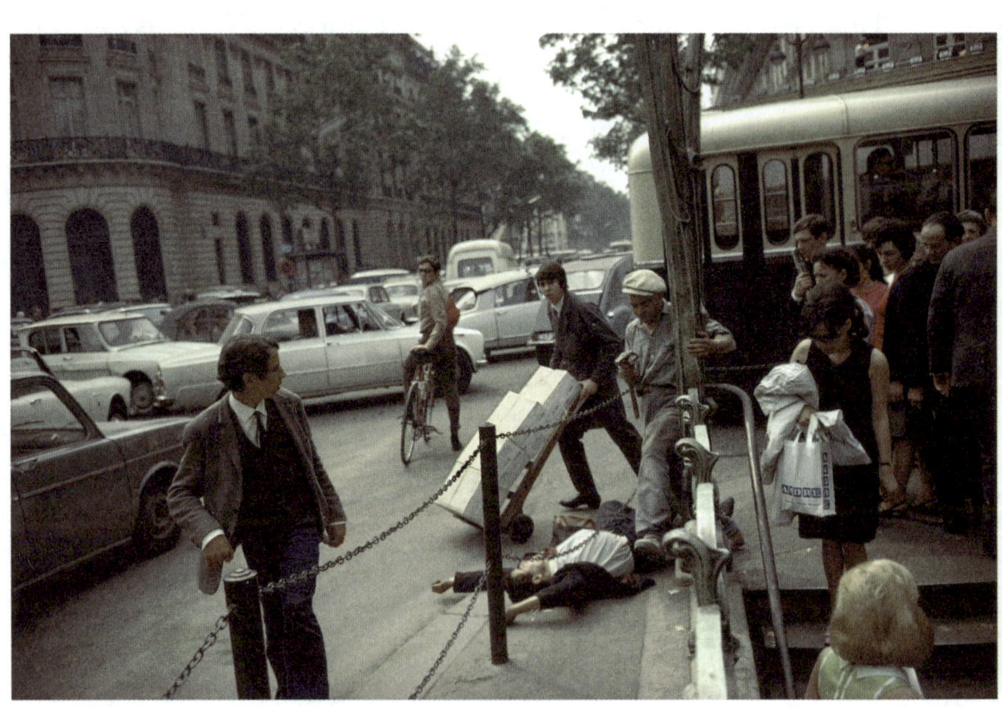

JOEL MEYEROWITZ
Paris, France, 1967

THE ARTIST AS AFICIONADO

Joel Meyerowitz

Introduction by George Prochnik

Your street is no longer your street,
Now it's just any street,
A road to anywhere.
– Flamenco copla

A man has fallen on the street, perhaps dead – possibly murdered. He lies splayed on his back outside a Paris metro station at a busy intersection; eyes shut, arms flung above his head, pale hands curled as they jut from his dark suit jacket. A workman, capped and booted, powdered with dust and clutching a hammer shaft in one fist, steps over the body, peering down grimly as his other palm clasps the vined, patinaed stalk of an art nouveau station sign. Pedestrians clustered by the metro entrance stare toward the prostrate figure with consternation. In the foreground, a well-dressed adolescent boy twists his head back to watch, lips parted, brow taut – shocked. A young man in a dark smock and tie, shoving a dolly piled with white boxes just behind the body, glances up over his load disapprovingly, scrutinizing the unseen crowd from whose perspective this view is manifest – perhaps glaring at the photographer himself.

You see it all in that split second: drivers planted in their snarled cars against rows of uniform stone buildings girt with black iron railings; hunter-green trees lining the sidewalk; milky sky; a two-tone bus (its colors echoing the hazy air and foliage) bisecting the metro entrance, while – by a trick of optics – apparently right above its steel roof, a window cleaner carries on his trade.

When the photographer Joel Meyerowitz selected this image from 1967 for the cover of *Where I Find Myself*, the survey of his life's work published in 2018, he chose it both for its intrinsic drama and for what it says about the principles of his practice: the cardinal asset of serendipity, together with perpetual preparedness. The need to trust instinct while in pursuit of undetermined subject matter – maintaining a kind of vibratory alertness to the imminence of meaning, the coming instant in which the disparate elements before one's eyes cohere into some charged constellation. Here that stance engendered a scene in which the 'whole ballet of the street' was revealed, he says, a spectacle of 'incredible beauty' notwithstanding the afflicted person on the ground, the suggestion of violence, the panoply of moral questions surrounding the onlookers.

Meyerowitz's career began with the premise that the street could teach him everything.

At the beginning of the 1960s, after studying painting, art history and medical illustration, he started supporting himself by working as an art director at a New York advertising agency. One day Meyerowitz's boss sent him downtown to observe the photo shoot for a booklet he'd designed for *American Girl* magazine. 'It was about two pre-teenage girls doing after-school stuff,' in his remembrance. 'Homework, playing, snacking, applying makeup – things that I see now were really about seducing the next generation of consumers, but to me back then they were seemingly innocent activities.'

The photographer that day was Robert Frank, and though Meyerowitz knew nothing about Frank's photography at this point, he realized that he'd never seen a camera used the way Frank was handling it. What separated Frank's approach was twofold: how he interacted with his subjects and the moments when he saw fit to press the shutter. Almost without speaking to the girls, Frank 'freed them to just be themselves, and then silently and effortlessly he bent and swayed and slid in and out of their activities which continued on in real time and real life,' Meyerowitz observed. Each time he heard Frank's Leica click, he realized that the sound came at the most revealing moment of the unfolding action. In one instance, this was the second when a girl applying lipstick seemed to metamorphose into a woman. Until he watched the session, Meyerowitz had assumed 'that to make photographs, you froze everybody before the fact'. Now he saw that rather than arresting them you could join in the dance. It had never occurred to him that photographers could move inside the scenes they were observing – passing through something like the proverbial fourth wall of a theater.

When Meyerowitz left the shoot and returned to the street, the entire world appeared transformed. Every gesture and interaction seemed radiant with potential: 'a hand shooting up for a taxi, people hugging goodbye, a mother bending over the stroller to fix her baby's hat, and then the look that came over her face. Everything woke me up!' By the time he made it back to his office, he'd decided to become a photographer.

That pivotal photograph he took in Paris five years later marked the moment when he felt he could 'step away from overt drama toward forms of image-making that didn't depend upon a central incident or story.' Meyerowitz dubs this latter style 'field photography' – packed urban scenes with multiple narrative thrusts. With this work Meyerowitz was 'trying to empty the center, so that the action would not be the main focus anymore,' he said. 'I wanted the surprise and chance of the street to play on something that was *becoming*, something that was suggesting itself to me, which would have a non-referential partner.' He thought this decentralized focus might advance photography beyond the more formal, decisive moment aesthetic established by figures like Cartier-Bresson, toward work attuned to contemporary fragmentation and instantaneity. 'I was hoping that I could make the viewer enter the moment and look around in it.'

Over time, Meyerowitz's idea of field pictures led him away from street photography to portraits, landscapes, and still lifes. When he's returned to the streets in recent years he's found it almost impossible to frame the sorts of dense tableaux, rich in fertile contrasts, that his street photography once exhibited, and which mirrored his actual experience of the animated, communal atmosphere of the Bronx neighborhood where he spent his childhood. This has less to do with shifting priorities in the medium of photography than with changes to the environment. The wider, demotic forum of the street, in which one doesn't need a central focus point since everyone can draw attention, has itself been crowded out by corporate interests. The streets where Meyerowitz learned to see have shrunk into the hand-held device and become dwarfed by giant big-brand advertisements. 'When I do street photography now,' Meyerowitz says, 'I often feel the pictures appear to be *about* the phone, because that's what people are consumed by.'

Meyerowitz has from the beginning maintained a spirit of chameleon-like experimentation, but in his early years as a photographer he didn't feel he could move forward as an artist until he first explored what would happen to his viewpoint in unknown territory. A week-long well-paid advertising assignment at the end of 1965 gave him the means to act on a long-held wish to travel to Europe. 'As soon as I got that money I decided: *I'm going to run away!*' he laughs. He persuaded his then wife, Vivian Bower, that they should rent out their apartment and take off for a year. They sailed from New York harbor in August on the SS *France* bound for Southampton. Over the course of the next twelve months, they drove some 20,000 miles, not only in Europe but also across Turkey and Morocco.

There are echoes in this project of the far-ranging road trip that gave birth to Frank's *Americans* – and Meyerowitz acknowledges Frank's influence – but the resulting image sequences are worlds apart. Frank's subjects often seem defined by elegiac isolation in spaces of expulsion. Whether actually solitary, or in the midst of other figures torn away from their own stories, they appear to be staring past the forlorn present.

By contrast, Meyerowitz's subjects frequently appear enmeshed in some variegated social context where anything might happen. His early work celebrated the parade of street life – and sometimes intercepted actual parades or their unfettered aftermath. Take two men he caught in fancy marching-band uniforms striding jauntily down a New York sidewalk in 1963. It takes a second to spot the pair of shiny tubas they've apparently abandoned by a No Parking sign a few meters to their rear. Instead of lamenting the loss, their swagger sings, *Good riddance*, so becomes a dreamy gesture of emancipation.

True to this spirit of spontaneity, his European journey itself included an unplanned detour that proved determinative: for half his year abroad he left the road behind and settled down in Malaga, where he spent much of his time in the home of one extended family. It was those six months that Meyerowitz credits for his coming of age as an artist and a man.

At the start of his road trip, Meyerowitz met an American from Brooklyn named Paul Hecht who was living in Malaga, where he was writing a book about flamenco. As part of the project, Hecht was collecting traditional gypsy flamenco songs from across Andalucía that hitherto had only been transmitted orally. Hecht encouraged Meyerowitz to visit him when he came to Spain. The gypsy families, he said, had taught him what it meant to subsist '*actively* within time', as opposed to being enslaved to 'clock time' the way he'd been in New York. Hecht had arrived in the world of flamenco as a stranger, and its practitioners immediately invited him into their lives.

Meyerowitz showed up in Malaga a few months later, and Hecht introduced him to the Escalonas, a multigenerational family of flamenco artists who lived in one of the city's poorest neighborhoods. The patriarch, Antonio Escalona, was a highly regarded guitar player who as a young man had accompanied Lorca at poetry readings. The whole family was committed to upholding the flamenco tradition in which, as Meyerowitz came to feel, the bitterness of the music, at once lyric and acerbic, was counterpointed by the warmth and grace of the surrounding human interactions.

When Meyerowitz discusses his first experiences of being with the family and hearing them make music, his voice conveys an undiminished passion: he knew from the start, *this is it, the real thing,* he says. But it took time for him to be able to articulate what made the scene so captivating.

Eventually, he came to see that it was the exchange between flamenco performers and their audience (specifically the devotees known as *aficionados*) that catalyzed the art's revelatory moments. Night after night, he watched the *aficionados* 'push the singer to go deeper and deeper until an instant came when they'd say, "*Throw it from the inside, pull it from the inside, (rompe la voce!), go there*" – trying to draw the sound out from them, as if it were a birth,' Meyerowitz recalls. 'At this point you heard something emerging like a cry from within, not a refined, channeled tone, but something burning its way out' – longing, love and love's frustration, loss, tragedy and the soul – that together conferred 'a transcendent quality on the music . . . You knew then you were in the presence of authenticity, and at this instant you would hear the *aficionado* burst out, "*Olé!*".' The exclamation would rip out of them the same way the song was torn from the singer.

In this symbiotic trade between expression and reception, Meyerowitz found something germane to his understanding of photography. 'One has an instinct and you just go for it, and the form is shaped by your reach in that second.' That action too, he decided, represented a kind of *Olé*.

A picture Meyerowitz took at the time depicts a large group of people with dark hair and strongly etched features laughing in a small room painted pink and cyan, hung with family photographs. Other images show the Escalonas dancing, making music and attentively observing one another in that same setting. They're lilting, lively scenes – rough, shadowed, slanted, often partly blurred. One photo shows two young men dressed in black and white, a singer in mid-utterance, eyes fluttered shut, the other performer gazing down at his guitar while a woman in a gold-peach blouse, smiling delightedly and clapping, tosses her eyes back over her shoulder. A third male figure stares intently in her direction. The crisscrossing sight lines make an ocular concert of individual perspective.

At the start of one flamenco session around the Escalonas' kitchen table near the start of his stay in Malaga, Meyerowitz rose up on impulse, interrupting the recital to go retrieve his tape recorder. He plugged it in, hung the microphone from a lamp above the table, and the singing recommenced. After a while the singers stopped and asked to listen to the machine. 'I watched everything in their faces then,' Meyerowitz remembers. 'The study, their excitement, their surprise at the way they sounded.' *They'd never heard their music played back to them.*

From then on, the door of the Escalonas' home was always open to him. Meyerowitz and his wife dined with the family and attended all their musical performances. Vivian started studying guitar with Antonio. Daytimes, Meyerowitz wandered all over the streets of Malaga taking photographs. It was the first time in his life that he'd been able to go out completely on his own day after day without the company of his New York street photographer comrades-in-arms (Garry Winogrand, Tony Ray-Jones and Tod Papageorge, in particular). He became a familiar, accepted character around town, whom the locals nicknamed *El Ojo*: The Eye. '*El Ojo, Venga!*' they called, inviting him over to their cafe tables and market stalls to see what they were up to, opening their lives to his camera.

Meyerowitz narrated the streets to himself as he walked – describing what he saw now, and what might happen next, as if he were reading a text replete with clues about when to click the shutter. He thought of that voice as his own interior *aficionado*, pressing him to enter deeper into the fabric of the action, guiding him to *go there*.

Along with that inner *aficionado*, Meyerowitz recognized his larger vocation as an *aficionado* of public existence, photographing the transient flares of emotion and surreptitious congruences that once defined civic spaces, imbuing them with dynamic unpredictability.

Meyerowitz remembers feeling totally alive during his months in Malaga. The city was a revelation to him, not only on an aesthetic level, but also as a human being. 'My identity was cohering in Malaga. I watched the way Spanish men handled themselves, the kind of interaction, the boldness with which they related to each other, their conversations, their arguments. There was a flexibility and solidity to them and I thought, there's something for me to learn here. I needed that. When you understand that you need something, it's an opportunity to let go of the original version of yourself, to watch that shell break open while you emerge into the world with a new understanding of who you are and what you have to say.'

Although it was an idyllic time for him personally, he wasn't under the illusion that the situation in Malaga itself was halcyon. There was severe poverty in the barrios, along with a surge in the construction of high-rises and hotels that heralded the rise of the tourist industry. But the pressures on tradition seemed to increase the urgency of the music, just as the omnipresent menace of Franco's armed militias patrolling the streets, doing all they could to constrict Malaga's communal life, added to the poignance of the Escalona family's expansive generosity. A handful of Meyerowitz's photos show Franco's men posturing around town with imperious pomposity, as if the streets belonged to them. These uniformed interlopers embodied the 'real, unified presence of the state,' Meyerowitz said. They cast into relief the spirit of freedom that the general population exhibited in public, which seemed a testimony to their authenticity.

In our last conversation, I pressed Meyerowitz to specify what he meant by this idea. After all, he'd spoken on numerous occasions about the authenticity of the Bronx world he grew up in, with its compelling immigrant stories and vibrant street markets. If he came from an authentic place, why did he need to go searching for another, second authenticity?

'That was all disappearing in New York, even when I was a young man,' Meyerowitz said. 'Those markets were being replaced by supermarkets – chains. Before that, the bakeries, the fruit and vegetable stands, the pickle stores and shoe shops – they were all geared toward people who lived in the neighborhood. It's different from a generic store or a commercial block in Midtown, which is either for people who work in the skyscrapers or who go there to shop in high-end places – that glossy, universal consumerism.'

The delocalization of businesses helped drive a greater depersonalization of street life, Meyerowitz suggested. It represented the antithesis of what he'd tried to achieve in decentering his photographic images, pursuing pictures where every element could become an axis point. This was why it was so intensely evocative for him to find markets in Malaga that shared features with the shopping thoroughfares of his youth. But a second, deeper parallel between Malaga and his old neighborhood emerged as we spoke.

Meyerowitz began talking about the Bronx of his past. 'In that neighborhood, wherever you went, if you grew up on those blocks, everybody knew you,' he said. 'They knew who your parents were. "*Hey Joel, tell your mother hello,*"' Meyerowitz laughed. 'So it was all, "*Hey come here, try this.*" "*See what I have here, Joel.*"' He began mimicking the voices of a suite of beckoning characters from his childhood. 'The feeling you get when you're part of an environment like that is the feeling of being part of a whole, larger social network, and that's amazing. There was this extraordinary knitted-together thing, but then as I moved downtown and as time moved on . . . That's the thing that, you know, as one gets older one gets distanced from.'

I thought he might break off there on that snow-globe image of a vanished village, but instead, after a beat or two, Meyerowitz began again. 'So what it was then to find myself invited in as I was by the Escalonas . . . To rediscover that welcoming feeling of my youth in Malaga, in the barrio – it brought back to me the ease with which we all moved in and out of each other's apartments as kids. The doors were always open, you know. You just walked into the other person's apartment. You tapped on the door, "Hey Mrs Nassau, where's Danny?" "Hey Joel." It's like *that.* "Try this, Joel." That's what the Escalona family was like – even Malaga in general . . . After a time photographing there, people recognized me. "Oh, here comes *El Ojo.* Oh boy, try this!" I loved wandering around in an atmosphere that was totally foreign, yet totally familiar, just watching life . . . I had this incredible drifting, dreamlike day, day after day.'

'*Ojo.*' 'Joel.' The words themselves in his enunciation carry a loosely doubling ring. In Malaga, Meyerowitz found another iteration of the spatial porosity that had made his childhood enchanting – even as he rediscovered his youthful sense of being seen. Whereas the sentimental position would be to fetishize the lost neighborhood in which every door was open to a kid who'd had the luck to grow up there, a different, political sensibility comes into play on registering how locals *chose* to open their doors to unknown visitors – making strangers feel at home. This humane welcome is a willful expression of our commonality.

Meyerowitz had the fortune to be able to reinhabit a semblance of the lost space and time of his childhood. These made for dreamlike days floating through the streets and into the home of fellow artists who treated him as one of them. 'I was living as fully as I could what life has to offer,' he says. 'I realized this is the life I yearned for.' But what distinguishes his project is that rather than submerging himself in this restoration of the past, Meyerowitz set out to shape a new aesthetic ethos. He came to understand hospitality as its own form of artistic expression. Artists like Joel build a house with their work that you can walk inside of. There are different rooms, different chapters, but the spirit of hospitality is always there, inviting you onward, stimulating your own engagement with the world. ∎

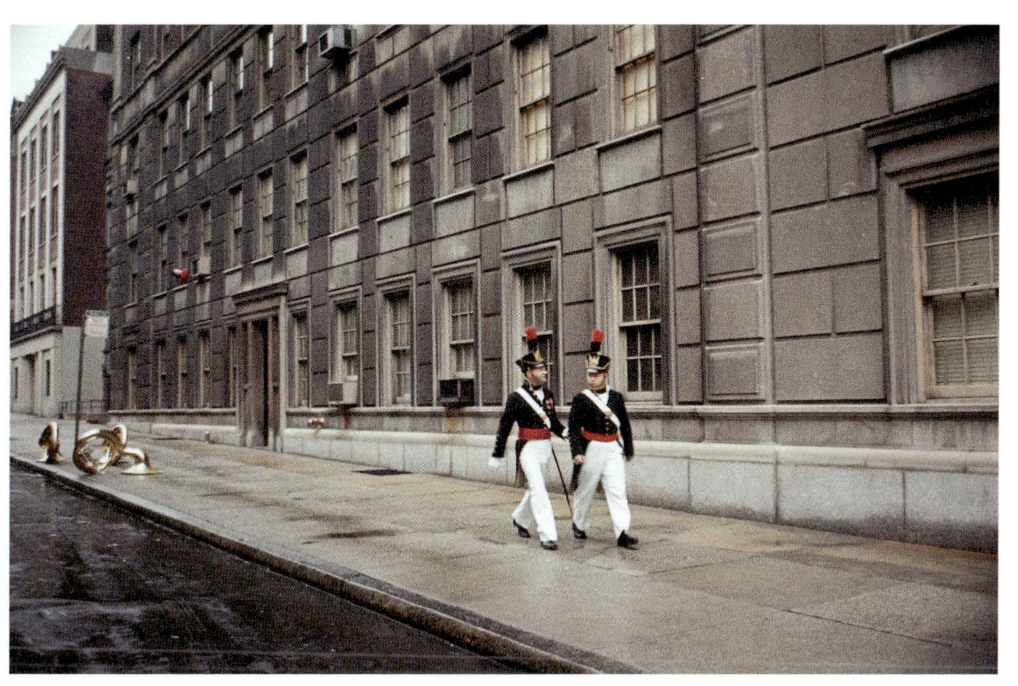

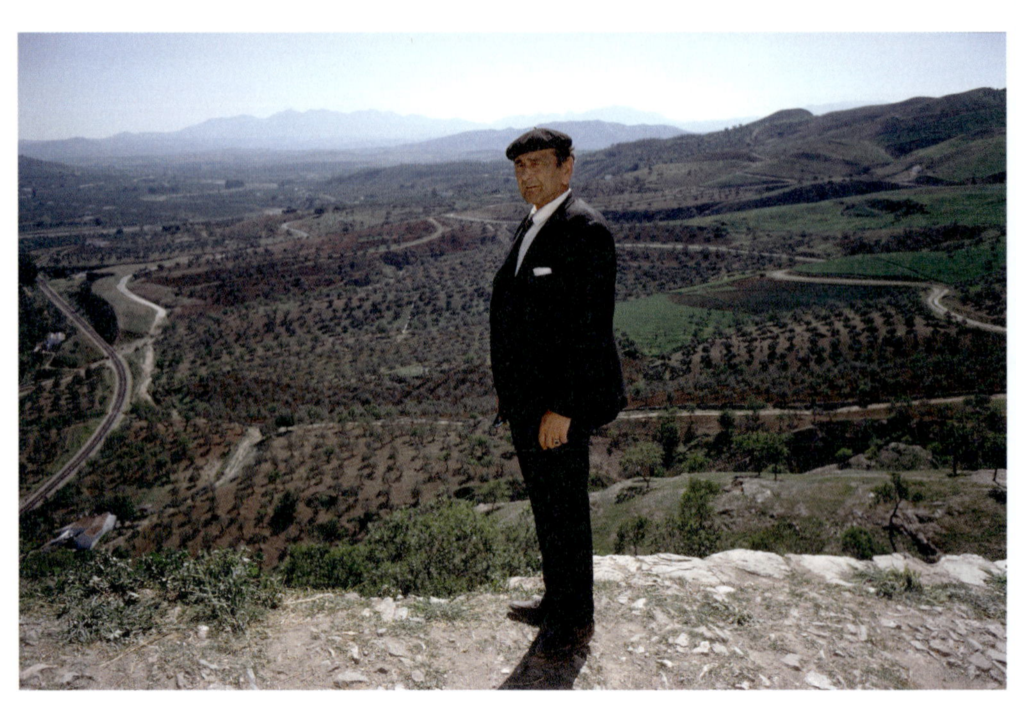

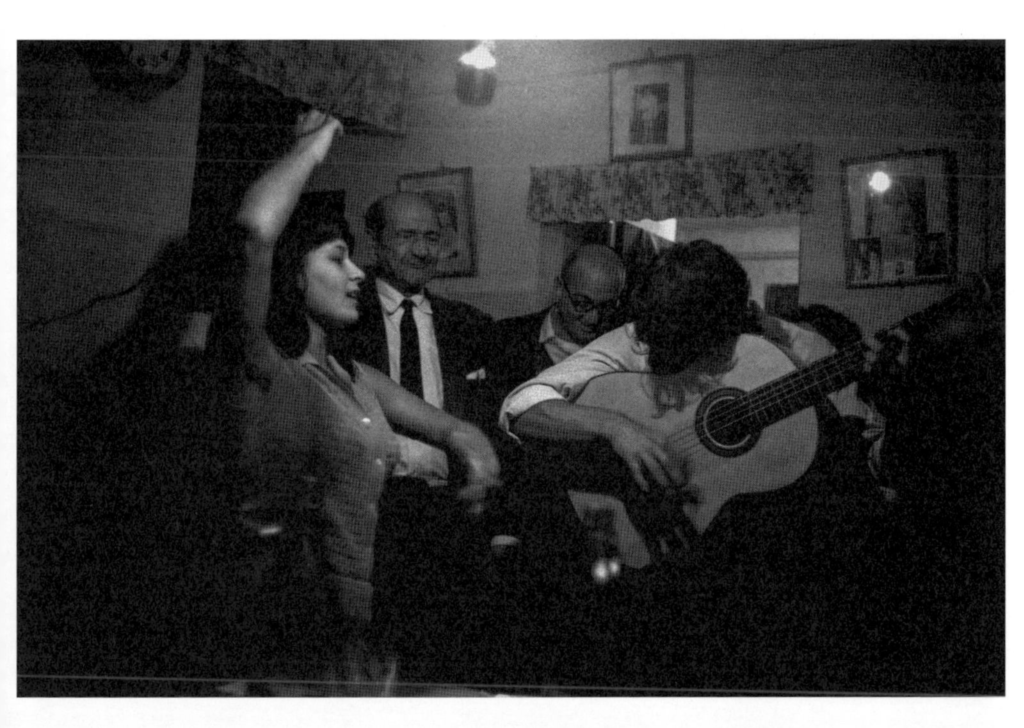

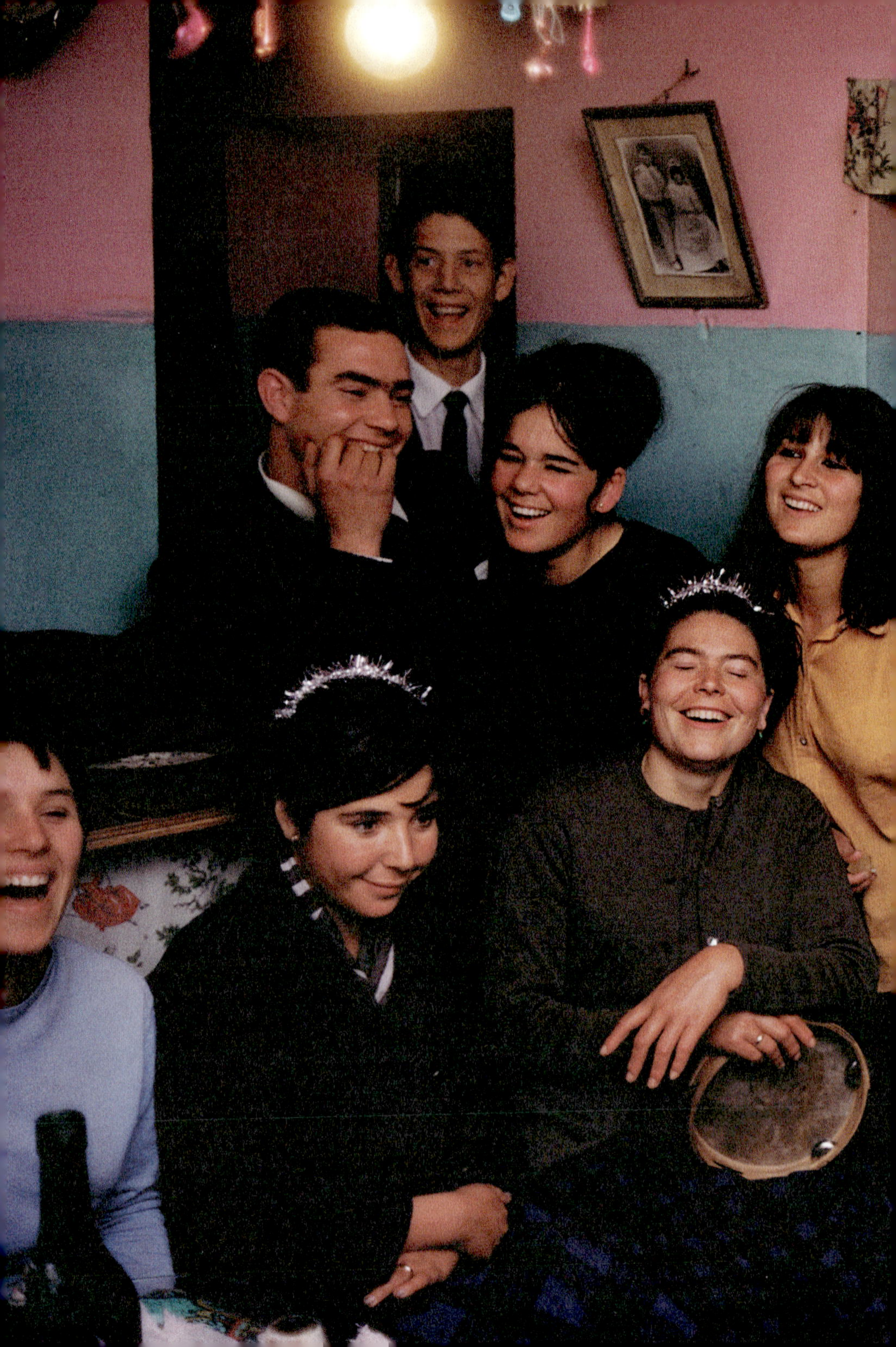

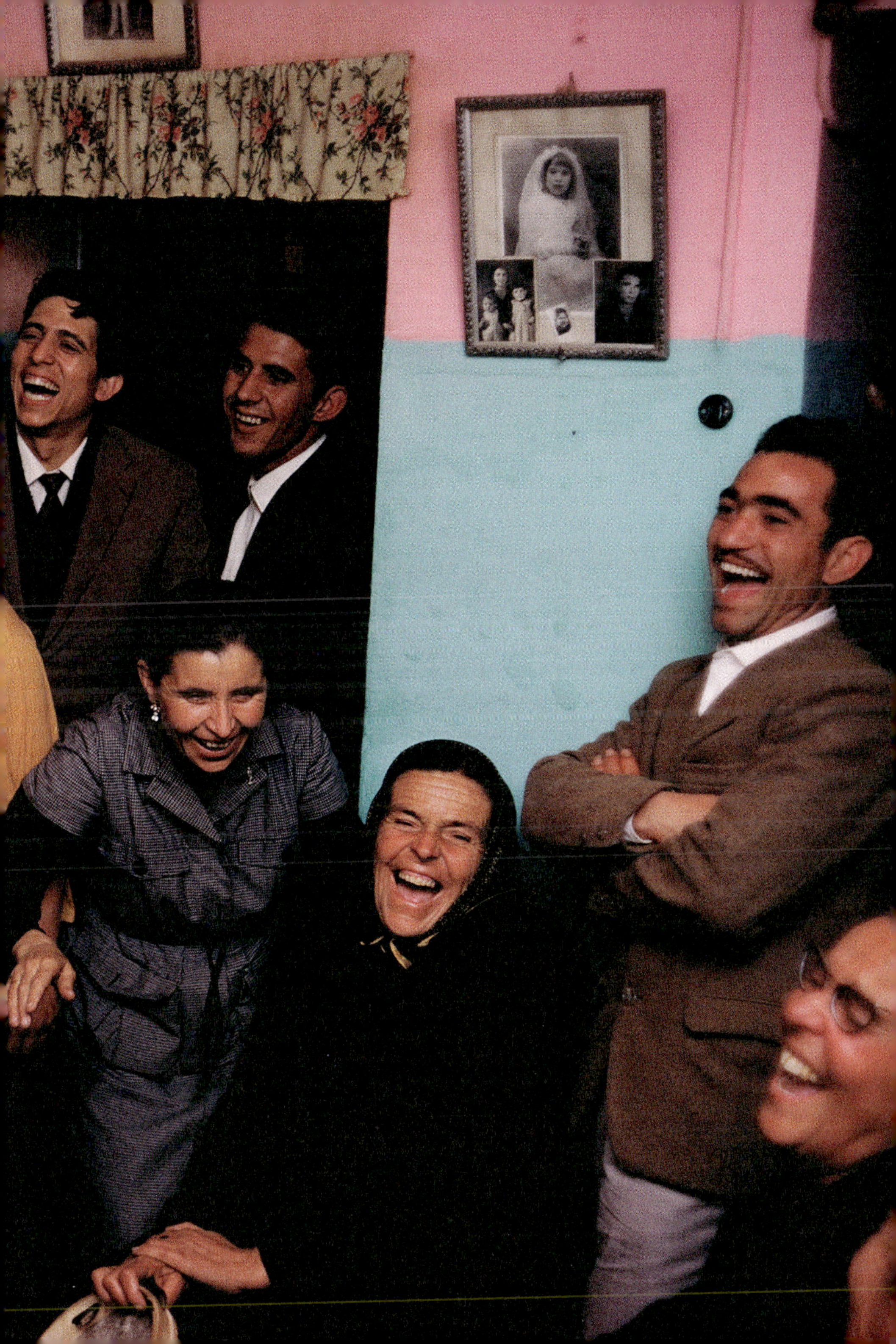

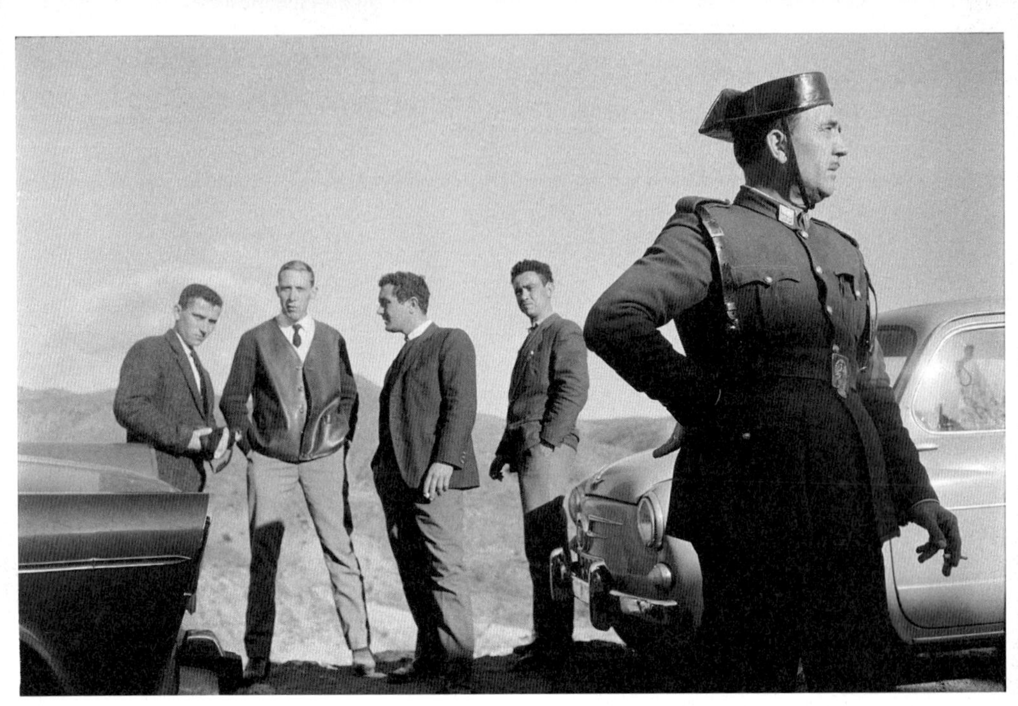

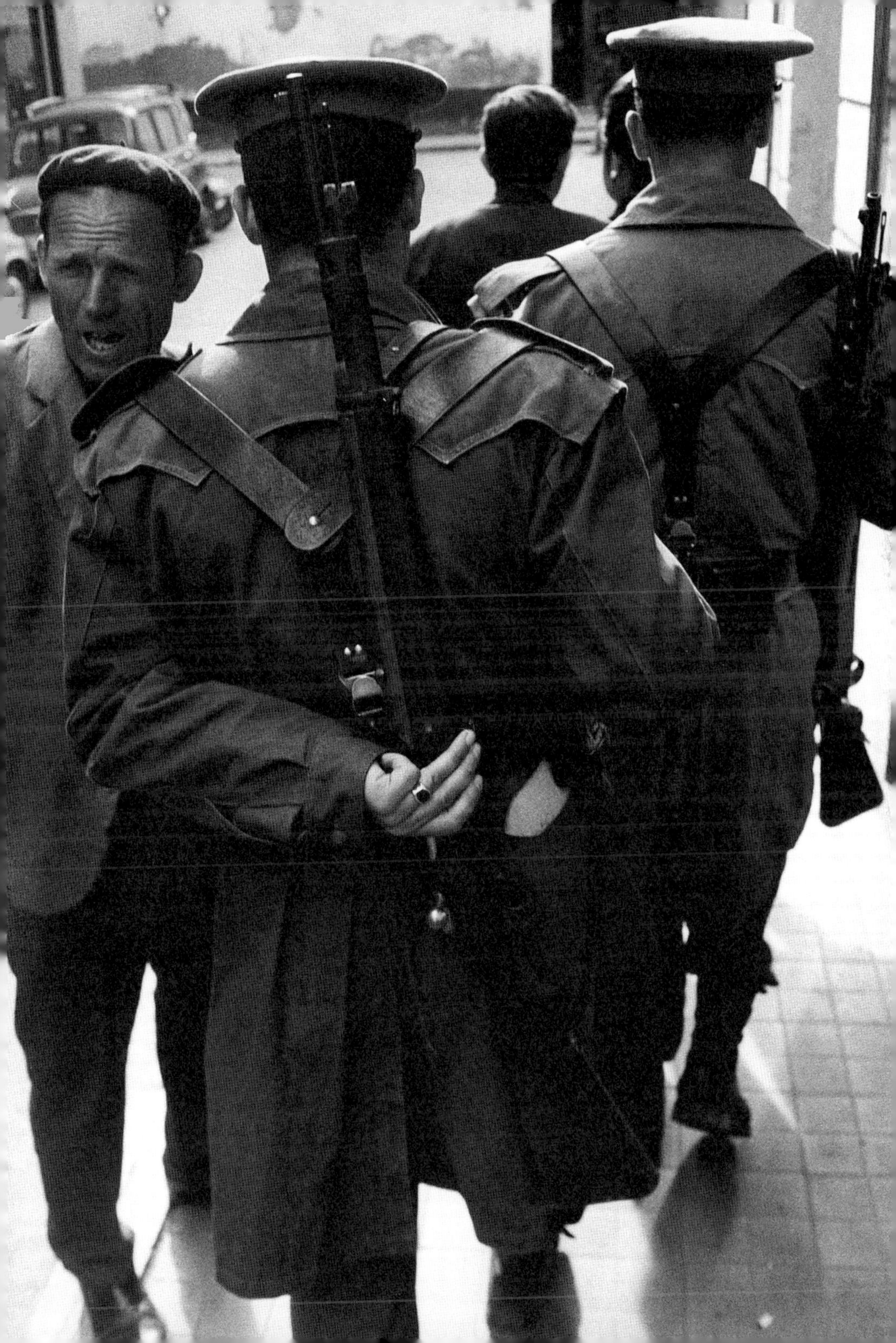

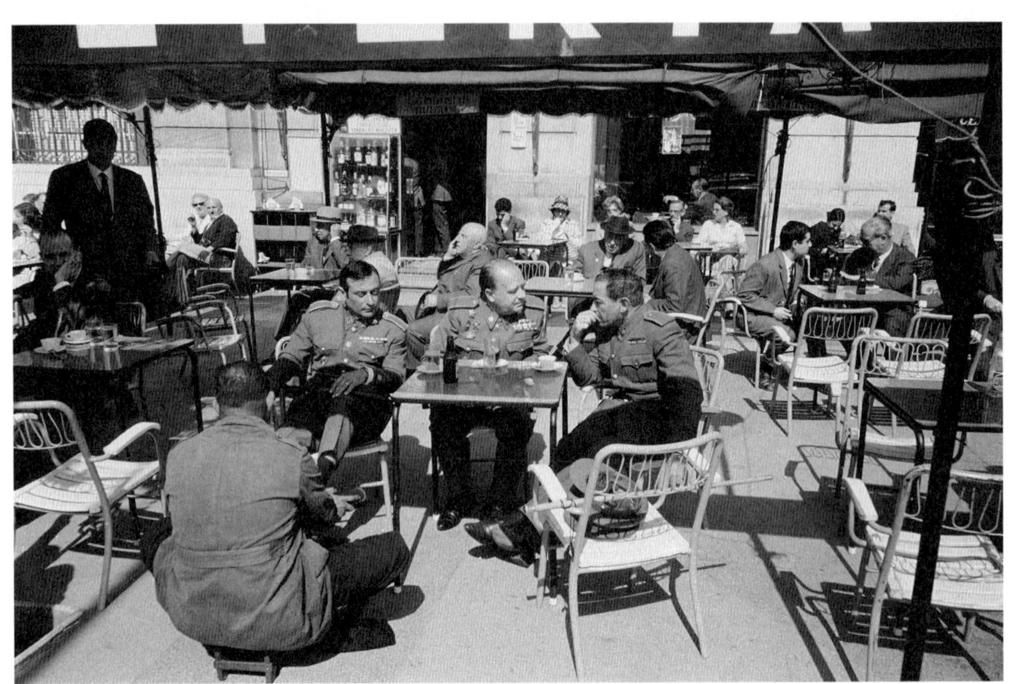

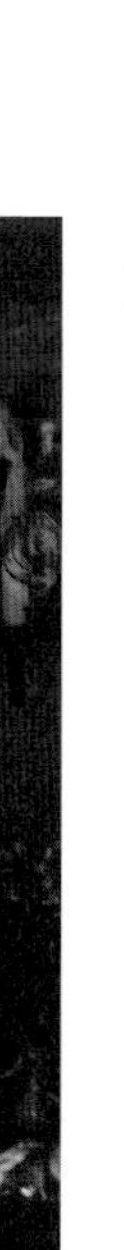

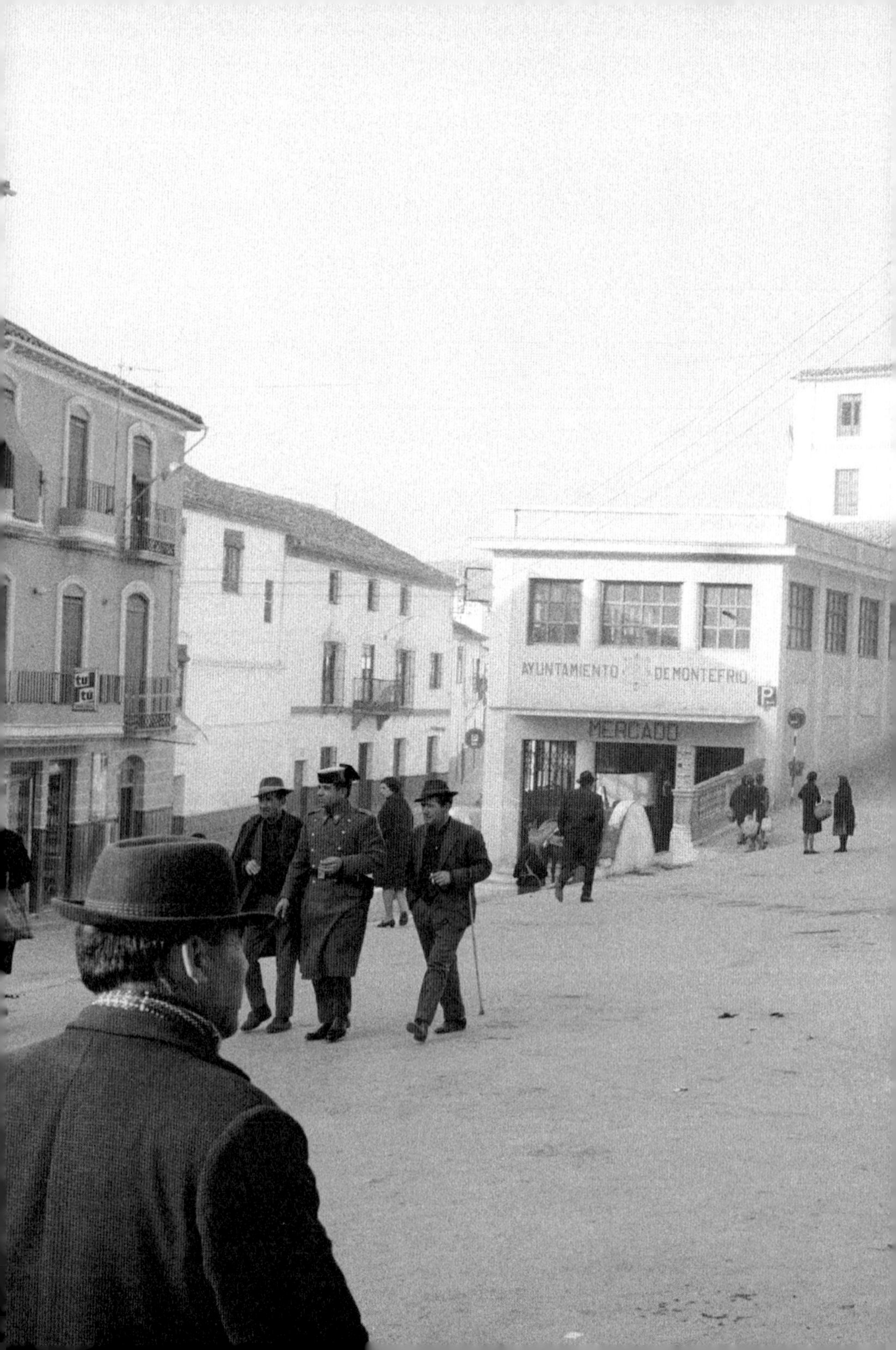

tu
tu
AYUNTAMIENTO DE MONTEFRIO
MERCADO
P

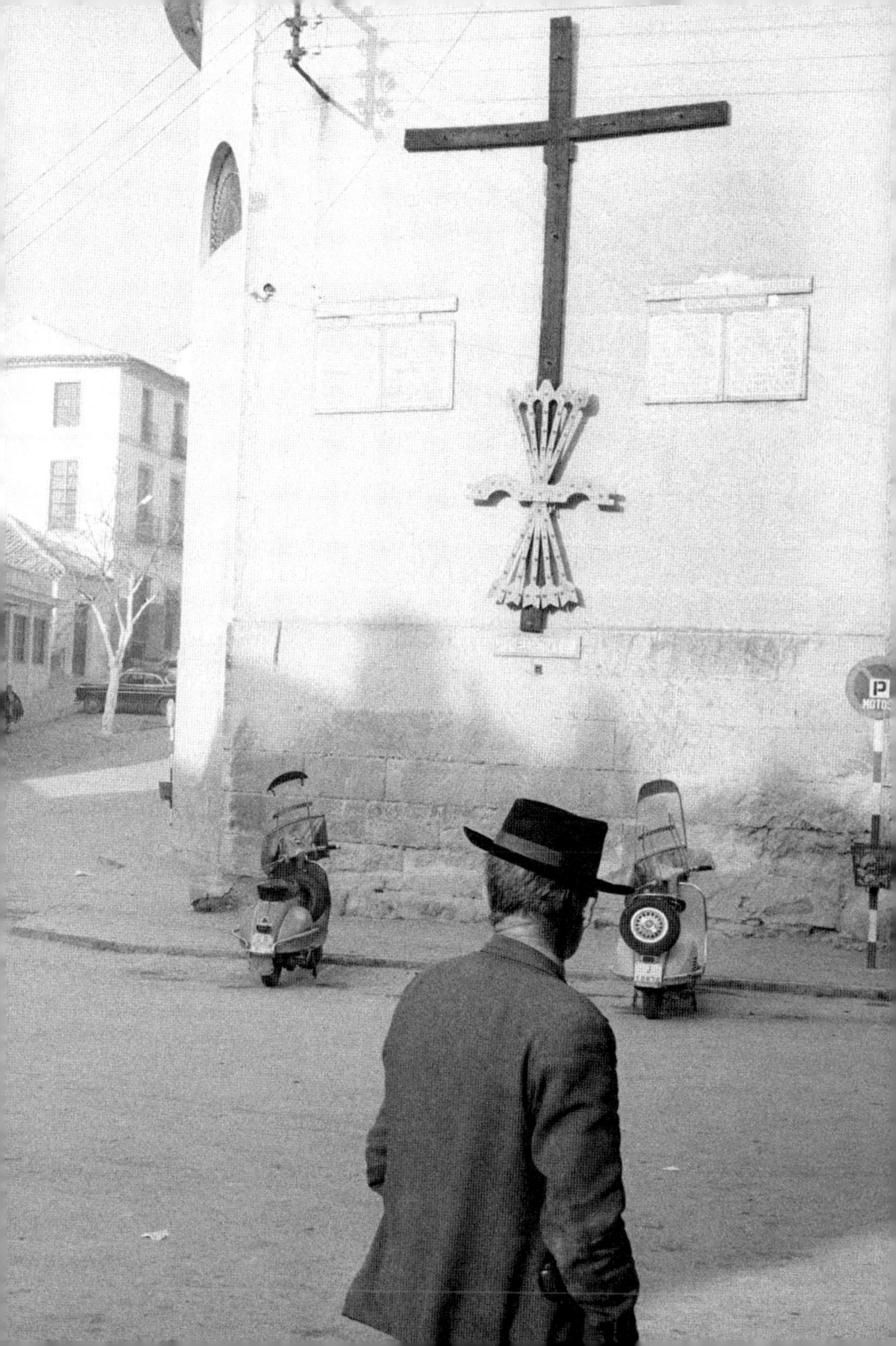

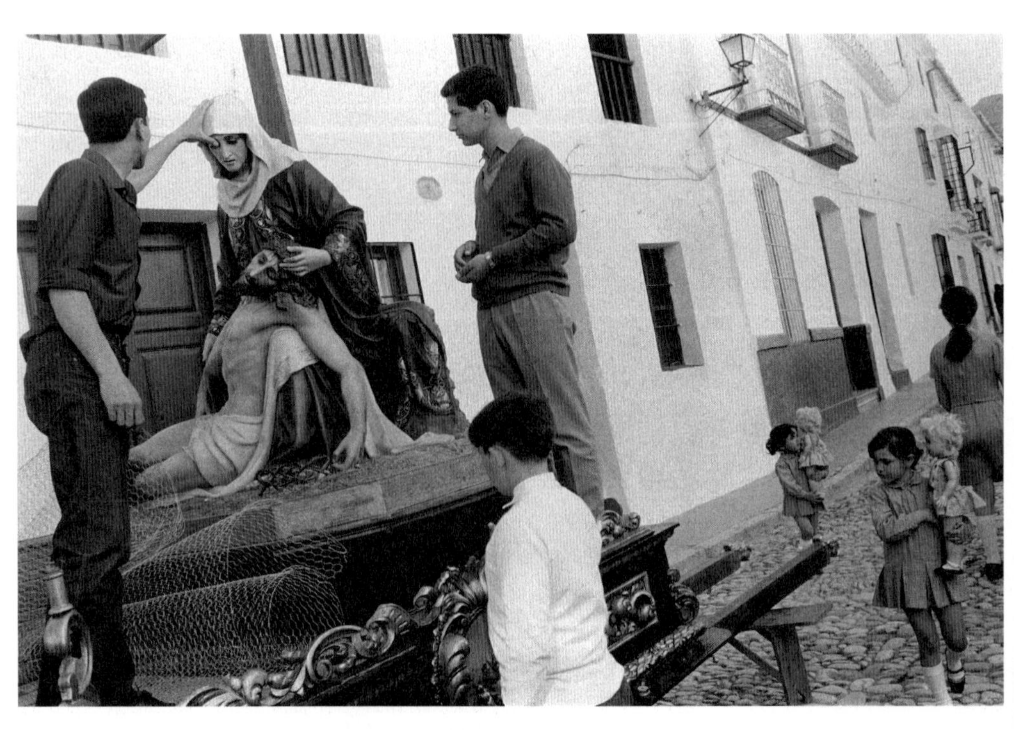

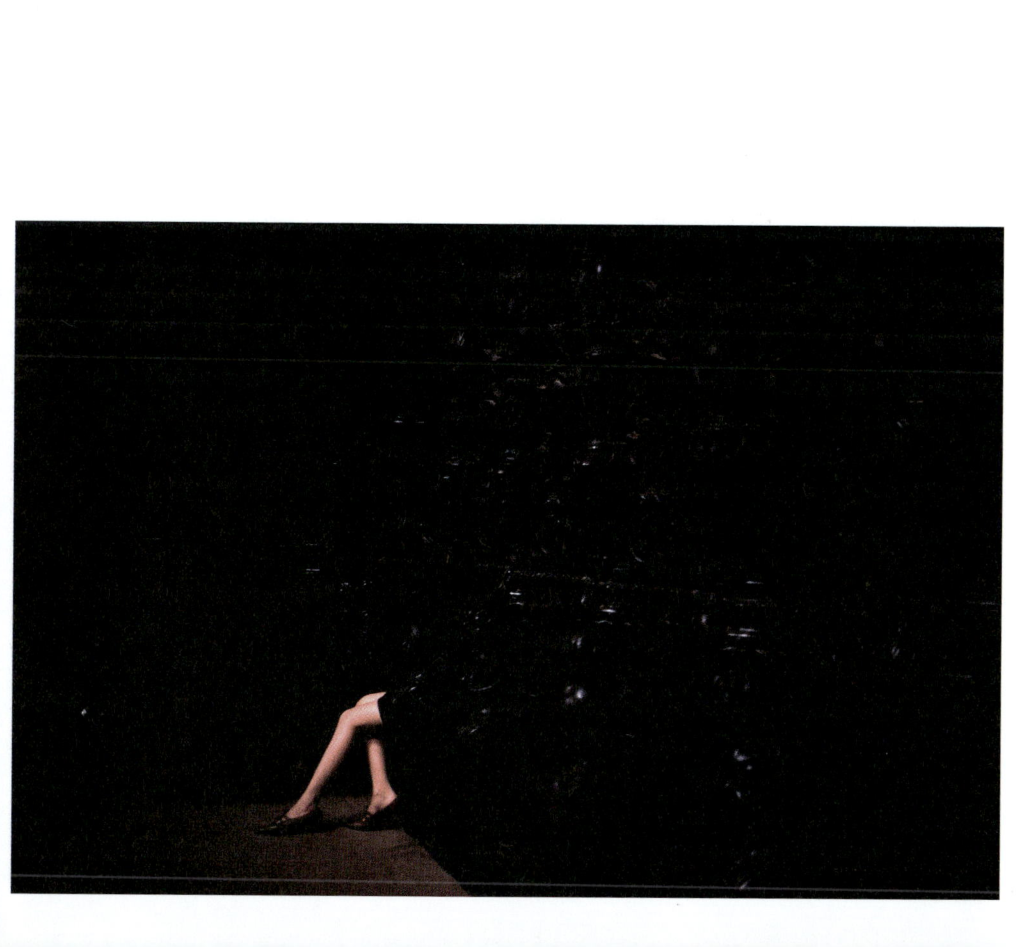

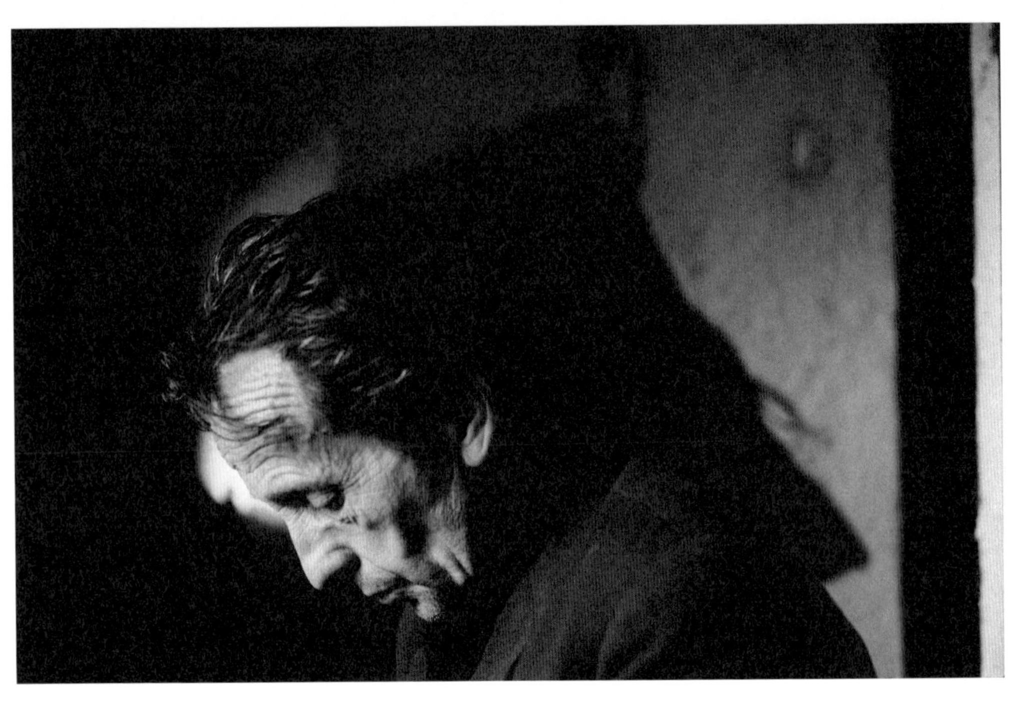

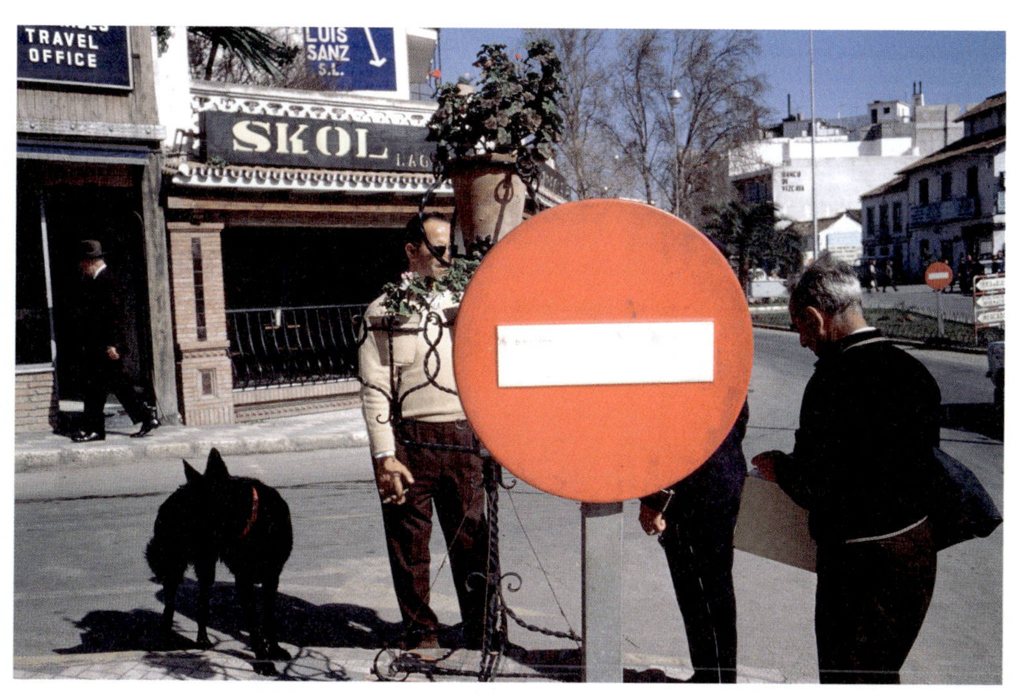
TRAVEL
OFFICE
LUIS
SANZ
S.L.
SKOL
BANCO DE
VIZCAYA

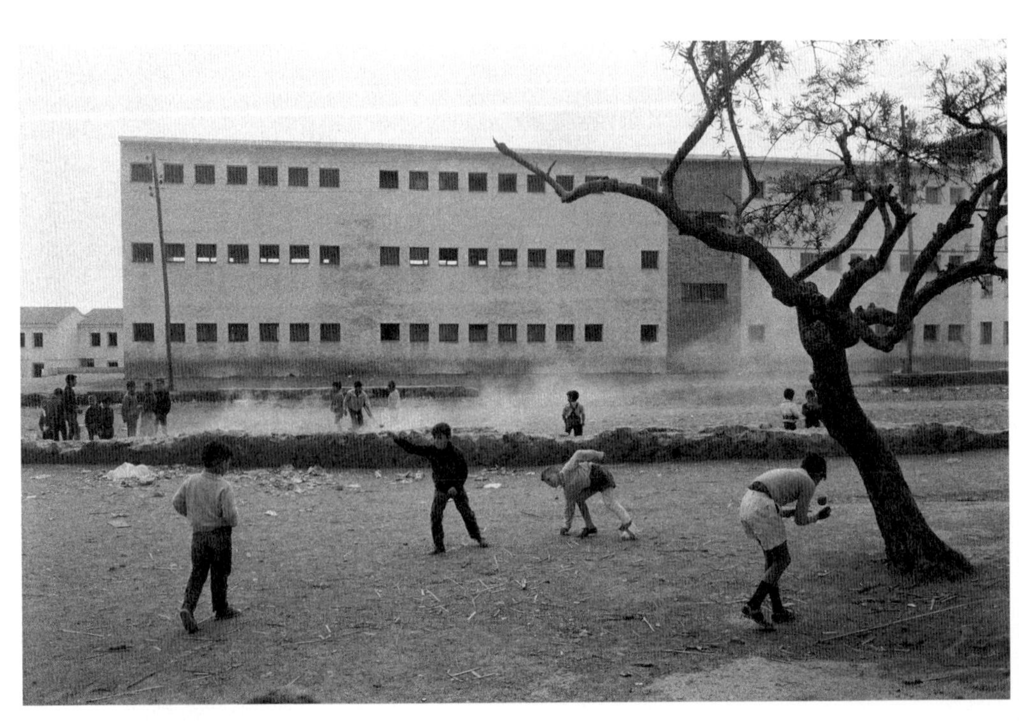

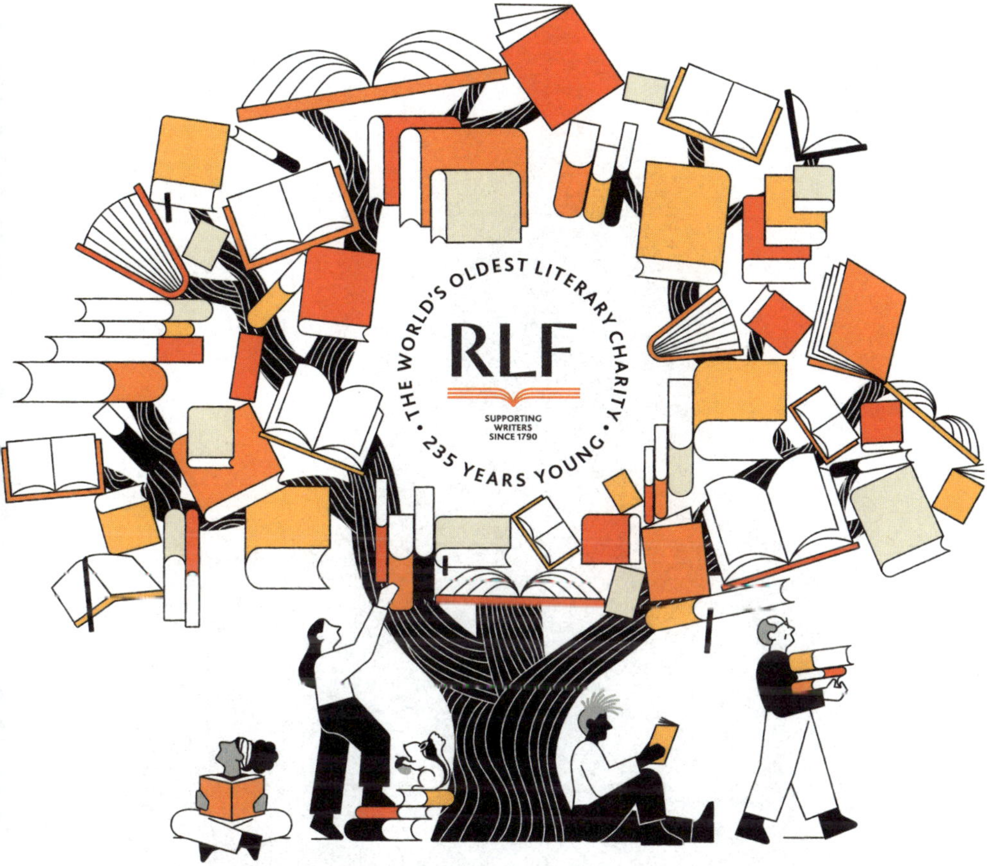

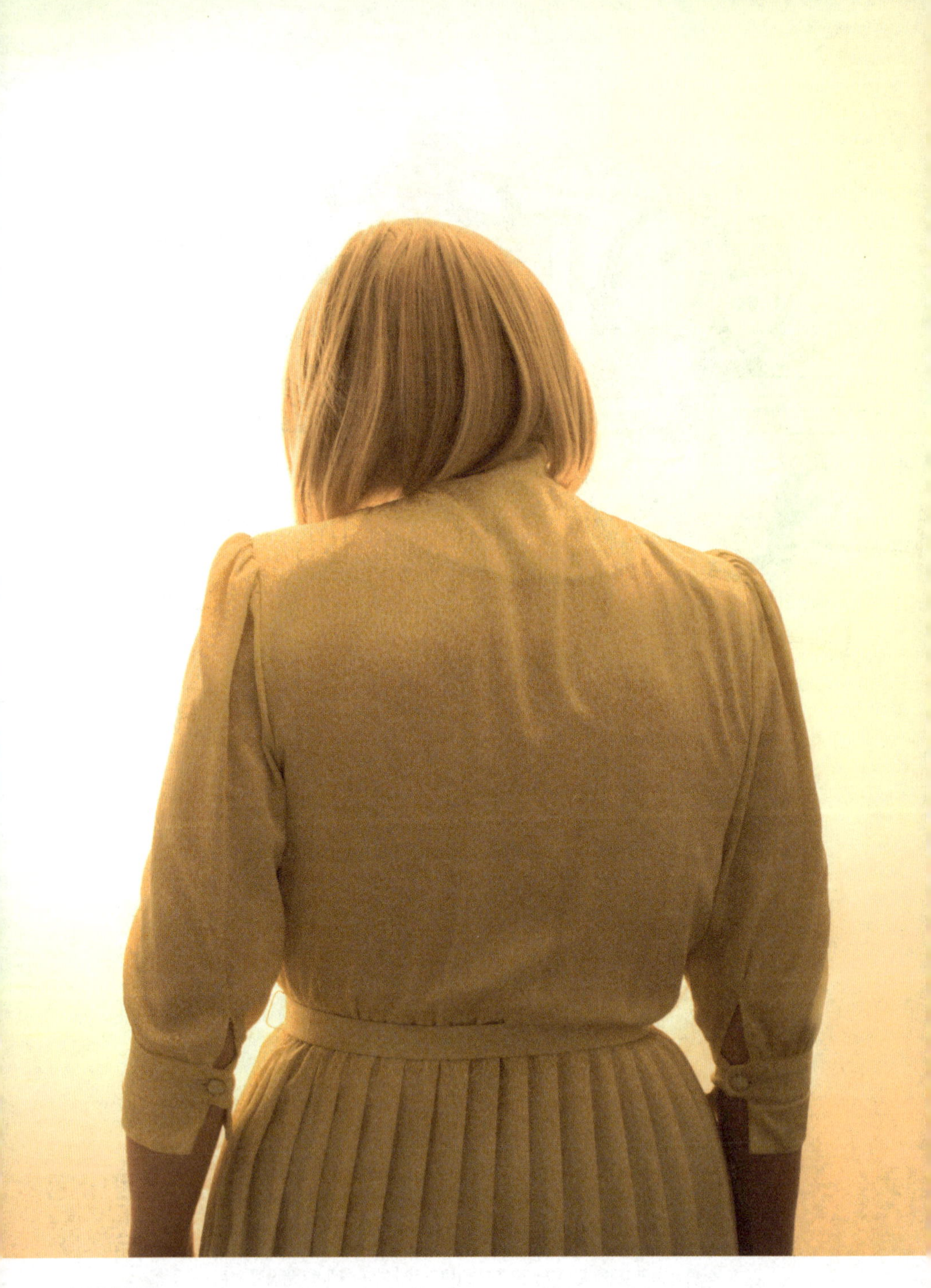

ELIZA BOURNER
Golden Hour, 2020

CAROUSEL

Leopold O'Shea

What was I saying. I am putting my face on for the second time this morning. My brow, my cheeks, my chin receding into the featureless landscape of the unguents. I am drawing on the eyebrows, which have largely vanished after years of preening. Hurrying this time. The sun has left the bathroom so I move, following a line of orange colouring marker on the skirting boards that dips and rises to our daughters' old bedroom, where I bend awkwardly for a small, round mirror. I have found an eyelash on my cheek. I dab it with the end of a middle finger, holding it erect for a moment, then close my eyes, and make a wish, to please keep the aircraft in the air today. And blow as on a birthday candle.

I will have to find a new wish now, I am thinking, looking for the eyebrow pencil. Now I have retired from the airline, I could change the make-up routine. Try plum or lilac. I am looking around the dresser for the pencil I was holding a second ago, my annoyance only half drawn on as I look in the drawer of the nightstand.

Has my husband, sitting in front of the television, seen a pencil, I am asking on all fours, looking under the armchair. An eyebrow pencil, brown, about this long. What are you watching. Maybe I took it to one of the other mirrors, I am saying, letting the question trail off into the television's applause. My husband, who retired from the welfare office a year ago but continues to dress in his office clothes and to rise at seven on weekdays, has fallen asleep in front of the game show, which means it is later than I thought.

When the face is a mess, as we say to juniors, the rest follows, things begin to slip. But a face put together feels no fear or tiredness or anger. Bright smiles hold the plane in the air, I am always saying.

I am looking around the bathroom, on the floor, on and around the sink. But unlike my husband, I do not lose my head when things disappear. I have come to accept that sometimes you are holding something and then it is gone. You are writing a list, you put the pen down and then the pen is gone. No matter how hard you look it is as if the pen had flown away. My husband says I have a talent for making his things disappear. It has become a source of despondence to my husband when I put things away and forget about them, which he says, is the same as deliberately hiding them. It is as if an entity living in our house were slowly moving things out of our reach. One day, my husband says, I will misplace him and it will be like falling through a hole in the world where at least, he says, he will be reunited with the charging cable and his reading glasses, the Blu-Tack and the good pen. But if my husband would let me finish, a while later when you are no longer thinking about pens but looking for the television remote, which has somehow fallen out of existence, it turns out you are actually holding the pen. There, in your other hand, as in a magic trick. And so there is no reason to get angry, I assure my husband, for though the remote is lost, is not the pen regained, and if something must first be lacking, is not everything found that once was lost.

I am looking around the sink in case the pencil decided to reappear when I had my back turned. And then my phone starts ringing. Our eldest daughter is calling as I search for the reading glasses without which I am always stabbing the wrong part of the phone and declining people's phone calls. Please wait, please hold on, I am saying, as I hurry down the stairs, looking around the catchall, the pockets of my coat, letting my hand fall to my side in mock despair when the ringing stops.

I am standing for a moment in front of the game show where contestants open boxes. Whatishecalled is speaking through a red telephone to an entity who dispenses cash prizes, and because of Jenny from Manchester's enormous gums, I have forgotten what I was looking for. Still, I am turning over the sofa cushions so that by looking I may remember what was forgotten, maybe under the sofa or somewhere around the room, my hands on my hips, so that no one will say that I wander into rooms forgetting what it was I was doing.

Everyone is praying for Joan from Middlesex who has selected the box in front of Andrew from Cardiff. The number of the box is the same as her son's birthday and she is holding to her lips a small stuffed tiger that once belonged to him, its ears and stripes worn with fondling.

I am worming my hand under my husband in case he is sitting on whatever it was I was looking for, until finally I take my glasses off, put them on my head and drop my arms in defeat, letting go of whatever it was that was probably nothing, leaving the room with the same assurance I have learned from years of smiling into the distance, even as the oxygen masks are dangling and the duty-free is rolling along the aisles, and clings to me wherever I go, obliging and never complaining, impeccable in every detail, appearing always busy, unperturbed by strange noises and sudden drops in altitude.

As I climb the stairs, I think is it possible that I did not lose anything. As when I leave the house with the feeling that something is missing or forgotten or undone, but after checking all my pockets or turning back find that everything is where it was. Maybe you cannot remember, because no one can remember what they have not forgotten, I am thinking, putting away the suitcase from the France retirement holiday. My husband insists he will put the suitcase away, but it has just been lying on the floor of our bedroom since we got back a week ago, reminding me of this holiday he thoughtfully organised to celebrate my retirement and which I would like now to forget. The whole time he called me Madame, for he knows I love France and everything French. He said I would never pick up another suitcase as long as he lived, but I wish he was less rough with our luggage and with things in general which, he says, are not made of glass, doing a mincing impression of a French homosexual, but was in fact a retirement present from the airline and now the retractable handle is broken and you have to bend down to wheel it in front of you over the quaint but uneven cobbles of Chapeau, causing him to sweat and gasp in front of the French, who never gasp or sweat. I wish my husband would close his mouth when we are on holiday, and not stick his tongue out at the slightest effort. I wish he would stop breathing in front of women on deckchairs, in front of children in swimwear who cannot help watching the spectacle of my husband eating ice cream cones. Still, it is important to me that he performs these gestures, such as carrying the luggage, showing that he thinks of me, and that I continue to exist when I am not in the room.

Before I put the case in the attic I will use it to store the summer clothes and some things I have found in the closet, like the cushion shaped like a fish which admittedly was very funny at the time but now you do not know what to do with, and some lewd souvenirs from Chapeau which my husband thinks are extremely funny and wanted to give to people and which I put away when we came back and we have not been able to find since. I am moving some old video cassettes that we have been keeping in the girls' bedroom to the suitcase lying on the bed.

I am sitting on the small single bed opposite the bunk beds in our daughters' bedroom, young men with hair gel and abdominals looking on dreamily as I leaf through some old copybooks from a cardboard box that once contained an under-desk bike exerciser and now is full of all kinds of rubbish, sports-day medals, communion medals, ribbons, CDs, spare memorial cards from our daughter's funeral, things you do not even know what they are. The orange marker that goes around the skirting boards comes into the room, loops over the window frame, runs up the bunk bed and swirls and expands under the top bunk where it begins or ends, and now leaps on to the copybook where the youngest of the three has done a crude drawing of her father which, you must admit, looks like the male member smiling at you with bird's wings and flaming orange hair. Our eldest, it must be, has written, I am doing your hair the colour of the holy spirit in quotes and the date.

Hmm, I am thinking, wandering out on to the landing. I am like a coin that has not yet fallen on one side or the other. But then I start moving towards the bathroom, where I catch myself unfinished in the mirror. I had to put my make-up on twice this morning because I cried all over myself like a papier-mâché head left out in the rain and now I am behind on the day.

I almost never cry, never once went on strike. But this morning I called our eldest daughter, whom I am usually careful not to disturb, about something I cannot now remember. Now, as I apply the contours of the nose, heightening the cheekbones, foreshortening the top half of my massive forehead, lining the airline's stipulated red smile, I am thinking about how I started shaking with tears this morning and had to hold on to the kitchen counter as if to stop myself from falling. I am remembering the long rope of weeping that reached almost to the floor, until by the fourth or fifth ring of the phone I suddenly fell quiet, like a baby that has cried itself out, and whatever it was fell right out of my head and I hung up before our daughter could answer. I am taking the pencil from the edge of the sink to complete the ponderous expression, thinking what it could have been that I forgot. No trace of the storm that carried my face away, only the quiet optimism which you feel on some level is all that is keeping the plane in the air.

Pulling the shopping trolley behind me on the pavement, I wish I did not have to experience the tedium of the walk to the Lidl supermarket. It is mostly pebble-dash, except for the statue of the Virgin which they have had to put behind chicken wire to stop children throwing stones at her. Once you are in the Lidl supermarket it is not too bad but then there is the return which is arguably worse, where you pass the Virgin again, missing her hands and nose, baring her terrifying wire armature, where the plaster has fallen away. Sometimes I wish the shopping could be done as in a montage.

Much of life, I feel, should be as in a montage. The effort and tedium edited out, the wheelless, seatless bicycle tied to the lamp post edited out, the young men on bicycles, and the wet mattress clinging to a lamp post edited out, leaving only the nice parts, and maybe some light piano music. Surely they must be working on something like it. How is it that one minute you are on the pavement going to the Lidl supermarket sighing at the eternity of the pebble-dash and then somehow you have returned, and where does the time between the one and the other go. Does it fall out of existence, I am asking my husband as I survey the road between the curtains of the front-room window, or does it remain, not in an actual room, not in a literal room, but somewhere, I am saying, sucking my teeth at the smear on the shoulder of my blouse, where a series of beige chins accumulate. My hand falls with a despondent slap of my thigh at the stain on the fun and different pineapple blouse where I must have caught my face this morning.

I am wetting my finger on the way to the kitchen, wiping urgently at the stain which you must address as soon as possible, like mutinous junior flight staff or an unfamiliar lump. Quick, the fun and different pineapple blouse is new, its jumble of pineapples is very me. Quick, I am thinking, rubbing harder. Wiping the pineapples with some soap, I notice that my husband has pulled sheets out of the Lidl supermarket magazine and laid them in front of the wall where he has started painting over some orange marker. When my husband retired he started seeing orange marker all around the skirting boards of our house. For a second the shadow of what I was crying about opens its arms to me and I try to hold the memory by rubbing harder with the soap and sticking my tongue out a little. Our daughter died a long time ago and you feel it is okay to paint over these things now, to get new appliances even if they have orange marker on them where our dead daughter tried to colour everything in the so-called colour of the holy spirit. I am doing a sad weeping face and thinking of our dead daughter in case that was what it was this morning, but then the kettle grumbles to a boil. I do not remember putting the kettle on but it has a cup next to it with a teabag inside, which I drown in the water. Then I go back to rubbing the blouse with the soap, looking around at the floor in case the tears are there waiting to be cried again. I am trying to remember the first two notes of this memory which is like a song that will not come back or a bird that has flown back out of a window, leaving me in the hallway, thinking, where am I going, until the hot tea I am holding takes me, as though by the hand, into the front room where it is set before my husband.

Andrew who works at an Argos warehouse is weeping and has to be comforted by Jill from Northampton and Noel from Antrim, and eventually, everyone joins in to comfort him, including Joan, the woman with the stuffed toy, because of how guilty Andrew feels about the contents of the box that was randomly assigned to him. I am standing for a moment, hands on my hips, sucking my teeth and shaking my head, then turn to the door and go upstairs where I had started packing.

But I must have drifted off. Like when I am reading and pages later I have no idea how I got here, in this woman's body, sitting on the lid of the toilet, under the open window, eating biscuits as the cars on the motorway rock back and forth in the rain like the sea.

The way I have drawn my eyebrows is as if I were thinking very hard about something, but actually I was gazing into space remembering the restaurant in Chapeau when he insisted on shaking the chef's hand. He had to congratulate the chef on the food. He got angry because I would not try the mussels. Kept saying how talented the chef was, and I had to try and calm him down. People looking, waiters asking him to stay seated, a fight almost breaking out. It comes back in waves of clenching embarrassment. Then, later, watching him apologise to everyone profusely with a French accent to make them understand, tears in his eyes. My husband is always crying and saying sorry. Before leaving, I went to the bathroom, and when I came out he was doing his magic routine, his expression full of wonder, theirs polite and embarrassed, a napkin folded into a dove perched on his arm and then vanishing.

I am wearing one of the dingier bras and still almost-skin-coloured underpants that sink into rolls of fat like bread dough, thin blue veins scrambling like fireworks and petering out over bristling thighs, painted toes staring back like fat pigs from a nursery rhyme. The biscuits I am eating come from behind the plastic bath panel that my husband has still not sealed to the tub. This is where I hide the biscuits from my husband but I have no memory of pulling out the plastic bath panel or only vaguely, or it was a different time.

I was about to remember what I was doing here, but our eldest daughter is calling again and by the time the glasses are on the end of my nose and I am holding the phone, close at first, then farther away, close and far away, back and forth like this, taking aim with a red fingernail and the tip of my tongue sticking out, our daughter has hung up.

Hmm, I am thinking, trying to match the puzzled expression of the eyebrows with a pursing of the mouth, what is the kettle doing on the floor.

Suddenly, I am remembering to lock the door in case my husband comes in, asking why am I sitting naked on the toilet, eating biscuits and so on in the middle of the afternoon.

But the door is already locked.

My husband and I never lock the door though, I am thinking, eating another biscuit, thinking what was I doing in the upstairs bathroom.

Suddenly my irises widen. My heart flutters. But it turns out to be nothing and I sit back down again, shaking my head at myself and this stupid idea I just had.

Back on the toilet seat, I notice the orange marker again, this time in the grouting. Our four-year-old's most concerted effort with the marker took place behind the television which we moved to cover it up. This meant adjusting the sofa which we forgot had been covering up another spot that she had been trying to fill in with the holy spirit, but which, it turned out, was roughly the shape of the CD rack, and then when CDs were no longer a thing, became a cheese plant.

I am listening to the vascular throb of the television downstairs, wondering what my husband is watching. Soon it will be time for my programme, and then I realise, with sudden brutal clarity, why it was I came up here. I slap myself on the forehead but when I stand up and examine this new realisation, it turns out to be the first realisation, in all its abject stupidity, for the second time.

Soon it will be time for my favourite programme about a depressed English detective. It is getting cold and dark and quiet in the bathroom and I wish I would stop eating the biscuits which are beginning to turn my stomach. I know it was a stupid idea, but still, I cannot help feeling hopeful about this idea I once considered extremely stupid. I am standing at the mirror, taking the hairbrush from the edge of the sink, and brushing my hair. I am brushing my hair in case that was why I came up here but how, I am thinking, can the brushing account for the kettle or the nudity or the lock on the door or the biscuits. Still, I continue to brush my hair in case it takes a while to take effect.

Our eldest daughter is calling but I just remembered why I locked myself in. You become so accustomed to the shouting and crying and recriminations in this house that it becomes a kind of routine in the middle of which you drift off listening to the hush of the motorway or thinking of Chapeau. Some things you do so many times, I always tell my juniors, you can forget you are doing them. I could work through an entire flight, thinking about something else, or perform the safety demonstration, sometimes thinking nothing at all, and have almost no memory of the flight taking place, or the memory of that flight would be the memory of some earlier flight. So now, I cannot remember the precise details of this argument with my husband, but which has all the signs of many previous arguments and is the only way to explain the lock on the door, which he could easily break through but is held back from for fear of damaging the frame. And though I cannot remember all the particulars of this argument, the whole situation is very distressing, which is why I console myself with the biscuits and keep boiling water to throw on my husband should he attempt to tear through the door's flimsy locking mechanism.

That is why I cannot answer my phone. There is a lot our eldest daughter does not know about her father that her mother keeps behind closed doors. Soon my husband will come out of the front room and call my name from the bottom of the stairs. I will refuse to come out of the bathroom, and may well have to leave my husband for good this time. After a minute or so he will lose patience and go back to the television. Then he will rise from the sofa with something that has occurred to him, stirring things up again, and so on, until, at the end of a long silence, the stairs will ache under my husband's weight. I will refuse to open the door and will not believe any of my husband's words which are empty. What has pushed me to the edge this time and so many times is how routine the whole thing has become. The routine has changed and adapted in minor ways just as the in-flight safety demonstration changes and adapts, but always it is the same argument in essence, just as the planes are always largely the same. My voice then will crack with weeping, screaming at him to not come any closer and so on, I have boiling water and so forth. I cannot do it any more, for the last time I cannot do it.

It will not be long now, I am thinking, following the television for the time. My husband will let himself slide to the foot of the door, whispering there, as if our daughters were still here to listen. Who are you whispering for, I sometimes shout angrily. One minute my husband is shouting, the next minute he is whispering. But for whom, I ask, screaming. Then after a long silence it will be his turn to start crying, saying over and over again how sorry he is. My husband never used to cry when the children were around. Not until they were gone did he start crying, wearing you down until you drift off and eventually have no choice but to let him in.

It will not be long now, I am thinking. Because I am in love with France and everything French, my husband always made crêpes for our daughters after our fights, sometimes bringing a plate under the stairs where the two youngest would hide from the screaming. After the girls were gone, it was the only way we knew to bring things to a close and I am always careful to have ingredients, in case of an argument, always the same or more or less the same argument, usually on a Sunday, the only chance work ever afforded. I am not looking forward to the screaming, which is always exhausting, yet even now I cannot help smiling at the thought of the crêpes and the mystery of a dead body showing up next to a lake in Devon or somewhere. Eventually, I will unlock the door and sit back on the floor, eyes turned away from my husband, who, after a pause, will slide over to me, rest his head in my lap and cry as we listen to the lullaby of the motorway. I will stroke his hair until he goes quiet and later give him the rest of the biscuits, usually two-thirds to three-quarters, letting what is said pass into silence.

My husband thinks I will not notice that there are fewer biscuits behind the bath panel. He thinks I will not miss one or two, sometimes three or even four biscuits, which he sneaks out of the bathroom. He thinks I do not know he has found the hiding place, but I have always known. Imagine, I am thinking, how rapidly our marriage would have dissolved without the biscuits and ingredients for the crêpes, and if I let my husband do the shopping, what surreal assortment my husband would come home with if he was allowed to go to the supermarket. It is pointless sulking if there are fewer biscuits than usual. He should have taken less time to make things up to me, and in the first place, he should not be eating biscuits. I am shaking my head at my husband who thinks that by going unnamed, by remaining unspoken, the biscuits will not affect his diabetes. It is because of the diabetes that I must hide the biscuits, which, officially, are reserved for me, and are meant to be a secret, and, therefore, do not, strictly speaking, exist.

Pff, I am thinking, in the soft pink dusk of the bathroom, the water in the kettle could not burn anyone any more. What is going on in the mind of my husband. He does not call my name so I can shout back at him to leave me alone, to not come in here, and so on. I am worrying now about what he will say about all the biscuits I have eaten, even though he is the one who should have come to the door sooner, broken down in tears so we could move on. But instead I must eat my husband's biscuits which I do not even enjoy.

My phone lights the bathroom like a tea light in a church and goes dark again. A smile is forming on my lips even as I am sucking my teeth, for though it is always the same excuses, the same promises and twisting of words, I am looking forward to leaving the bathroom. But then it turns out to just be our daughter and my heart falls out of the sky.

Is it possible he is acting as if nothing happened, as if I had just been attending to the ordinary concerns of the bathroom, brushing the toilet bowl, changing the dried flowers in the ornamental dish, watching the television as if he had no idea of an argument, what do you mean, love, what did I do, what the hell are you talking about.

I am screaming. Usually, I would also be crying, but it is hard to get the tears going when you do not remember what caused them. The vein in the side of my head is swelling and throbbing, though I am held back by a kind of self-awareness and my heart is not really in it. The room itself swells and throbs with shouting, until there is no air left in my lungs, only a faint fading ring as the bathroom falls quiet again.

My husband knows it is Sunday and that my programme will be on soon yet he will not take responsibility. He does not care that I am in the bathroom screaming and, as far as he knows, also weeping. My husband, with whom I only stayed because of the children, is finally driving me to leave him forever. Now that our children have gone, each in their separate ways, finally, it is time to think about myself. Finally, I will pack a suitcase and I will leave forever, I have decided. It is the only way to put down the biscuits and get out of the bathroom, to get as far away as I can from my husband.

I am making sure to leave everything as it was before I came in, closing the window, pushing the plastic bath panel back into the tub with all of the weight of the years. The weight of the years makes a lot of noise scraping the floor tiles and I have to kick it into place a couple of times. Though in some ways it is true that I have not been crying, I wipe the make-up away from my face with the backs of my hands. I am emptying the kettle into the toilet and washing my face in the sink, rubbing it until it is red and swollen and ugly. Sighing for courage, I take a square of paper, drop it in the toilet and press the bigger of the two flushes.

I am standing, broken, in the doorway of our bedroom, for the last time. After forty years of trying, I am finally leaving my husband once and for all, just as our eldest daughter always said I should have but which I could not for one reason or another. Sometimes I think our daughter failed to leave her husband because of my failure to leave mine. The suitcase is waiting on the bed, where I started packing earlier but was probably stopped by my husband. Probably it is getting a bit cold for the dresses and flip-flops, I am thinking, I do not know what use I will have for a cushion shaped like a fish that beats its tail when there are batteries. Maybe to raise my spirits on dark days, I remember. That is why I have taken the children's old copybooks. The dresses, the fun and different pineapple blouse, and my passion for France, express who I am deep, deep down, far, far in.

I am slowly descending the stairs with the kettle and the suitcase and all of the years living with my husband. My steps are heavy and I am holding the bannisters as if weak with the years and the weeping. For though I am broken, I have not forgotten what my husband has done which at present I cannot quite remember. I am looking between the hinges of the sitting-room door, where I can see him pretending to sleep. I should have held my breath on tiptoe, I am thinking. Then I would have caught him watching, smiling at the television and moving back into position the way children do when you come back in the room. But I gave him too much warning, and now I will have to leave my husband for good this time.

My phone is ringing but I will be speaking to our daughter later when I need to find a place to stay. It will only be a couple of nights. I do not want to trouble our daughter, whose house is cold and dimly lit, you always feel you are in her way, and by then things will have sorted themselves out with my husband, who is not nearly as bad as our daughter likes to paint him.

But what was I saying. I am taking flour from the cupboard and eggs and milk from the fridge. I cannot remember when I first started taking boiling water upstairs, I am thinking, looking up at the time. Probably it dates back to when I did not know my husband as well as I know him today, like a safety protocol you have to point out for legal reasons but which no one really takes seriously any more. I am sifting the flour for my husband, making a little well at the bottom of the mixing bowl, to save us both some time. Pff, I am thinking, probably our daughter will take it as another reason to blame everything on her father. You cannot tell your daughter anything about her father without her telling you to leave your husband who has worked hard and has earned a break from her constant relitigation of the past. Our eldest daughter has an opinion on everything and uses these so-called thoughts as ways to not think about her own failures, her own husbands and children. I am heating the pan, looking up at the time. Children have their own individual characters, which you cannot set at the feet of their parents. Our daughter will see that eventually some of her children will move to Florida, some will die, while others will always be crying and complaining and relitigating. There is nothing you can do about these things, I want to tell our daughter.

I have made my husband's crêpes and we are watching my programme about English people winding up dead in enviable homes. There is lots of exposed stone and wisteria in this one and the investigator is particularly ambivalent about his job. His house, you can tell from his clothes and manner, is not as nice as the deceased's.

Every so often I tap my husband, asking is that not Whatishecalled, who plays the Youknowwhat, I am whispering behind the screen of my hand, in Thesomething, which my husband always confuses with Theotherone.

I am withdrawing my hand from my husband, who pretends to

be asleep because of something I must have said in the past which I cannot remember but which in its context was probably justified, and so I move to the other armrest. Maybe I will remind my husband that he snores but we are no longer speaking. At least now you can follow what is going on without a running commentary from my husband, even if what is going on is not as good as you remember.

I am drawing the curtains of the front room. I am taking my plate to the kitchen where I accidentally break wind, which I worry will make me sound cheerful instead of angry for the things my husband has said, which were far worse than anything I said. I am standing for a moment in the doorway, watching my husband in case I catch him smiling or taking a biscuit. He is not moving now but you can tell he was just a moment before, like junior flight staff going quiet when senior flight staff enter a room. Please turn the television off at the wall when you come to bed, I am asking politely.

I was going to unpack the suitcase after the crêpes, but now I will have to leave it in front of the bedroom so I am ready to leave him first thing in the morning. It is too late to leave my husband today and I have not spoken to our daughter about arrangements yet.

I am turning on to my side, away from his half of the bed, as close as I can to my edge without falling off, and letting one out. I have rolled myself in the duvet so he will not have any. I do not want him to touch me. I am closing my eyes, floating on tides of murmured television washing back and forth through the door, wondering in the warm vascular darkness what must I have said for him not to speak to me. I do not want to stay at our daughter's house, whose dog's name and gender you are always supposedly getting wrong. Admittedly, it is not unusual for one of us to take it this far, though packing a suitcase is usually enough to end it. Once I took it a step further and, after packing my bag, said goodbye to the children, lying that I had to go back to work, and the two youngest wept and hung on to my ankles and I parked on the other side of the block for a few hours, eating chocolate from an expired advent calendar. I did the shopping and, after a probationary silence, he made crêpes and the two youngest came out of their hiding places. The four-year-old wet with tears and my husband making the dove disappear.

And when I open my eyes, the sun is wincing in the curtains. My husband is up. His pillow cold to the touch, his half of the mattress empty, and the television already on. I am hoping he will not try to talk to me. He forgets that mornings are like jet lag for me, and then he complains that he told me something and that I forgot, even though I told him. I told him I am not there in the mornings.

I am dead weight. I lower myself down the stairs, one step at a time, shuffle to and fro in the kitchen until the water has boiled and lean against the counter, zoning out at a nest of orange marker I am noticing on the refrigerator, unspooling itself around the skirting boards and on to the dial of the washing machine. Since retiring I have started noticing things, primarily in the mornings, like the three freckles on the back of my husband's ear which I swear were not there before. We had to move the fridge around to hide our four-year-old's attempt to fill in this blank that resides in things. I am going to pour hot water from the kettle into a mug but I am already holding a mug, hot and beige and burning my lips.

I am putting my make-up on though I thought I remembered doing it already. I am putting the clothes from the suitcase back into the dresser, reminding myself to find something with which to take them to the attic, leaving the suitcase next to the bed for my husband to put away. I am not sure what I was doing in the front room but there is always something you can be getting on with while you remember so I am dusting the picture frames on the mantelpiece and around the retirement card which reads Bonne Voyage. I cannot help smiling at this as I dust, and at the kind words of my former colleagues, who I thought did not like me but perhaps just thought I was being French. People at work somehow got it in their heads that I liked France, and would use French phrases with me. I have no idea where they got this or who they could have mistaken me for. Friends and relatives also started working under this assumption, I remember, burning my lips, gazing out the front-room window. And eventually, my husband followed. I was always missing Christmas but I would come home to a lot of French-themed gifts and it seemed impolite to say anything, and eventually, it became a part of who I am, like the fun and different pineapple blouse, which it is true has something French about it. Sometimes I think I have gotten tired of France, tired of all the French-themed decor in our home, but actually it is that I never liked France. It is easy to forget that I have never cared much for the French.

What are you watching, I am asking my husband, who has fallen asleep in front of the antiques programme. Is it the antiques you are watching.

I am thinking we should get a new refrigerator, I am telling my husband, the old one works but probably it is time to get rid of it now.

My husband is wearing black leather shoes, a blue chequered short-sleeved shirt, grey flannel trousers open at the fly that bunch three centimetres down from the belt buckle. His head is cocked back, his mouth open, showing its glistening pinks, off-whites and reds. His tie is open and some of the buttons of his shirt have popped off showing some of his chest. One of your shoelaces is loose, I am saying, sucking my teeth, except that there is a knot where you can see he lost his patience and started pulling like a maniac. I am kneeling by my husband's shoe, trying to undo the knot but it is no use. I feel like crying at this knot in my husband's shoelace.

I am turning off the television. I am putting the television remote in my husband's shirt pocket as a joke about me always disappearing the television remote. I am caressing his thin, white hair and putting a throw over his knees, tucking him in, kissing him on the head.

I am standing, thinking what I will do next. I am opening the window to let the stale air out. Our daughter is calling but I cannot answer, unfortunately, due to the hoover, which is almost completely drowning out the ringing. I am not as careful with the hoover attachment around my husband's feet as I am around the furniture. Sorry, I am saying to my husband when it hits his foot. And again a second time.

I am catching my face in the glass of the picture frames. I have not done a great job of the eyebrows today, I am thinking, which look startled as if by something coming this way. I cannot always explain the placement of my eyebrows from one day to the next.

I am looking out at the road from the front window. I dreamed, I am telling my husband, I was flying, but the controls were written in French. Anyway, I am saying, flinching at the tea, though it is basically cold, flinching as I suck it in, as if it was burning hot, and scowl at the road from the heat of the tea. A sudden downpour of children's voices, screaming, school shoes smacking the pavement, a flash of coats and school bags, and the dead silence they leave behind them, like litter.

I am crouching under the window of the sitting room to avoid detection by our eldest daughter. Now and then you can hear the flimsy, metallic letter flap clearing its throat, her voice alternating with her daughter's and her husband's, Whatishecalled. No, not Whatishecalled, that is what we called the first one. Thenewone. Eventually, a key starts turning in the lock.

Our daughter is giving me a hug, then our granddaughter, whose name I am supposedly always getting confused with my youngest daughter, and I smile affably at Thenewone who says Bonjour. Our daughter is asking me something but I hold a finger to my lips, gesturing to our granddaughter that my husband is sleeping in the front room. Our daughter is asking how I am and I take the coats. She tried calling a few times but I have to strain to hear what she is saying, cupping my ear, and she is speaking so low that I simply agree, smiling at Whatishecalled, Thenewone, who is quite handsome and likes to say things in French to me. France is my thing. I am winking at him and make a drinking-tea-from-a-cup gesture while orienting us to the kitchen.

I am explaining to Thenewone about the parking disc as the tea brews, and to be careful of his tyres. Watch your tyres do not get stabbed, I am telling him, with a stabbing motion. Our daughter says I called her yesterday morning and she was worried because I was not answering the phone, but I do not have any parking discs, I am sorry to tell our daughter's husband whom I am careful not to name in case I confuse him with the first husband, Whatwashecalled. I am offering him one of the biscuits my husband did not finish last night. I am showing our granddaughter the card I got from work. Not everyone makes it to the end, I am telling her. One colleague, years back, I am saying, laughing, after years in the company started panicking during the safety demonstration that there was nothing under our feet, and began struggling to breathe, shaking with tears and holding on to a bit of panelling as if she might fall. Haha, I am saying. She was never able to fly after that, I am laughing. Not once did I go on strike, I am telling our granddaughter. My girls always hit their targets. Where is our daughter, I am asking Thenewone, getting our daughter's name confused with our other daughters and then my sister and my mother until finally, I get the right one. Please, I am telling him, with a hand on his arm, do not leave valuables visible in the car. I am winking and smiling at him, nodding at something he is saying, and start pouring milk, remembering how once when I came home from work our four-year-old managed to kill herself with a Lidl shopping bag. This was especially depressing as people did not really go to Lidl at the time. People forget that it was embarrassing to be seen at Lidl, to have German-labelled gherkins or biscuits, as this meant you were poor and shopped from bins, as we used to say. Their biscuits are very good though. My husband, who you know, I am saying to Thenewone, had to break down the door of the bathroom and when he got in the room was empty, as if the four-year-old had flown away. There and then not there, created and uncreated. Actually she was at the foot of the house outside, I am saying, shaking my head disapprovingly. The bag was tied to a string, I am saying, tied under her armpits in a sort of parachute. Now it is perfectly acceptable to shop in Lidl. Everyone does. I am trying to think of something else to say to our daughter's husband in the front room where his wife is having some kind of meltdown. Still, I am saying, I find the bags a bit depressing so I usually bring a shopping trolley.

For a second I was worried I had forgotten the purse I usually take for the shopping, its weight missing from my left coat pocket, but actually this is normal as I am standing next to a coffin laid on a pair of trestles in an alley of the cemetery, with our daughter, and Thenewone and their daughter and others. I am beginning to notice a certain pattern with our children. Though we have three daughters, it is always the same daughter I have the least to say to who is always calling or linking arms with me, looking mournfully at me, or rubbing my back. Our daughter in Florida is sorry she could not make it, because of the dogs, which you have to say is fair enough, but sent a wreath. How true to life that the daughter I have the most in common with, the one I have the most to say to and would welcome a phone call from at any time, is the one who jumped out the bathroom window. And the daughter I have the second most in common with, who feels like an old friend you have drifted away from but still welcome a catch up with from time to time, at least is not dead, but still is very far away, has children who sound American, and almost never calls. And that finally, the daughter I have nothing to say to, the one who has nothing but the most trivial, empty things to say because she never travels and just stays on her estate, a couple of estates from here where they have exactly the same things happening, is, contrary to the first two, always calling me, and calling round to our house, and at the most inopportune times, when I am holding more things than I have hands or when I am trying to remember something perching its weightless anxious body on my shoulder and that the slightest movement will scare away. She scares it away.

The man in charge of the ceremony is wearing a black suit and white shirt and asks if anyone would like to say a word. He makes you feel awkward, this man, that you did not dress better for the occasion, or are not sad enough and do not have poignant words to say. At least he is not a priest, I am thinking. You have to say, looking at this man, that the country has come far. There is some awkward looking around at our feet, some holding of breath, clenching of jaws. A cousin of my husband is about to say something but closes his mouth again when the man moves on to the next bit. I want to laugh at my husband's cousin, who as soon as he opens his mouth someone else is talking over him. The officiant is unfolding a sheet of paper from his trouser pocket and begins to read a poem. You have to wonder what else is in that pocket and what else that hand was holding today. A bus lurches past and I am wondering what number. I am standing the way people do, waiting for their luggage to come around. Our daughter keeps sniffling. I wish she would blow her nose but I do not want her to start relitigating the past.

Finally, the young men who were hanging around in a corner somewhere hurry solemn expressions back on to their faces and mount the coffin on to their shoulders. They too make you feel underdressed. There is a moment where the coffin looks like it might slip but coffins never slip. One of them has a stud in his ear. He is probably thinking about sex, I am thinking. My husband's cousin tries to rub my back but my daughter gets there first and he has to make it look natural as we look into the carpeted rectangle in the earth. Then, all of a sudden, I feel light with panic, as if I was falling or made of paper. I am digging around my pocket for the keys to the house, which are in the left pocket where I keep them. Then I think that I have lost my phone but it is in the right pocket. Our daughter, who is crying, is looking at me as if to ask what is it, and I am thinking that I have lost it, lost it forever, but then I remember that I am holding it, the umbrella, and wave her away. ∎

I walked past, not young, old elm trees that should have dignity.

That was one little flash of something that nearly meant something to me.

I was off to see Betty, but our ten o'clock plan was not realized.

I am very ashamed of myself for how long I have waited for Betty, considering that such waiting can result in confused thinking and irritability.

'She'll be down,' I was told. 'Do you want anything to drink?'

It tasted so good. The coffee I was served might as well have been cocoa.

Once, weeks previously, Betty had spoken to me from her stair landing. It was as if she were presenting an important address from a balcony! – with her hands gripping the banister, and that may have helped me.

I want an outlook on life, a plan for my life. I want to feel like an excited dog.

I heard today what sounded like a dog's tail being stepped on, coming from her kitchen, while waiting – also, the doorbell – and two boys dropped off a plate of cookies for Betty, iced with slapdashed-thick-white frosting.

And I said, 'She won't like those.'

The boys were dressed identically, but one's face was happy and the other's sad. I could say one face was ecstatic. I could say nothing.

But I say *this* in closing – today I waited for Betty for over an hour and a half, or two hours, and was not sent away.

A very little bit of Betty goes a long way, not unlike how the limbs of the ancient elms kink and then reach.

As I left her premises, there were so many birds flying at such speeds. Gulls.

Some were bumping into each other. They were overreacting to the wind – or just impulsively motivated or were they displaying agitation about a new project? – the sort of zeal I am always in need of. Or were they showing appetite for one another – I am going to *getch choo!* I'm going to *getch choo!* ∎

I was laughing the orgy off later. I had been curious enough. I was not then who I am now.

Maybe I went with somebody I knew, not very well – Lisa.

Hopefulness combined with bravery had gotten me to that place – a whole history could be written.

Two jumbo, gatekeeper-type porcelain lions stood at the entry when we arrived. Their legs, tails, paws and faces were painted blue. Their blue tails were curled over their backs.

There was a problem with the clothing – it was in a heap somewhere – my clothing, along with my money, and I knew I could not get at it when the lights went out.

I felt breath on the top of my head as someone dislodged himself, as people left the front room to find bedrooms.

I had not been invited and the only thing for me was this carpet, so I pulled it up – an edge – and it was dusty, and I was sweeping with my hand to get pieces of things out that were further in, and then I crawled under and fell asleep.

In that era, when I was a traveler, I found environments not very different from my own, where large numbers of people participate in festivals in the richest nation of the world; exclusive groups.

Please honor us with your presence – christenings, communions, weddings and surprise parties.

I still follow the trails of my friends – locating their camps and their ceremonies – first saying thanks to my father and to my mother for this day, before I go out most prayerfully, seductively. ∎

I got in behind him on the kitchen chair – as if we could share a ride on a motorbike – not nearly enough room.

That's Gideon. Silent and somber. My arms were around his front.

Back into my own proper place quickly – to take a drink of water. I aimed my full glass at and above my open mouth – and then poured, as if I had mistaken my glass for a pitcher. Not on purpose . . .

I had to mop myself.

After that I went out onto our porticoed porch and down the few stairs – where a stargazer I had planted appeared to notice me.

The bend in the road I followed led to the house with shutters that are commonplace, as are the clapboards and one wraparound veranda.

I try but cannot describe such sights in a particular way – the old-style houses that should brace and inform me, *if they only would!*

In the evening, does it matter when? – I was so often doing this – I was rubbing a dinner serving bowl with a soapy brush and conducting the marital conversation: *Na-ah. Ah. It's all right*, and *I don't know* – said three times.

I grew up in an old stone house with a walled garden to the rear. I often climbed the wall, and that was never easy, and I sat on it.

There was not much more I could do with the wall.

I did kick at it with my heels, the memorable chance to feel cruel, to hurt myself too. ∎

Afterward, the man, who appeared confident, was looking and looking, but not at me – the man who added a flurry to the mix of the objects all around us, out of which his head and face seemed to pop.

I had a stomachache, but had consented to intercourse, because I did jump at every chance – with him.

But none of this is controversial – nor had been the man's modest request.

Then I was downstairs at the point of leaving Hank Hardy forever, because he had decreed it.

It is worth noting that at that time I had the same teakettle that Hank had (not on purpose). Not on purpose – I owned the very same carpet that Hank had – small enough to be used in any part of the house! The background was gold.

*

So even after decades have passed, I find that I thoroughly ache for Hank, and I would love to see Hank's face as he now appears with old age creeping in on him.

What I look like now . . . heavy eyelids dominate my face and I am as near as may be to slightly rotund.

*

Out on an errand, I walked close enough to an elderly couple to overhear the woman say, 'What can I do with them?'

'Do all you can do,' the man replied, 'if it's not too much trouble.'

The woman slumped against the traffic-light post, holding on to it tightly.

When the light turned green, the man continued on without her, so I offered her my arm, as she was still latched to the post. She is frail.

I might as well say this was Ann Lenihan and her husband. They're my neighbors.

And while we both dealt with the difficulty that the uphill sidewalk presented, a hulk of a woman swung by us.

A toddler, seeming to be on his own – was many paces behind this person I took to be the child's mother.

He was hauling a backpack that caused him to hunch like an old man, although he'd been outfitted like a teen with shades on, with a visored cap. A sort of beast of burden, or a beast of a burden likely.

*

Today I managed to waylay a robin by whistling in a manner that a robin might take to be bona fide – because I was careful to repeat the phrase with no alteration.

I sounded a bright note up, a bright note down, and followed those with a rolling sound – over and over again. How many times do you kiss? – pet somebody? – fuck . . .

The bird chirruped and remained rooted to the ground – did not tire of me, because I had successfully wooed him.

Then I flagged, I quit, I left – all of which counts, suffice it to say, for something. ∎

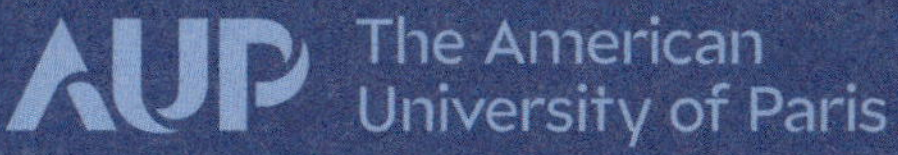

Master of Fine Arts in
Creative Writing

Discover Europe's only two-year, interdisciplinary graduate program in creative writing. Students are taught to hone their craft across multiple genres, languages, and cultural traditions, so they can tell their stories in the ways they need to be told.

The MFA in Creative Writing at The American University of Paris has a global focus. Students engage with writers from all over the world and read both works in translation from multiple languages and contemporary and classic works in English. Our curriculum encourages students to challenge traditional divisions between fiction and poetry to move into new realms of self-expression.

We welcome students from all backgrounds, including mature students with strong portfolios, regardless of their previous academic pursuits.

Scan here to learn more about joining our vibrant literary community in Paris

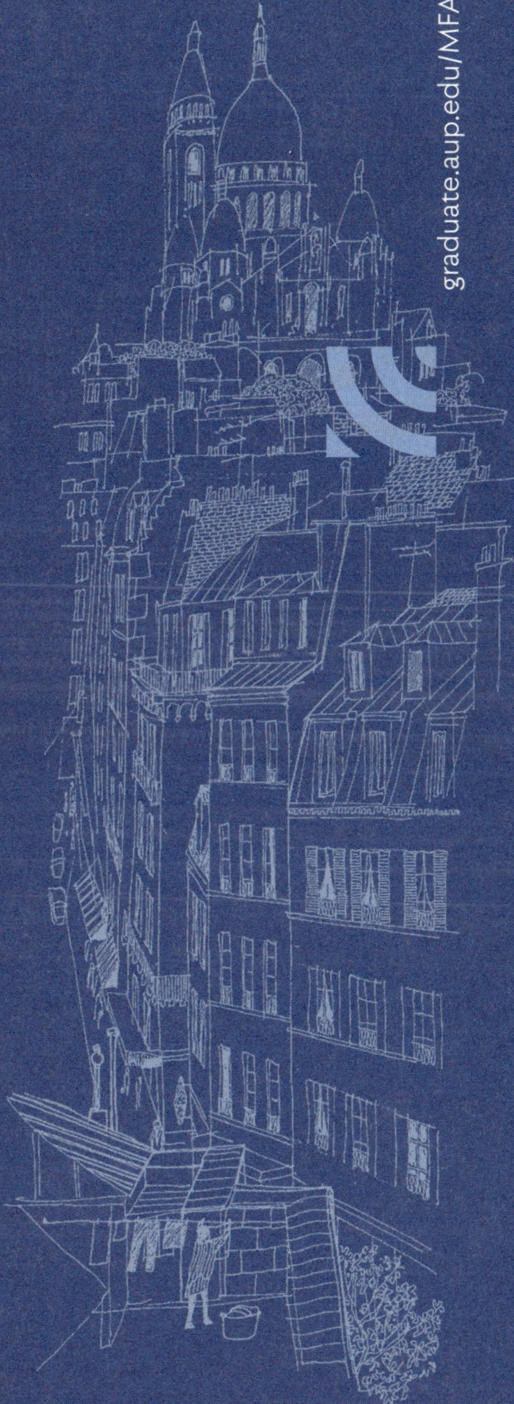

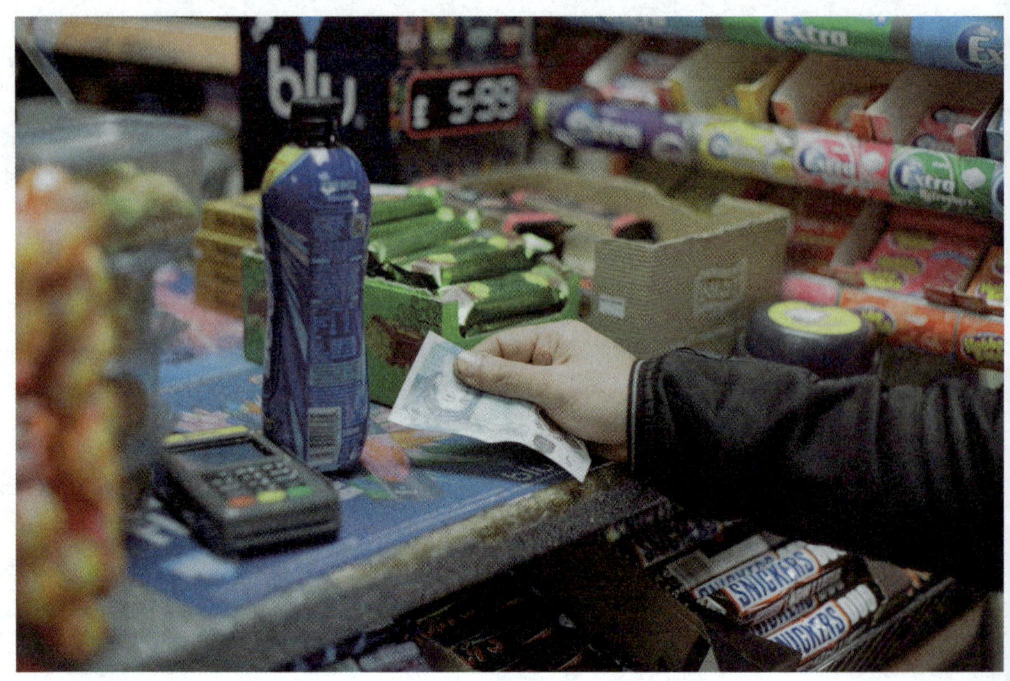

SANA BADRI

CORNER SHOPS AND BOSSMAN

Sana Badri

JERWOOD PHOTOGRAPHY COMMISSIONS

Corner shops feel like the final great equalisers in a neighbourhood. Regardless of age, class and background, everyone at some point will need to stop by their local corner shop. And everyone respects bossman. If you spend enough time hanging around a corner shop you observe a sort of choreography: gestures of care, social tensions, acts of survival and moments of humour. This is where a neighbourhood quietly (or not so quietly) performs itself.

Over the course of two weeks this spring, I photographed four corner shops in Kilburn, and two on Caledonian Road. I spent time in them during the morning commute, at the end of the school day, during very slow Sunday afternoons, and on weekend rush hours. On Saturdays, the city would wake up slowly, eventually arriving at the shop to get the milk needed to complete breakfast. It wouldn't get as busy as that again until the evening, when people hurried to pick up bottles for pre-drinks. To know this city is to constantly experience two opposing extremes.

Chatting to the managers and shopkeepers, I noticed the pride they have for their area. Often, they'd lived there for decades. When I asked one man about his shop, he spoke not so much about his business, but instead about the neighbourhood and its people. He'd had his shop for twenty-five years, he could describe the customers intimately. He told me he doesn't worry about people stealing from him, or being disrespectful towards him, because he knows that a regular customer will always intervene in his defence. He's watched people within the neighbourhood grow up from being young children to becoming parents and eventually bringing their own children to the shop. One afternoon he pointed out a woman as she left the shop, three young children in tow unwrapping their just-purchased ice creams, and said that he remembers her when she used to come and buy sweets for herself when she was a little girl, 'back when a Freddo cost 10p'.

I tried to photograph a range of 'types' of corner shops. Having grown up in London, and moved around a lot, I've become familiar with many. Of the four I photographed, there's the reliable, long-standing corner shop at the end of an estate, the impressively-stocked Kurdish corner shop that's almost a mini supermarket, the sad half-empty corner shop, and another that specialises in selling religious goods. In this one, there are crucifixes sold next to evil eye pendants, (you can get your cartons of black grape-flavoured KA and your holy water at that shop, too). I wanted to capture the claustrophobic chaos of some of these spaces, with Sellotape and syrups stacked to the ceiling, and the meticulous organisation of the shelves in others.

There is a comforting consistency in the outline of the corner shop. The flickering shop signs and the glow of the fridge act as a lighthouse. They are open when everything else is shut. My favourite is the one closest to me, not because it's the best stocked or has the friendliest staff, but because it's become a part of my daily rhythm. I have learned the habits of bossman and he knows mine. He has seen me at my worst and my best. The layout of this particular shop reflects the personality and efforts of the manager I have come to know well: careful and considered. Whatever the style of the corner shop, they all seem to communicate the same thing, 'come as you are'. ■

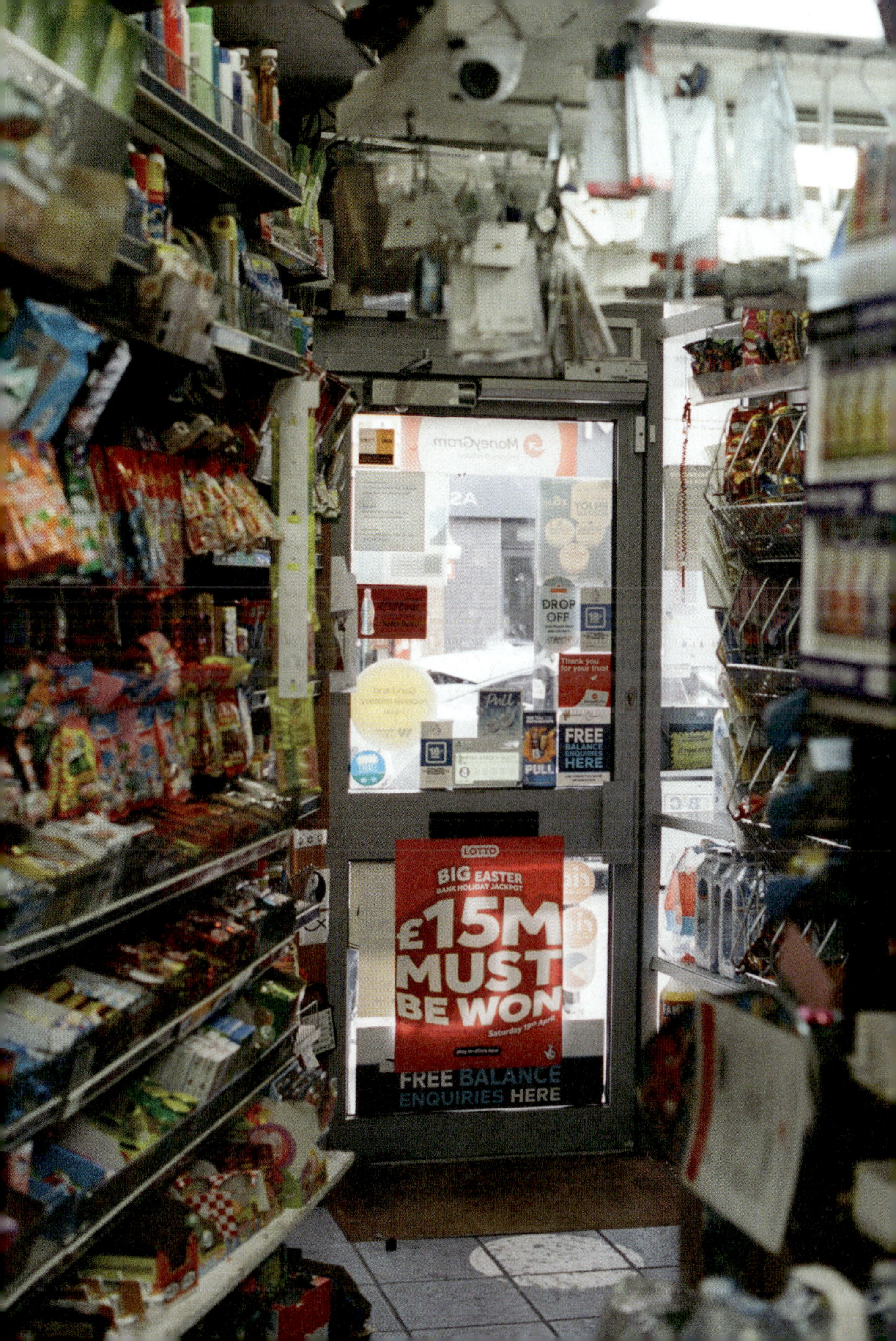
MoneyGram
DROP OFF
Thank you for your trust
FREE BALANCE ENQUIRIES HERE
PULL
PULL
LOTTO
BIG EASTER
BANK HOLIDAY JACKPOT
£15M
MUST
BE WON
Saturday 19th April
FREE BALANCE
ENQUIRIES HERE

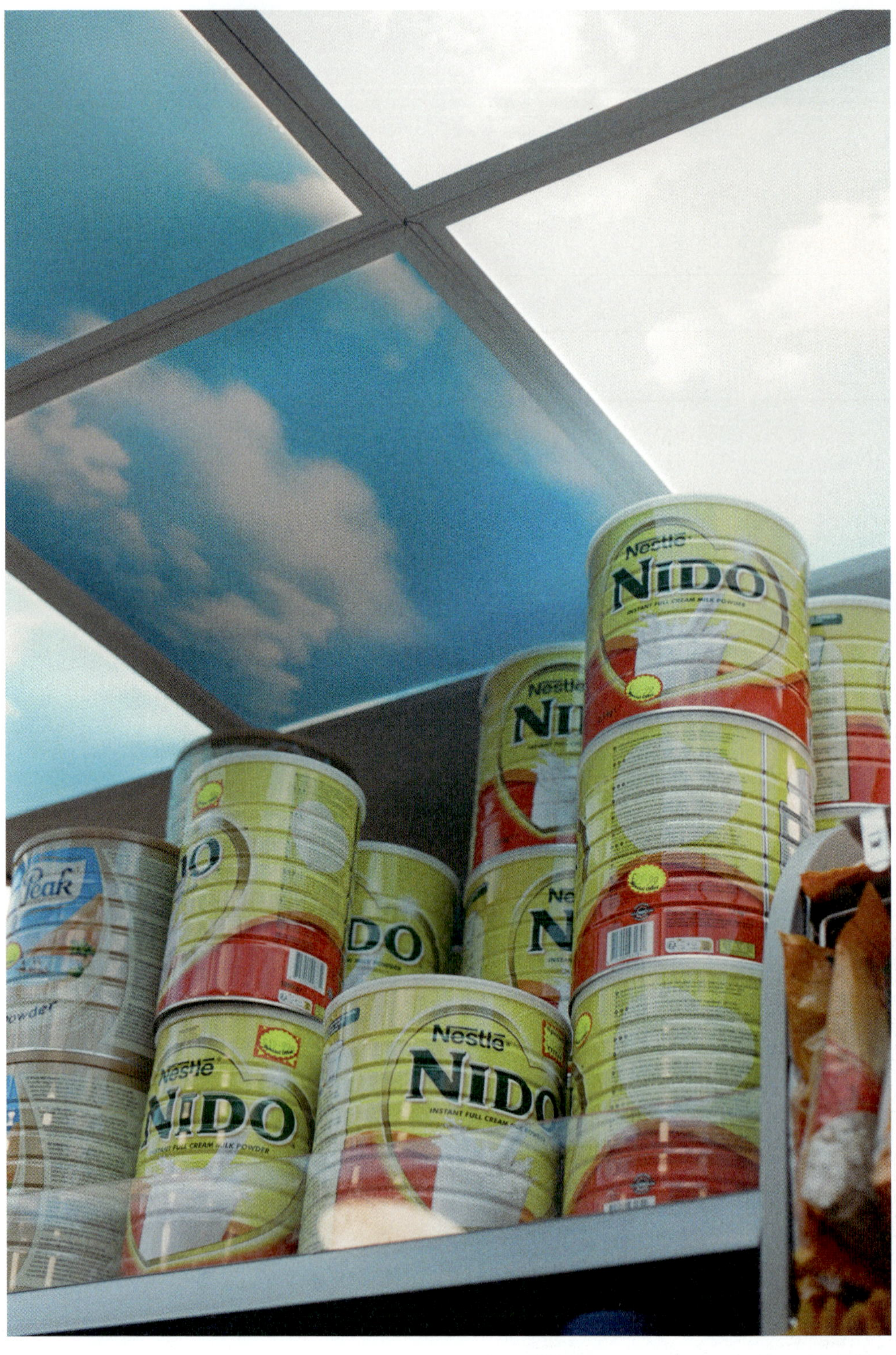

Nestlé
NIDO
INSTANT FULL CREAM MILK POWDER
Nestlé
NIDO
INSTANT FULL CREAM MILK POWDER
Nestlé
NIDO
INSTANT FULL CREAM MILK POWDER
Peak
Powder

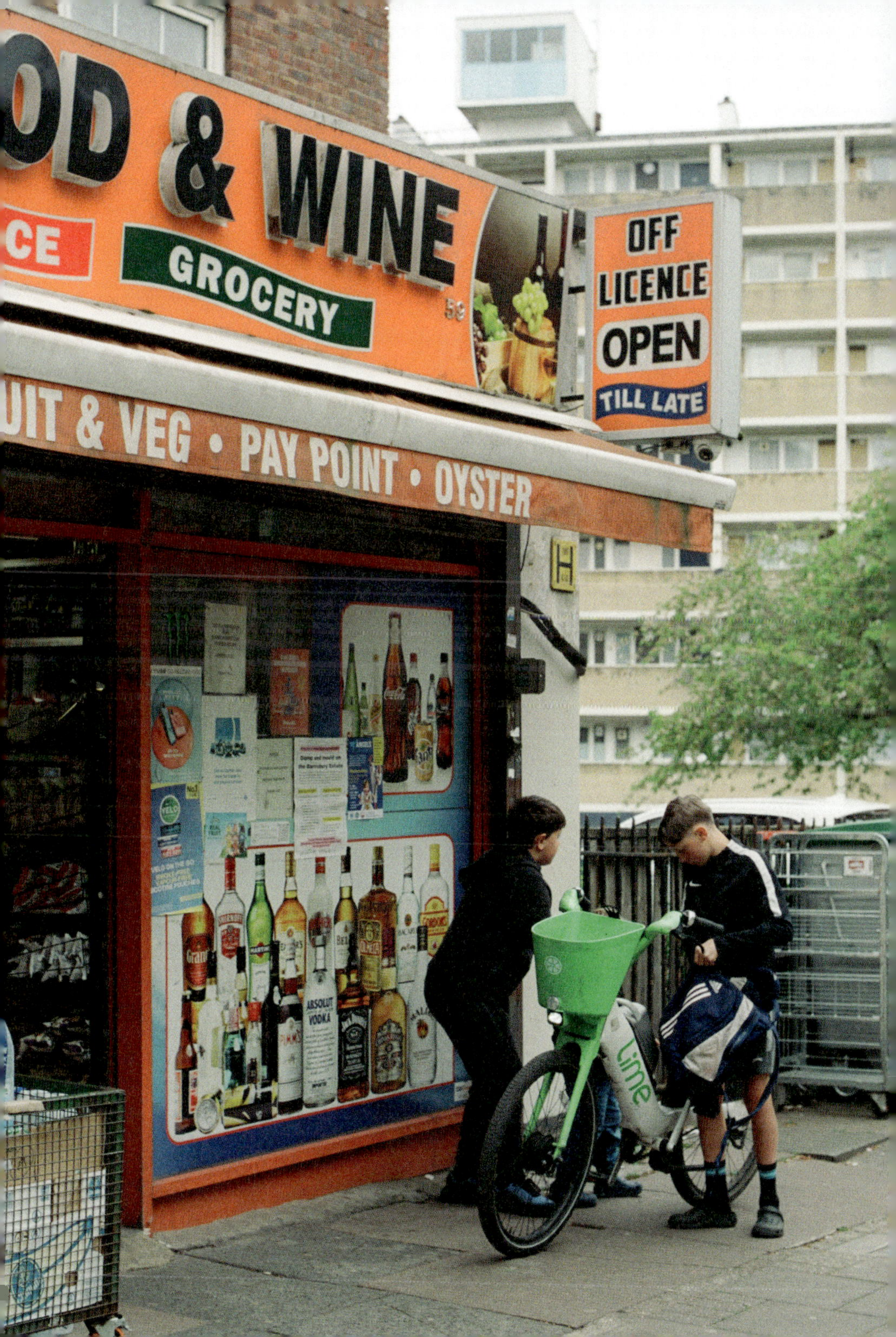
OD & WINE
CE
GROCERY
OFF
LICENCE
OPEN
TILL LATE
UIT & VEG • PAY POINT • OYSTER
ABSOLUT
VODKA
Lime

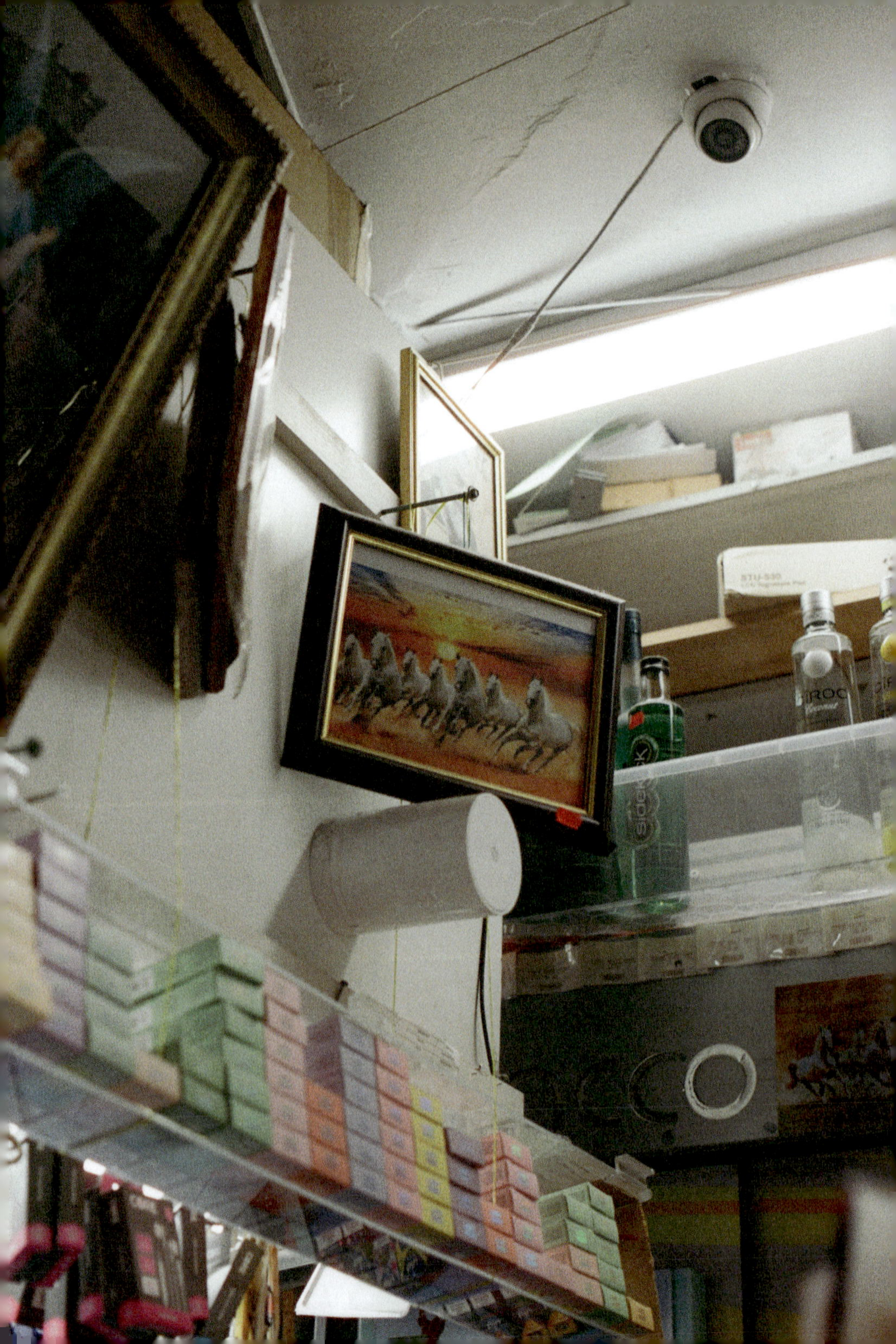

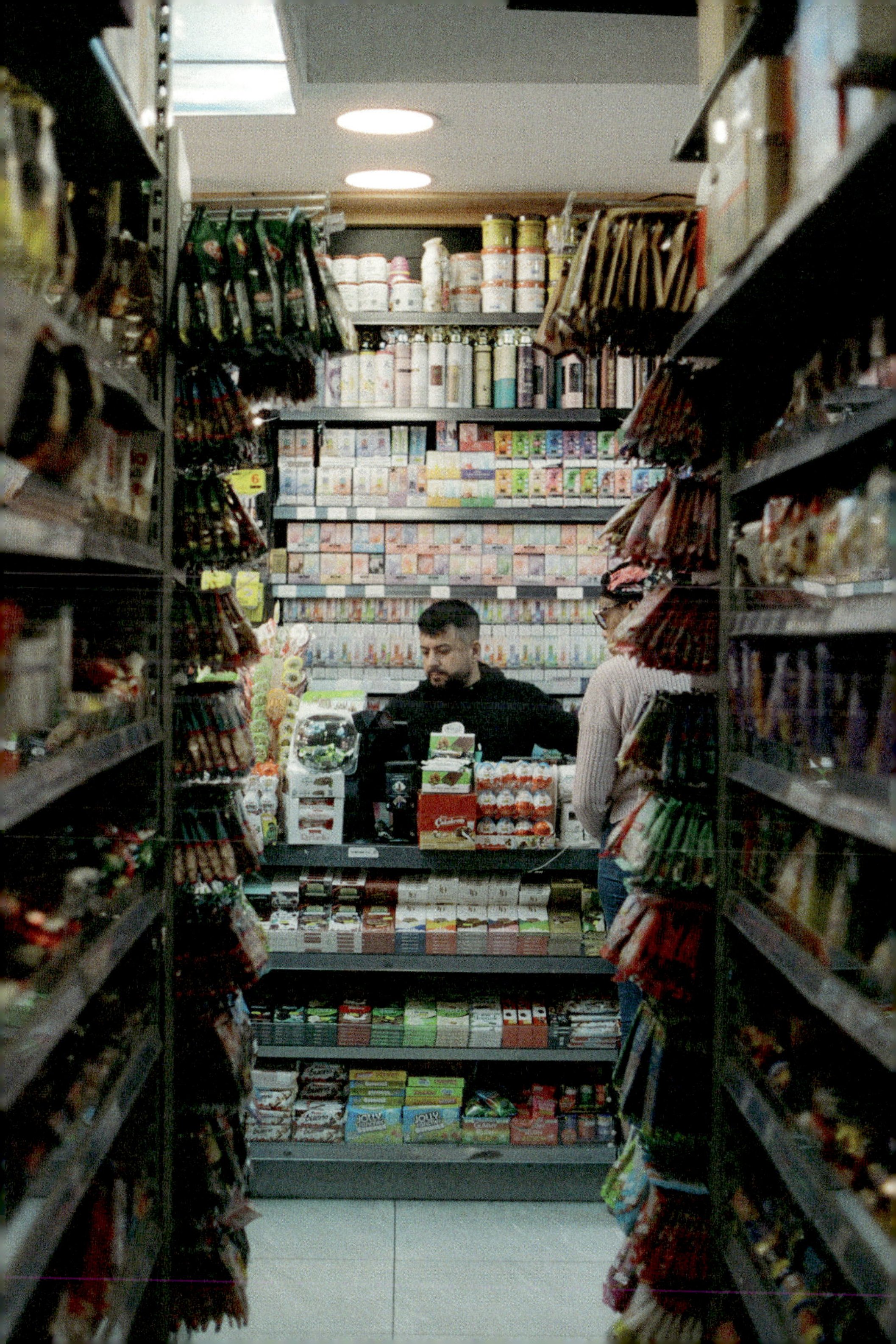

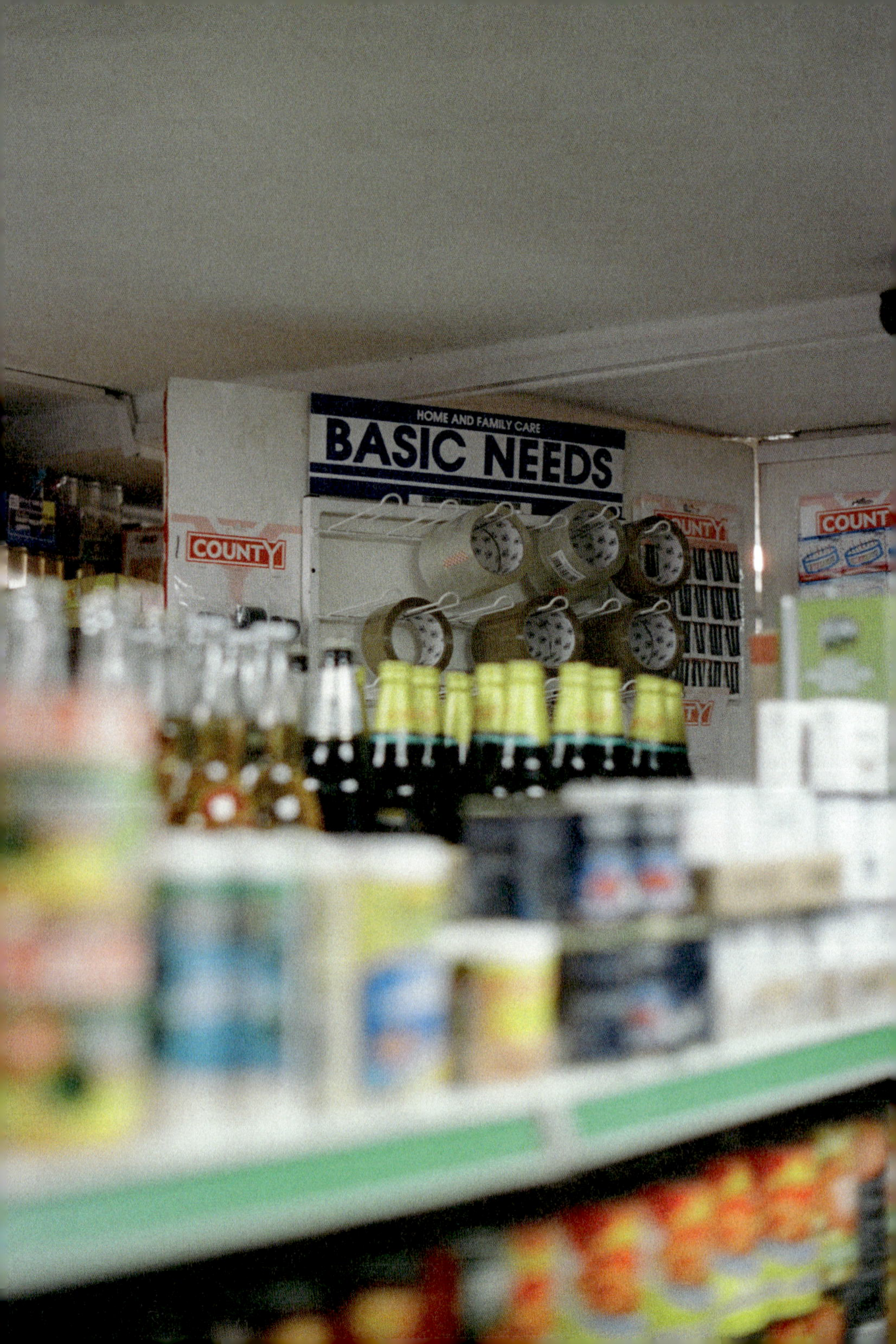

HOME AND FAMILY CARE
BASIC NEEDS
COUNTY
COUNT
COUNT

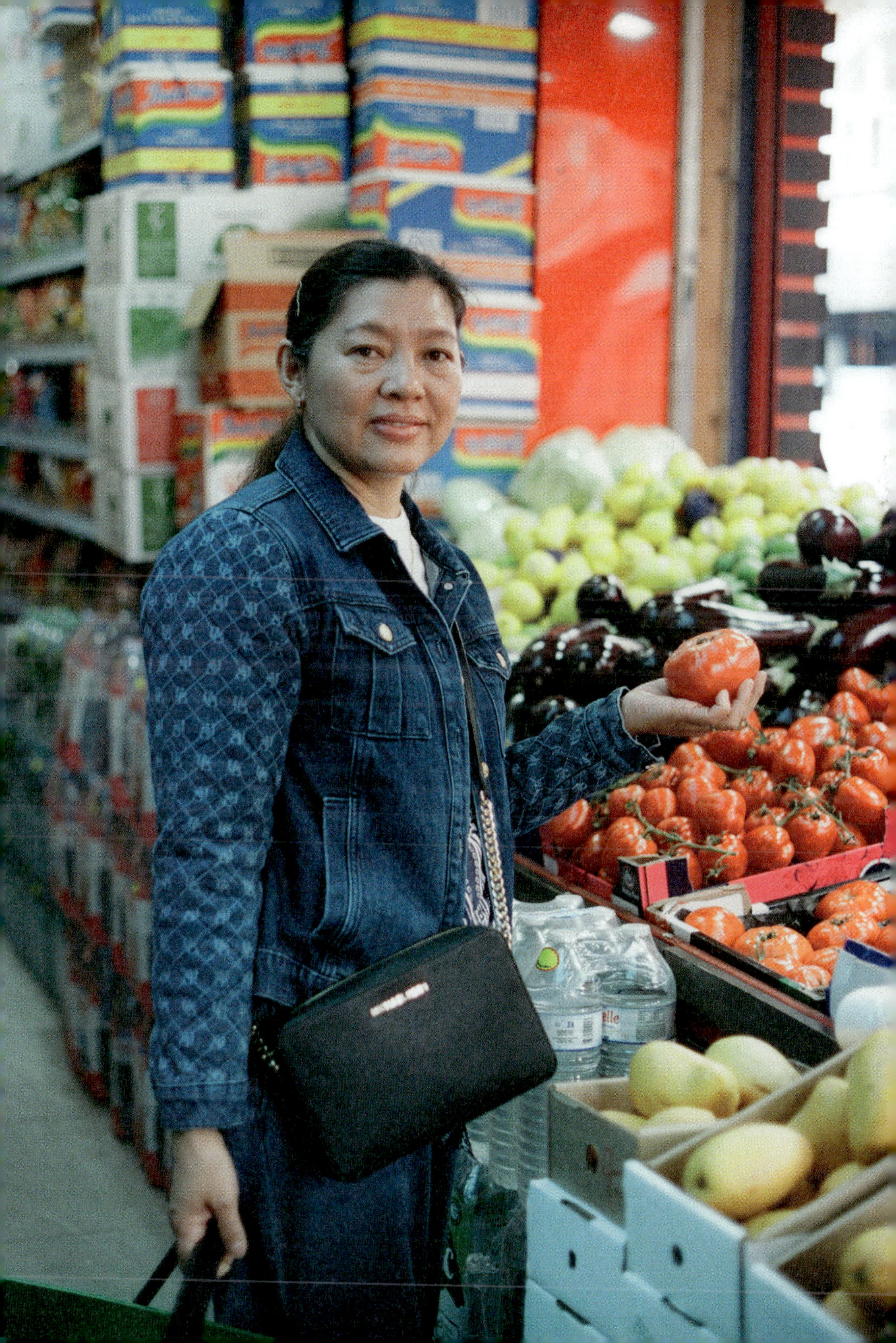

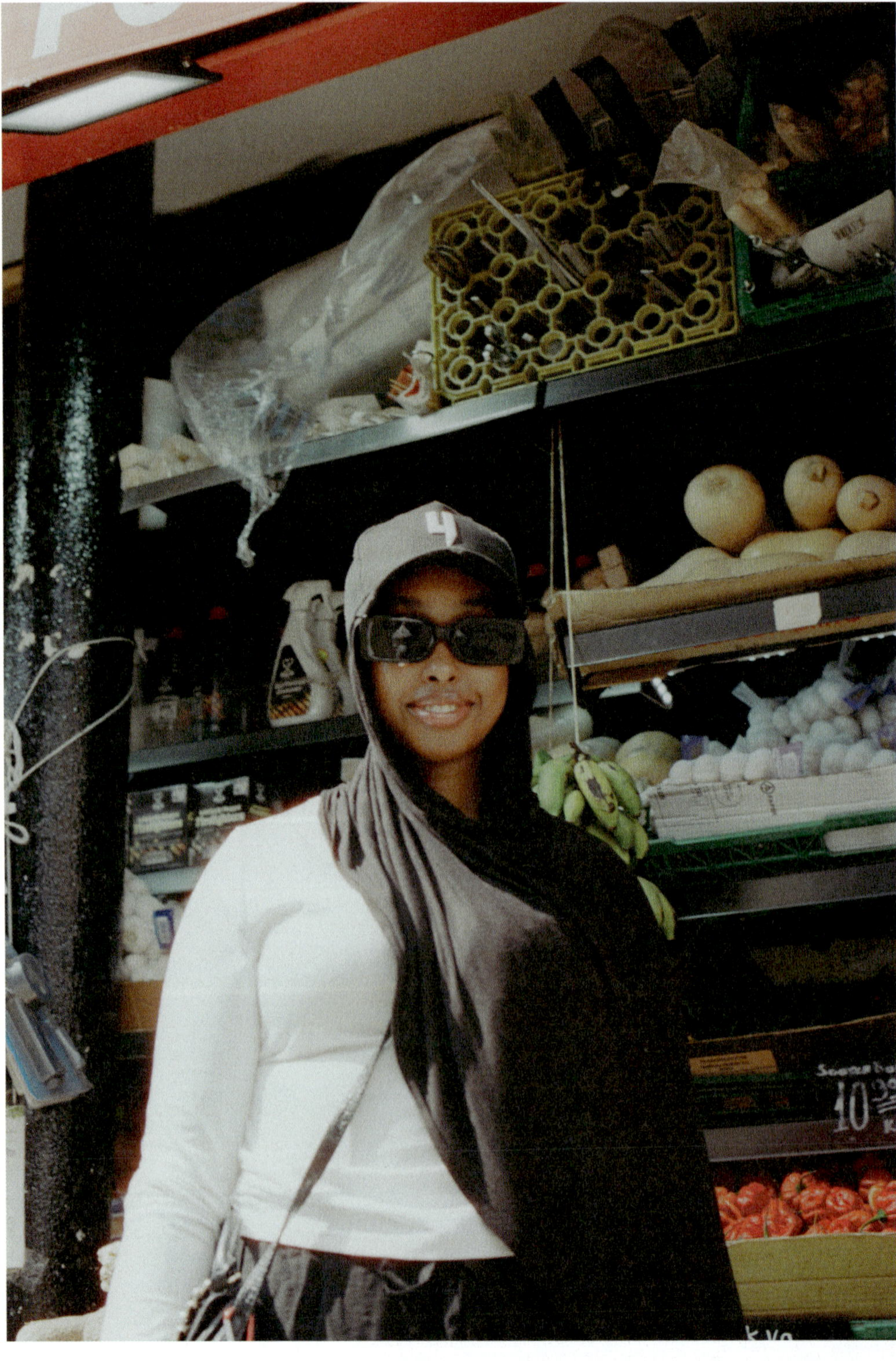

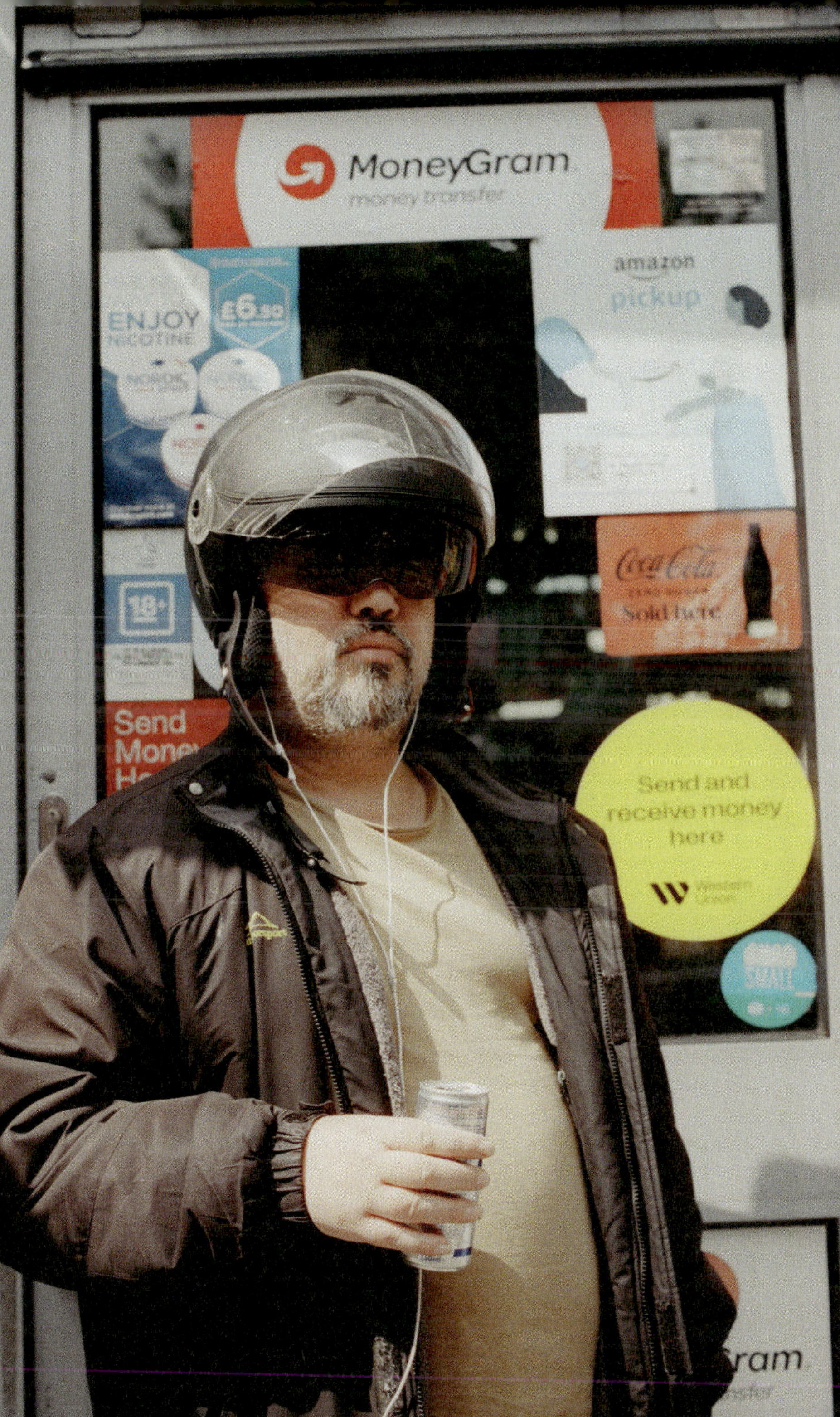

MoneyGram
money transfer
ENJOY NICOTINE.
NORDIC
£6.50
amazon pickup
Coca-Cola
Sold here
18+
Send Money He
Send and receive money here
Western Union
Gram

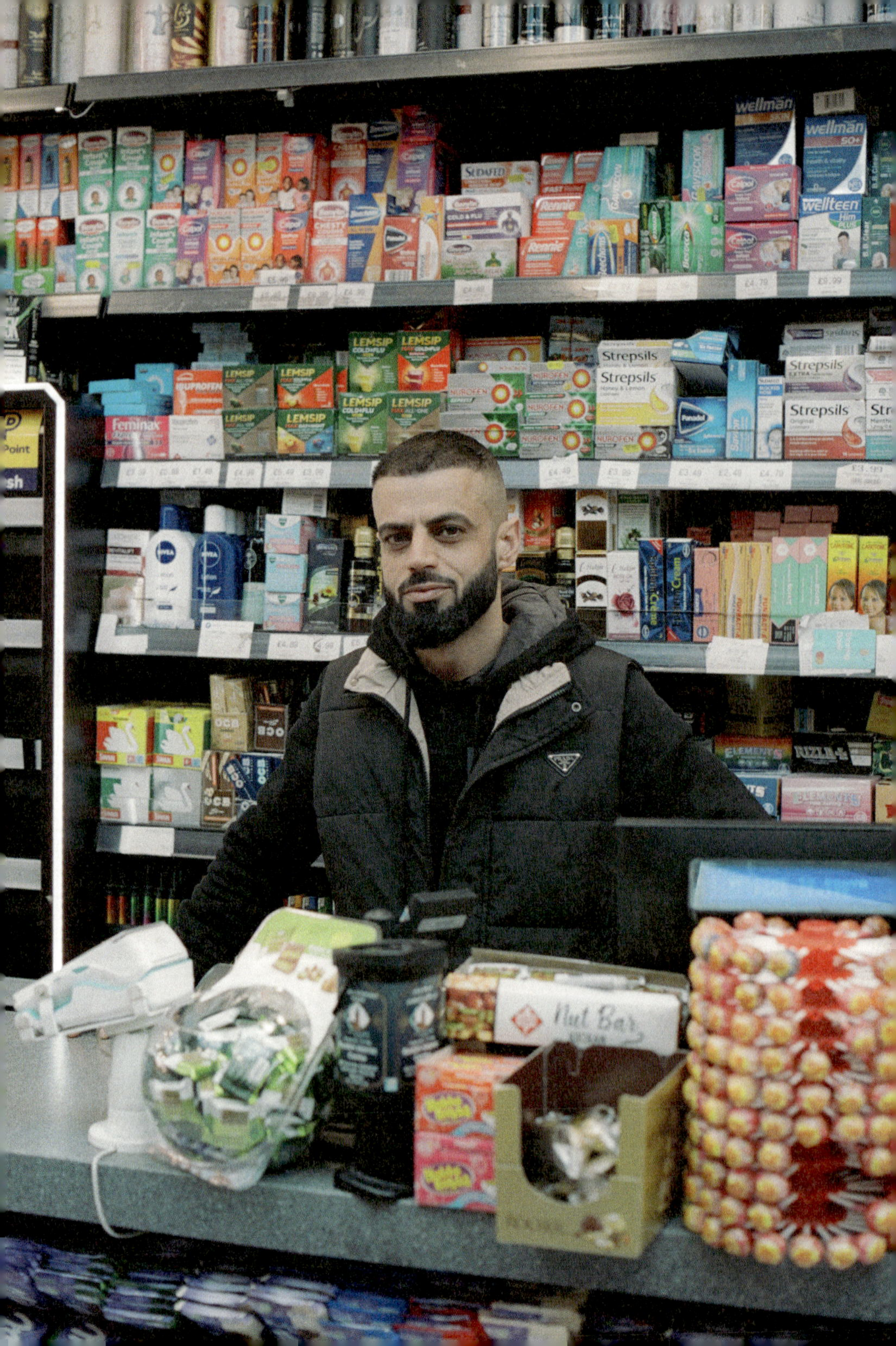

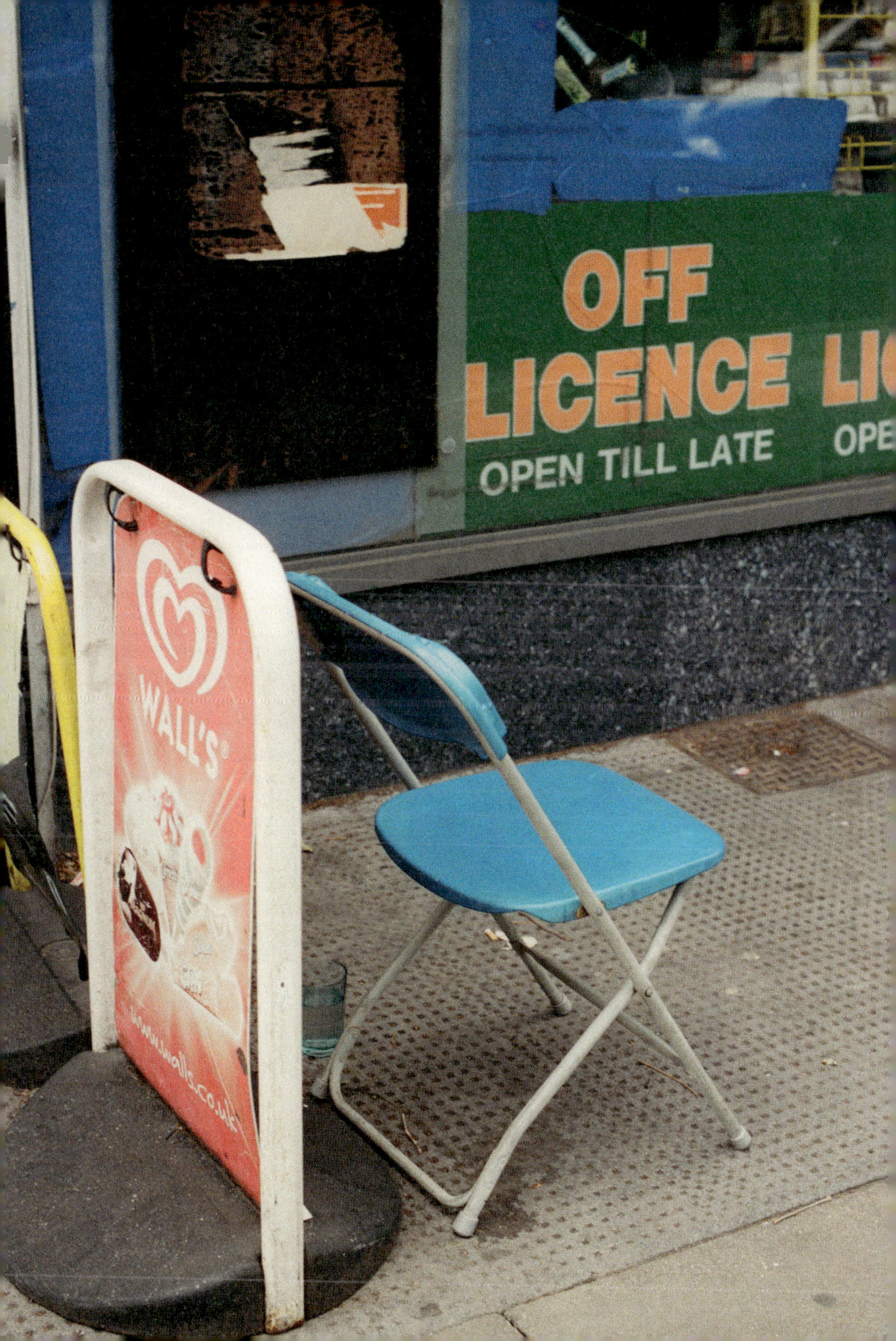

OFF
LICENCE LIC
OPEN TILL LATE   OPE
WALL'S
www.walls.co.uk

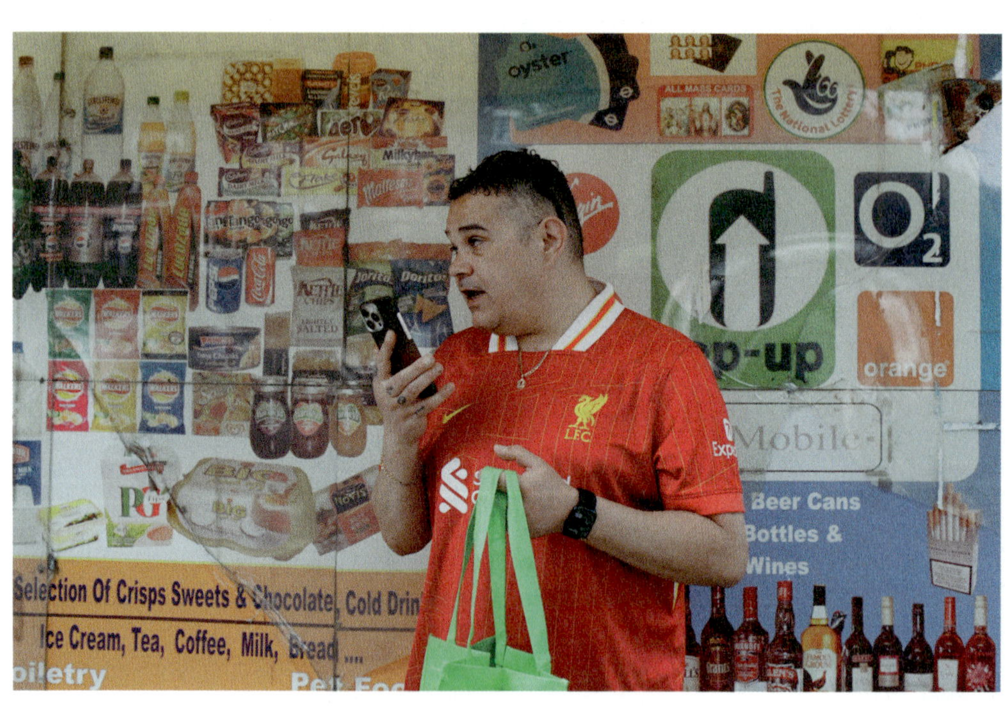

oyster
ALL MARS CARDS
The National Lottery
O2
pp-up
orange
Mobile
Beer Cans
Bottles &
Wines
Pepsi
Coca-Cola
Doritos
KETTLE CHIPS
LIGHTLY SALTED
WALKERS
PG
Selection Of Crisps Sweets & Chocolate, Cold Drin
Ice Cream, Tea, Coffee, Milk, Bread ....
oiletry
Pet Foo

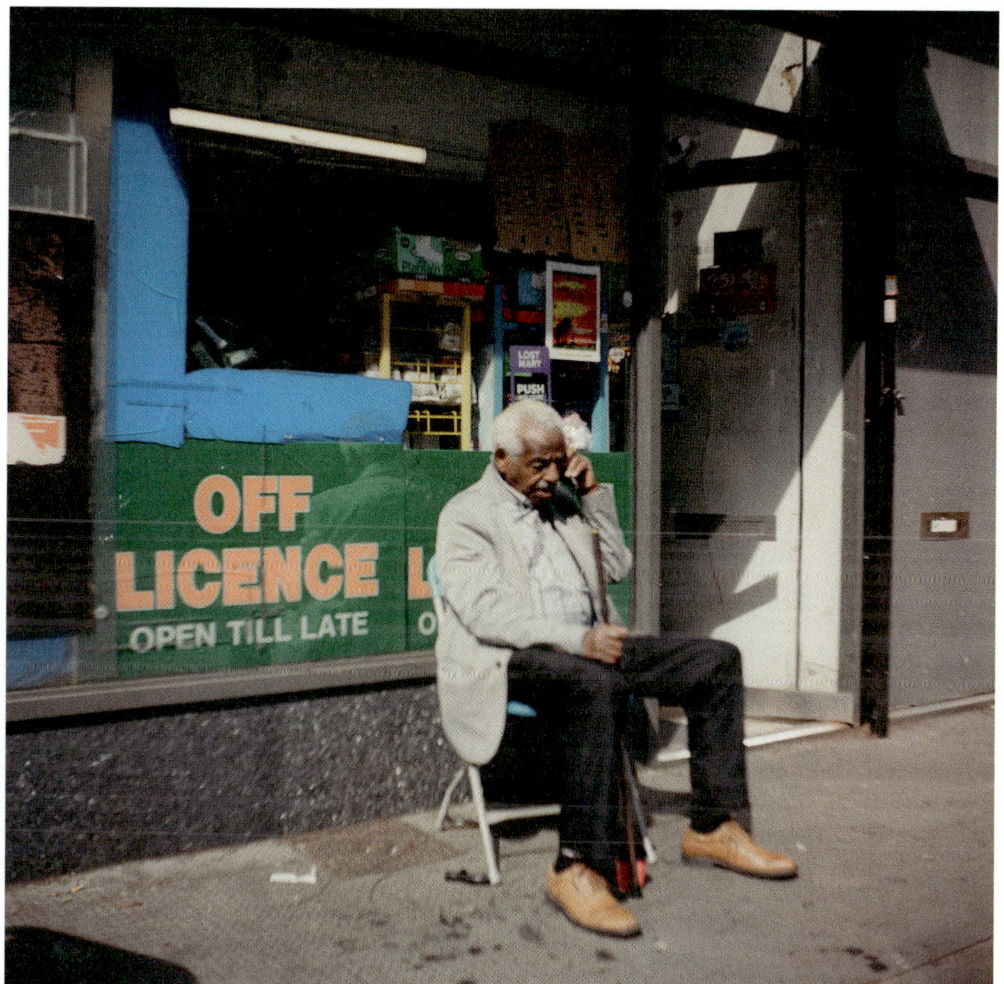

OFF
LICENCE
OPEN TILL LATE
LOST MARY
PUSH

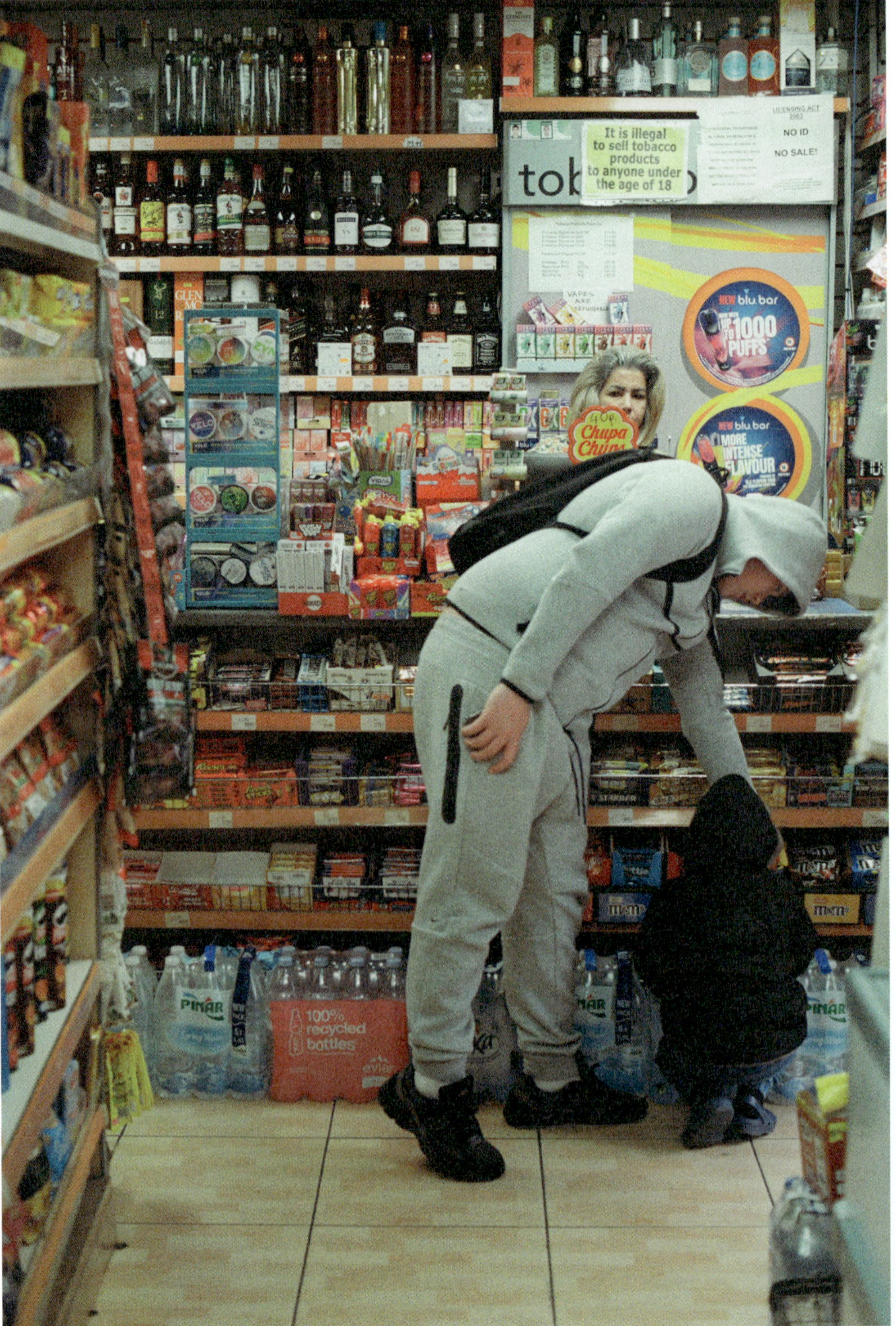

It is illegal to sell tobacco products to anyone under the age of 18
LICENSING ACT 2003
NO ID
NO SALE!
tob
NEW blu bar
UP TO 1000 PUFFS
NEW blu bar
MORE INTENSE FLAVOUR
VAPES ARE
Chupa Chups
PINAR
100% recycled bottles
evian

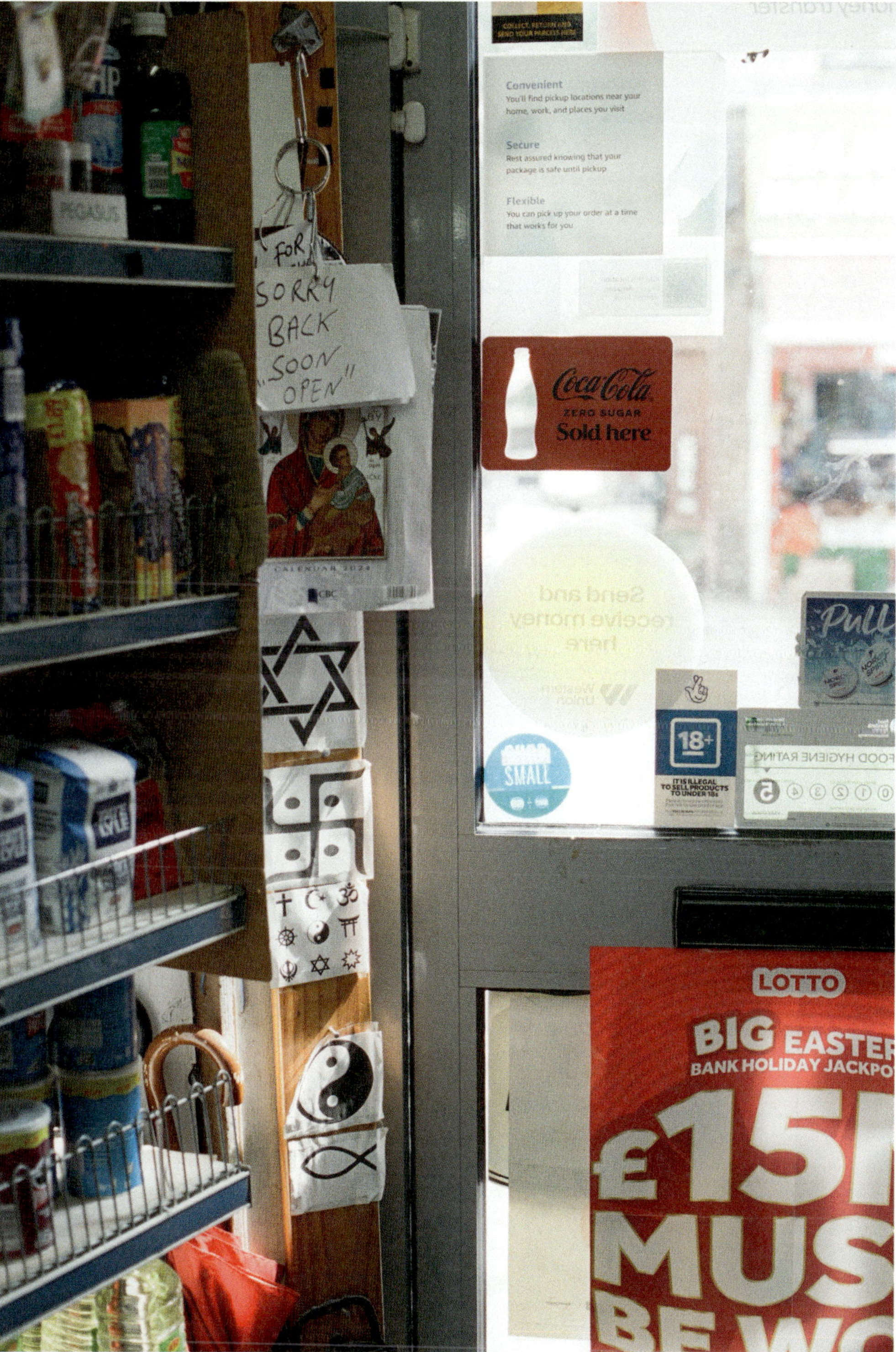
PEGASUS
FOR
SORRY
BACK
SOON
"OPEN"
CALENDAR 2024
CBC
COLLECT, RETURN OR
SEND YOUR PARCELS HERE
Convenient
You'll find pickup locations near your
home, work, and places you visit
Secure
Rest assured knowing that your
package is safe until pickup
Flexible
You can pick up your order at a time
that works for you
Coca-Cola
ZERO SUGAR
Sold here
Send and
receive money
here
Western
Union
SMALL
18+
IT IS ILLEGAL
TO SELL PRODUCTS
TO UNDER 18s
FOOD HYGIENE RATING
5
Pull
LOTTO
BIG EASTER
BANK HOLIDAY JACKPOT
£15
MUS
BE WO
LYLE

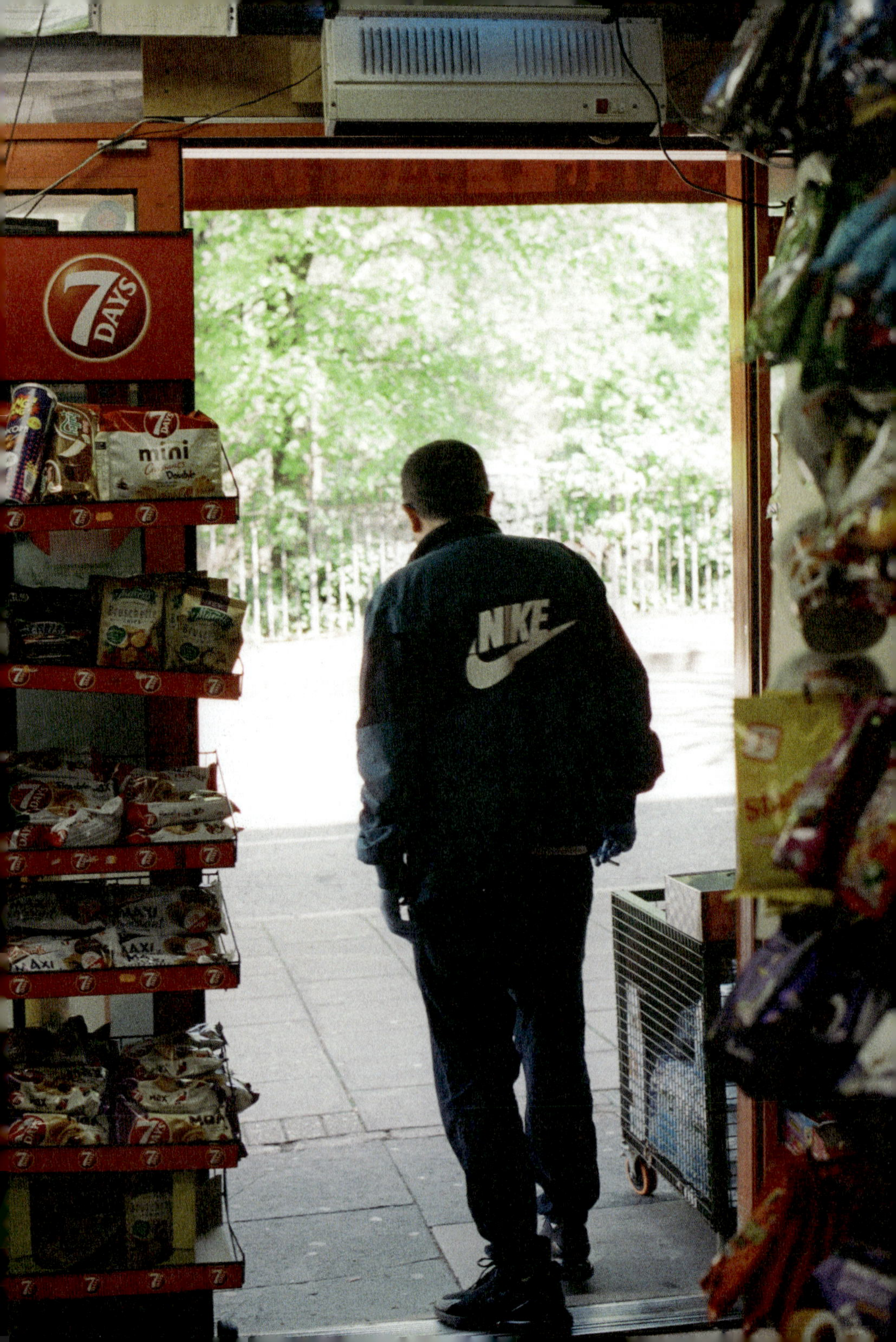

7 DAYS
mini
NIKE

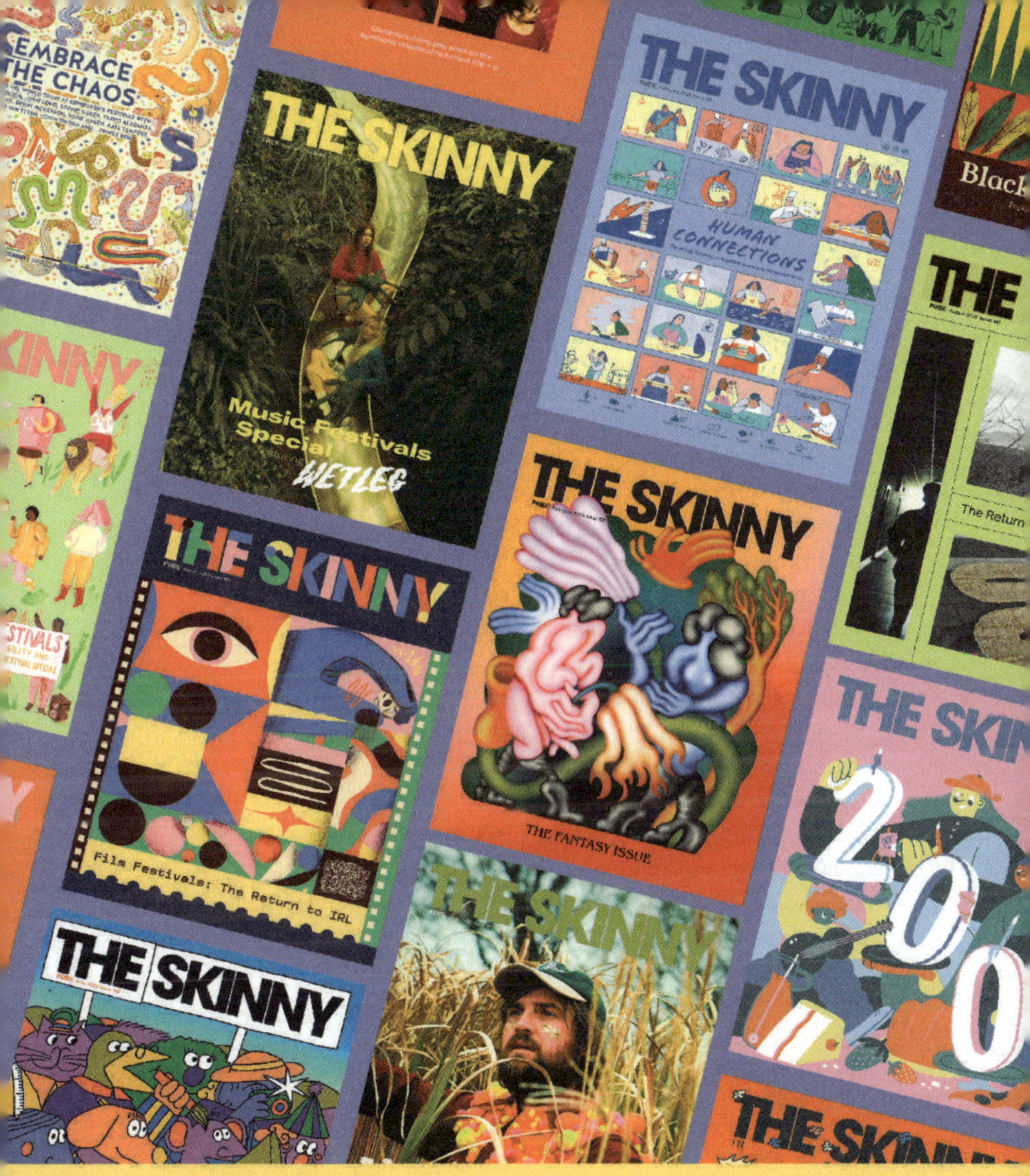

THE SKINNY

Independent cultural journalism.
Delivered to your door.

theskinny.co.uk

Frederick Seidel

The Desert Song

Hart Crane and Frank O'Hara are hitting on Donald Trump,
Not that they think he's one of them.
The poets strut and kick their heels up like in a chorus line,
Like it was Fire Island, arms over each other's shoulders,
And smile because both of them are dead and naked,
And because they genuinely like Trump-Trump-de-Dump.
William Blake and his buttocks are on a flight path
To land at Idlewild, as it was then called,
And will be met by Walt Whitman.
Pound will be there. Not Eliot.

The United States of America
Is a terrible disappointment.
Disappointment is an odd word to use.
The cockroaches are licking up the grease
They excrete, as if they were Virgil completing the *Aeneid.*
And everyone sings I don't have the time to grieve.
At least they're missing
The final days.
Poetry is winged speech licking up the grease
When you stomp on it barefoot.

Summer in St. Louis mothers me.
Summer heats my heart, beats my heart.
Summer smothers me.
I'm listening to an operetta at the outdoor Muni Opera
In the seats my family keeps, like our box at the ballpark,
Year after year.
The green perfume of Forest Park
Devours the audience in the lighted dark
Like the big bite of a white shark.
Succumb to art and sigh and hold your breath and die.

Operetta in the open air under the stars,
In Forest Park in old St. Louis near the private streets,
Inside a robe of humidity heavy as oatmeal,
But sweet-smelling as a gardenia.
It's the mile-wide Mississippi River pouring through the air
The crackling rumble of distant summer thunder.
But let it rain!
But it won't.
Eighty years ago or more before
Make America Great Again and President Donald Trump.

I'm turning eight,
And not yet old enough to date
The singer up there now, the lovely girl,
Now no doubt a long time dead,
I'm in love with.
Is this a turning point?
I hear the Muni Opera orchestra start
The beginning part.
The outdoor theater of businessmen and wives
In summer suits and summer dresses stirs.

A Berber uprising in the desert of Morocco
Against the colonial French, in 1925,
Inspired Sigmund Romberg's operetta,
The Desert Song. Thirty years after,
Next door in Algeria, Pontecorvo's
Movie masterpiece, *The Battle of Algiers,*
As real as a newsreel,
Stuck bombs in crowded street cafés,
Tearing off limbs. *My desert is waiting.*
Dear, come there with me.

The mother of a friend of mine
Was hit by an ambulance as she crossed the street,
Both legs broken, internal injuries,
Crossing 96th Street at noon,
Where it turned out others had been hit before
By ambulances rushing to a nearby hospital,
Which happens to be among the city's worst,
Presumably because of running the light,
With or without their siren on, in broad daylight,
And later died.

I can't connect the one thing to the other.
I'm sweating in my short pants at the opera.
I'm longing to teach you
Love's sweet melody.
The ambulance hits the woman.
I'm going home to the Sahara.
I'm going home with the soprano.
Blue heaven and you and I
And sand kissing a moonlit sky
Afterward, my father tips the cop who always parks our car.

The Desert Song thickens between my ears
And stupids me when *The Desert Song* appears
On stage and in the orchestra pit
And when after the show the cast bows and curtseys.
Applause draws blood back up to the surface where
My father tips the cop when the cop brings around our car.
St. Louis is a city of art and a great symphony orchestra.
And the outdoor opera and one police officer.
Back in Manhattan, the ambulance runs the light
And kills a pedestrian crossing the street.

How beautiful are thy feet with shoes.
Baruch ata Adonai.
How lovely are thy tits.
The Desert Song is a song sung at Auschwitz
By the rock and roll band Zyklon-B,
Offering the innocents Infinity
Who think they're lining up to take a shower.
Poetry climbs to the top of the tower
While, below, the ambulance runs the light
And kills Abraham Lincoln crossing the street.

St. Louisans of color expect
To drink the same water whites do
After World War II, but naturally don't get to.
Seidel Coal and Coke Co. supplied the shoe
Factories and big breweries with fuel to keep going
During the Depression
And now charitably delivers blocks of ice free of charge
In the unairconditioned summer heat
To the front door of the poor
And the soldiers, some of them dead, back from the war.

The happiest I have been in my life –
While I was still alive –
Was in Sagaponack, New York, on Gibson Lane,
Inches from the beach.
I liked Papeete in Tahiti,
I liked Denpasar in Bali,
But both places have hemorrhoids of tourists now,
And the Long Island potato fields that looked like Kansas
Under a wide blue summer eye of sky,
Have McMansions covering them like mushrooms.

The United States of America,
It's a fair bet, is going to die.
One minute the diaper is wet.
Then the sun is shining it dry.
Then Los Angeles is burning.
I climb on the motorcycle.
I climb the steps of the Capitol.
I'm speeding and bleeding.
But can't outrun John Wilkes Booth, and I've tried,
While helpless helicopters hover over.

THE MAGAZINE OF CHATHAM HOUSE. BRINGING GLOBAL AFFAIRS TO LIFE SINCE 1945

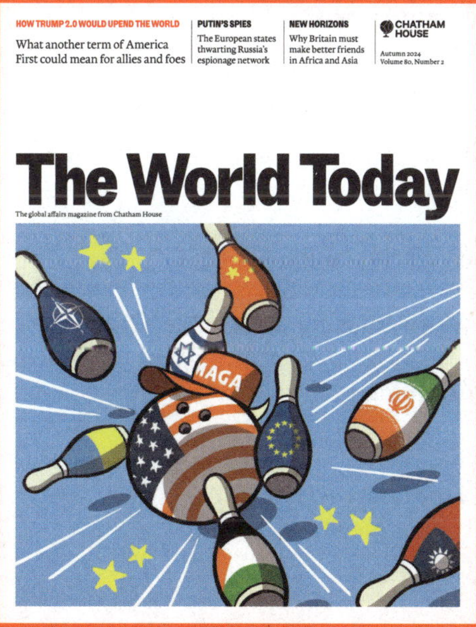

Commentary, analysis, reporting; Four editions a year; Online archive going back to 2000; *Subscriptions from £32*

www.theworldtoday.org

GRANTA TRUST

Granta would be unable to fulfil its mission
without the generosity of its donors. We
gratefully acknowledge the following
individuals and foundations:

Ford Foundation
British Council
Jerwood Foundation
Pulitzer Center
Amazon Literary Partnership
Sigrid Rausing
The Hans and Marit Rausing Charitable Trust
Anonymous
Bloomsbury Publishing Plc
SALT
Open Society
The Common Humanity Arts Trust
Jonathan and Ronnie Newhouse Fund

We also thank the following readers, including
those who wish to remain anonymous, for
their kind support:

Anonymous
Gail Anderson
Christine Bartels
Ria Bhavnani
Robert Cenek
Geoff Cohen
Alex Fardon
David Fobel
Monzurul Huq
Michael Isard
Patrick James
Hongnian Jow
Angie Libman
Helen Meads
Cristine Milton
Andrew Nugée
Luiz Otavio Ortigao
Marynel Ryan Van Zee
Laura Schwartz
Rob Shelton
John E. Simmons
John Sirek
Andrea Sydow
Dawn Walter
Lynnette Widder
Nancy York

If you would like to contribute, please make
a donation at granta.com/donate.

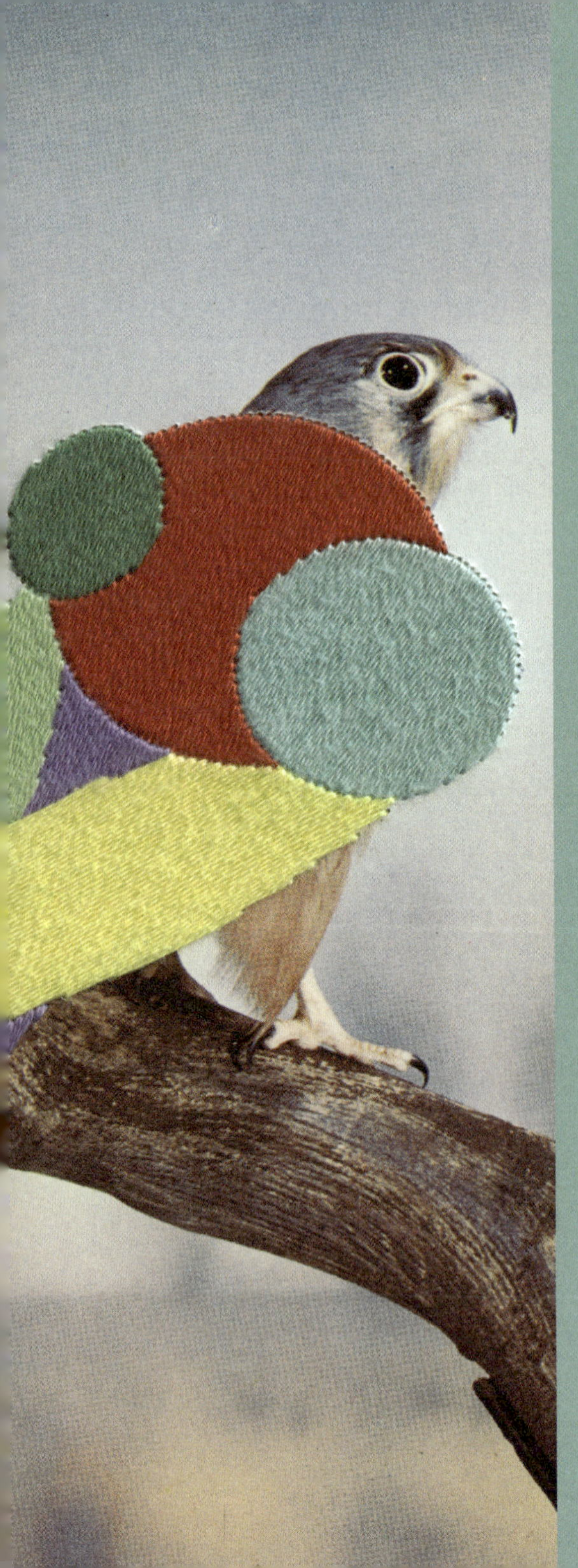

The Granta Writers' Workshop

**NATURE WRITING
SHORT FICTION
THE NOVEL
NARRATIVE NON-FICTION
MEMOIR**

'This is one of the most rigorous courses I've ever attended. A lifetime's knowledge of literature and writing, a compilation of enriching materials, videos, readings and references that will last a writer a long while.'
– MEIKO KO, COURSE GRADUATE

'Granta's course gave me the confidence and tools to produce, pitch, and publish long-form journalism for the first time. It's a fantastic opportunity for anyone eager to hone skills and guide ambition.'
– COCO PICKARD, COURSE GRADUATE

Image © Julie Cockburn

Sana Badri is a British Tunisian photographer. Her work is primarily focused on place-making and marginalised communities. She has been exhibited at the V&A and published by *Elephant Magazine*, *Splash and Grab* and *Huck*.

Annie Ernaux published her first novel in 1974 and has since written more than twenty books, including *Simple Passion*, *The Years* and *A Girl's Story*. 'The Other Girl' is an excerpt from her forthcoming book of the same name, published by Seven Stories Press in North America and Fitzcarraldo in the UK.

Rosalind Harvey is a translator of contemporary Spanish-language fiction, including Guadalupe Nettel's *The Accidentals* and Luis López Carrasco's *The White Desert*, forthcoming in 2026 with Granta Books.

Julián Herbert is the author of *Tomb Song* and co-writer of the TV series *La Máquina*.

Nasim Luczaj is the author of *Hind Mouth*. She translates between Polish and English.

Joel Meyerowitz is a photographer whose work has appeared in over 350 exhibitions in museums and galleries around the world. He has published fifty-six books.

Paul Muldoon is Howard G.B. Clark Professor at Princeton University. He is the author of fifteen collections of poetry, most recently, *Joy in Service on Rue Tagore*.

Brittany Newell is a writer and performer. She is the author of two novels, *Oola*, and most recently, *Soft Core*. Her writing has appeared in *n+1*, the *New York Times*, *Joyland* and *Playgirl*.

Cian Oba-Smith is an Irish Nigerian photographer. His work has appeared in the *FT Magazine*, *Time*, *Le Monde*, the *New Yorker* and the *Guardian*.

Sharon Olds's most recent books are *Odes*, *Arias* and *Balladz*. Her first book, *Satan Says*, will be reissued as a 45th anniversary edition in September 2025.

CONTRIBUTORS

Leopold O'Shea has been published in the *Stinging Fly*, and received the 2023 Stinging Fly/FBA Fiction Prize.

George Prochnik is the author of *I Dream with Open Eyes* and *The Impossible Exile*. He has written for the *New York Times*, the *New Yorker*, the *Literary Review* and the *LA Review of Books*. He is editor-at-large for *Cabinet*.

Frederick Seidel's books include *The Cosmos Trilogy*, *Ooga-Booga, Poems 1959–2009*, *Nice Weather*, *Widening Income Inequality*, *Peaches Goes It Alone* and *Selected Poems*. His latest collection is *So What*.

Natasha Stagg is the author of two collections, *Sleeveless* and *Artless*, plus two novels, *Surveys*, and the forthcoming *Grand Rapids*, publishing in 2025.

Alison L. Strayer is a Canadian writer and translator. Her translations include works by Annie Ernaux, Abdellah Taïa, Yasmina Reza and Virginia Woolf. Recent translations include *The Places of Marguerite Duras*, *Dreaming Out Loud* and the forthcoming *The Other Girl*.

William T. Vollmann's books include *Europe Central, Imperial* and the *Seven Dreams: A Book of North American Landscapes* series. His forthcoming novel, *A Table for Fortune*, will appear in 2026.

Stephanie Wambugu is an editor of *Joyland*. Her first novel, *Lonely Crowds*, is forthcoming in 2025.

Diane Williams has published eleven books of fiction. Her most recent is *I Hear You're Rich*. Her stories have appeared lately in *McSweeney's*, the *Southwest Review*, the *LRB*, *Harper's* and *Kismet*. She is the founder and editor of *NOON*.

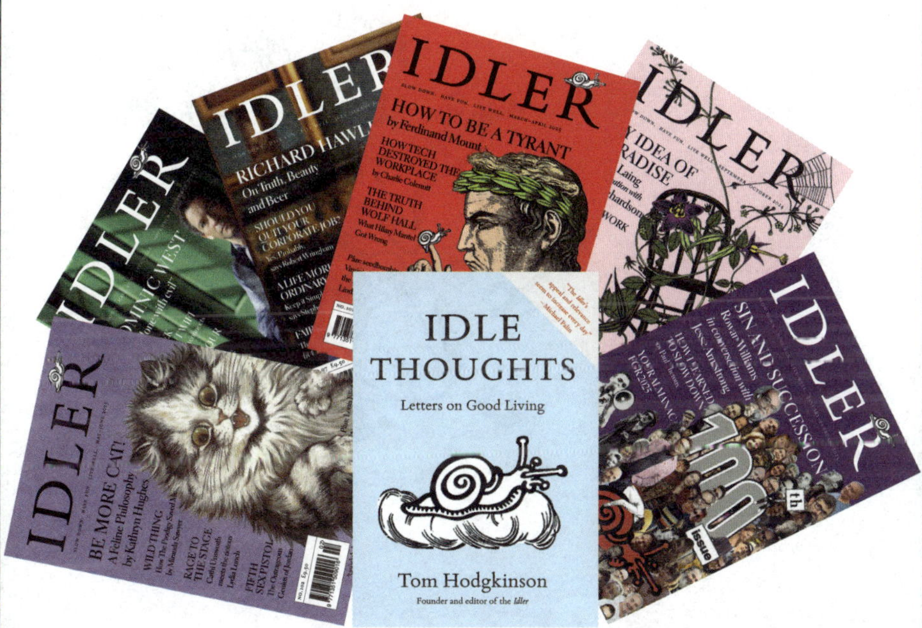

IDLER
SLOW DOWN, HAVE FUN, LIVE WELL.
IDLE THOUGHTS
Letters on Good Living
Tom Hodgkinson
Founder and editor of the Idler